MW01618680

JOSÉ CISNEROS—
AN ARTIST'S JOURNEY

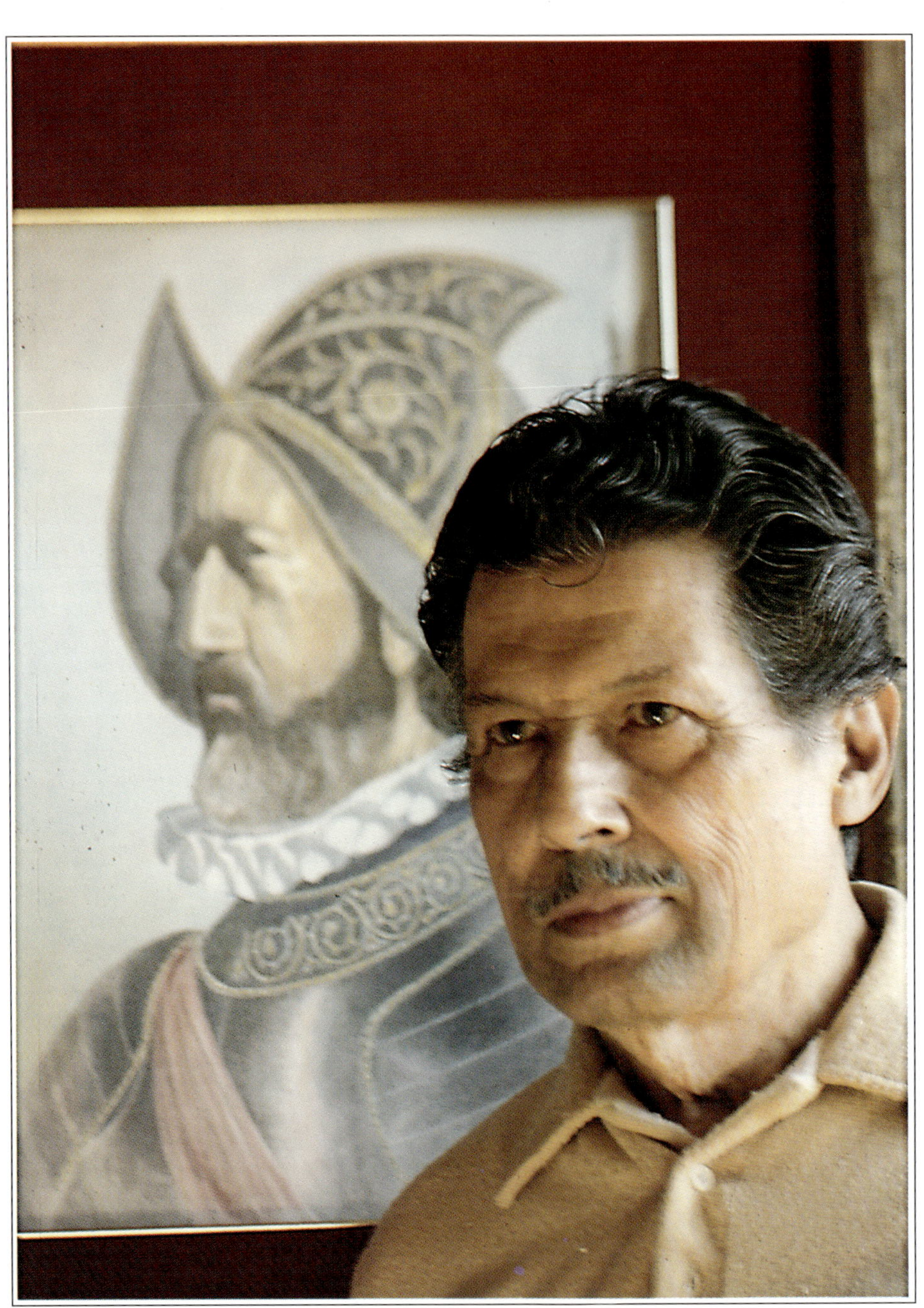

JOSÉ CISNEROS—
AN ARTIST'S JOURNEY

by John O. West

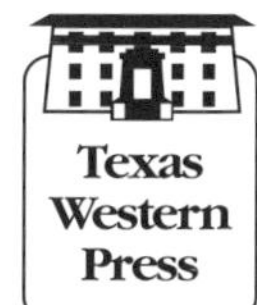

The University of Texas at El Paso
1993

First Edition
Library of Congress Catalog No. 92-083743
ISBN 0-87404-231-3

∞ All Texas Western books are printed on acid-free paper, meeting the guidelines for permanence and durability of the Committee on Production Guidelines for Book Longevity of the Council on Library Resources.

Dedicated to
Vicenta Cisneros,
loving wife and supporter for over half a century,

and to the memories of
Carl Hertzog and Francis Fugate.

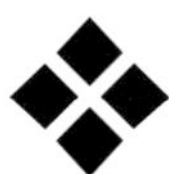

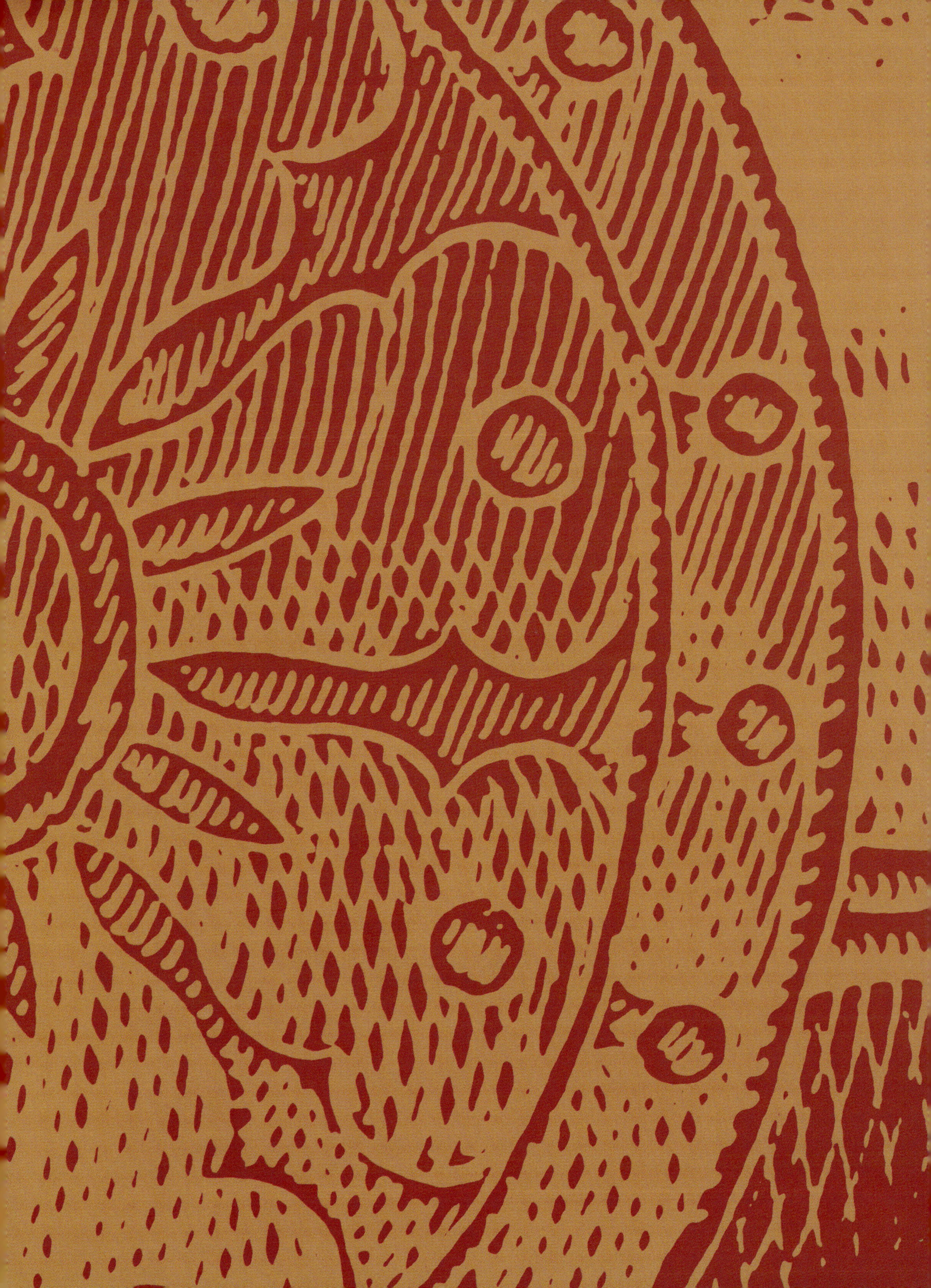

Contents

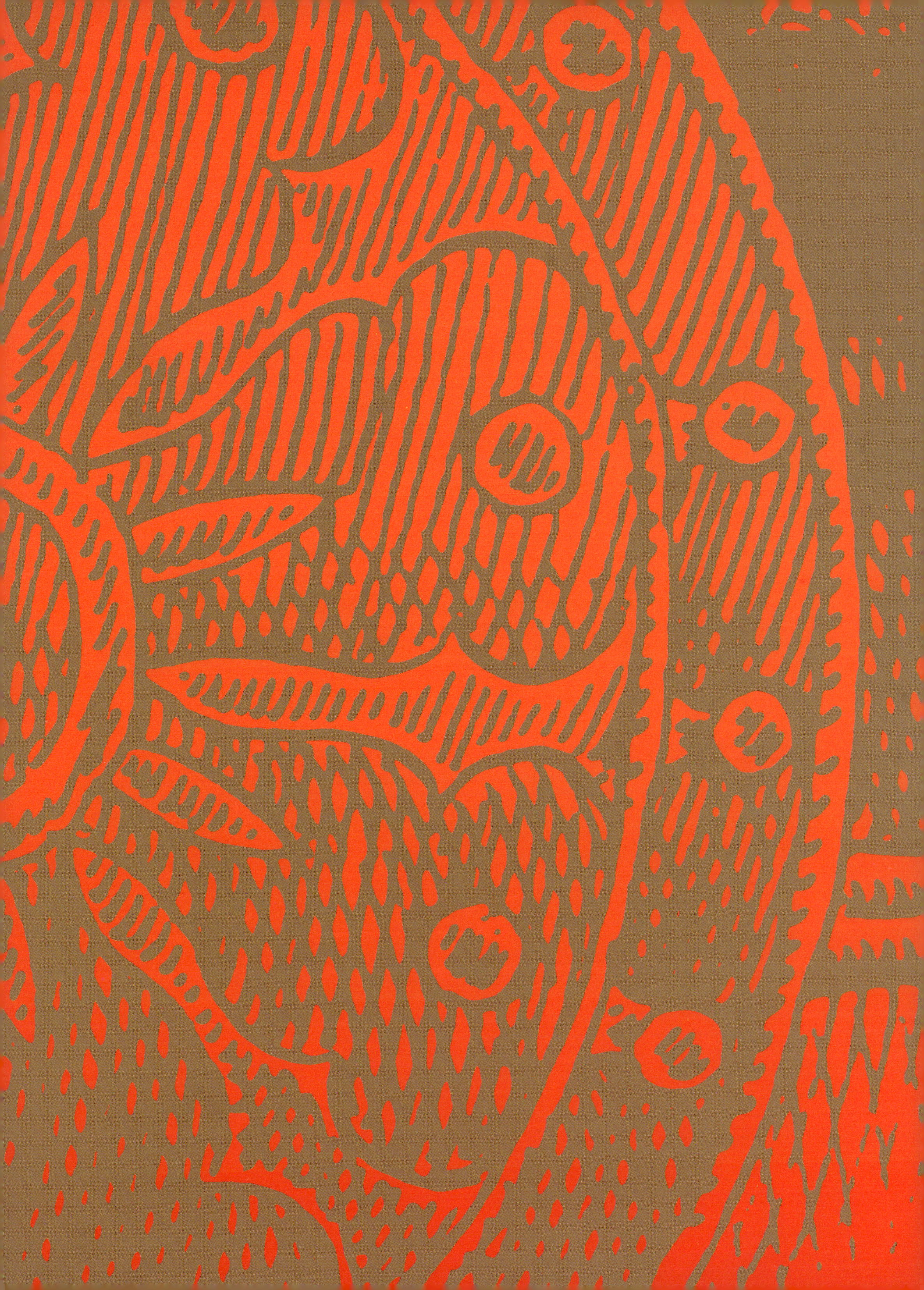

The Journey Continues

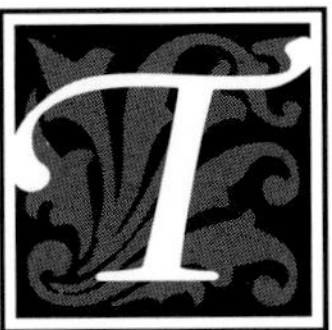

This account of the life and work of José Cisneros speaks strongly of the strength of the human spirit. Self-taught and self-motivated throughout most of his life, Cisneros has achieved recognition and honor as an artist in his adopted country after an unpromising beginning in his native Mexico just as the revolution there turned his family's world upside down. With no formal training he has become a renowned specialist in drawing historically accurate riders and their horses. In addition, he has branched out over his lifetime into even broader fields, creating statues in wood, plaques in bronze, designs in leaded glass, exquisite calligraphy, and incomparable maps. From early childhood he has been driven by the need to excel; he taught himself to read, to draw, to use watercolor despite being color blind, and to research the history of the Spanish Southwest. His book and magazine illustrations number in the hundreds; his historical accuracy is unchallenged—and unequaled.

His story rivals the novels of Horatio Alger, but the story of José Cisneros is a true one.

My own friendship with this modest artist goes back nearly thirty years, to a meeting of the El Paso Corral of the Westerners. Our mutual friend, C. L. "Doc" Sonnichsen, arranged to introduce us, and I felt honored that evening to sit beside this man who had already achieved great distinction. I was astounded to find that *he* felt honored that a brash new Ph.D. had wanted so much to meet *him*. Since that night our friendship has grown stronger each year. At his request I have written several items about his horsemen. When he was asked by Dr. Haskell Monroe, then president of the University of Texas at El Paso, to bring together a collection of his drawings for a major book (eventually to be called *Riders Across the Centuries*), he consented, on condition that I be asked to write the introduction. The honor was one I accepted without hesitation.

Working with José Cisneros over the years has increased my great respect and admiration for the man and his work, and the more I have learned of his artistic journey, the more I have been impressed with his achievement. He, on the other hand, calls me his greatest fan (although his adoring and supportive wife Vicenta is truly due that honor). He also calls me—only half in jest—"The Keeper of the Flame." Without the friendship and mutual respect between me and this remarkable couple, which I treasure, the challenge presented by this book would have been impossible to meet.

Over the years, Dr. Robert Bledsoe, chairman of the University of Texas at El Paso Department of English, and Dean Carl Jackson of the College of Liberal Arts have generously lightened my class load at vital times, for which I am indeed grateful. Al Lowman generously opened his Carl Hertzog research files to me, and the Summerlee Foundation provided funds for an invaluable research trip. My wife Lucy, besides encouraging me to keep going, has relieved me of other duties and pressures that would have diverted my energies—and always came up with the right word or phrase when my muse deserted me. Dale Walker, director of Texas Western Press, who insisted that it was time for this book, has been a great asset in making me keep my eye on our goal. Other friends and associates have been generous with time and advice: Ann Massmann of the Special Collections division of the UTEP Library; the many research people at that library who have been patient with my many questions, for which they always found answers; historian Dr. Félix Almaráz, Jr.; artist and friend Tom Lea; my departed *compadre* Francis Fugate, who shared his store of memories with me; and the late Carl Hertzog, who kept such rich records of his association with Cisneros. Will Wilson, former State Supreme Court justice and Attorney General, and his son Will II, generously provided me with three drawings from "The Shape of Texas"; Arturo Vásquez, Kathleen Rogers, and Gerónimo García were true kindred spirits in the design and preparation of this book, working to make it worthy of its subject. Also, the support and care of Lisa Ewart and Marcia Daudistel, of Texas Western Press, have lightened many a chore and relieved the tension that creating a book can produce. Without the help and encouragement of these supporters I would never have been able to complete this work. I thank them all for their generosity.

–John O. West

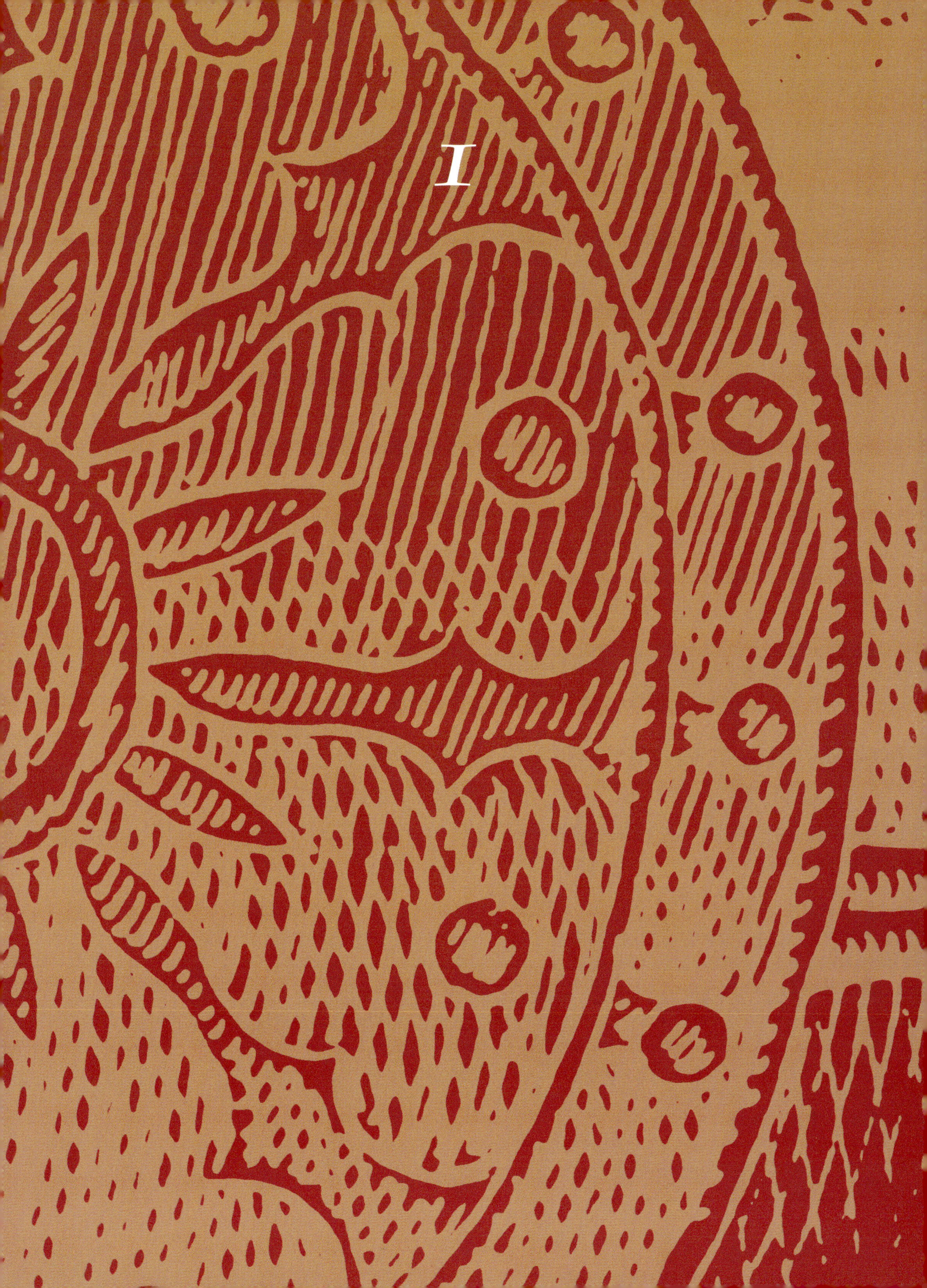

I

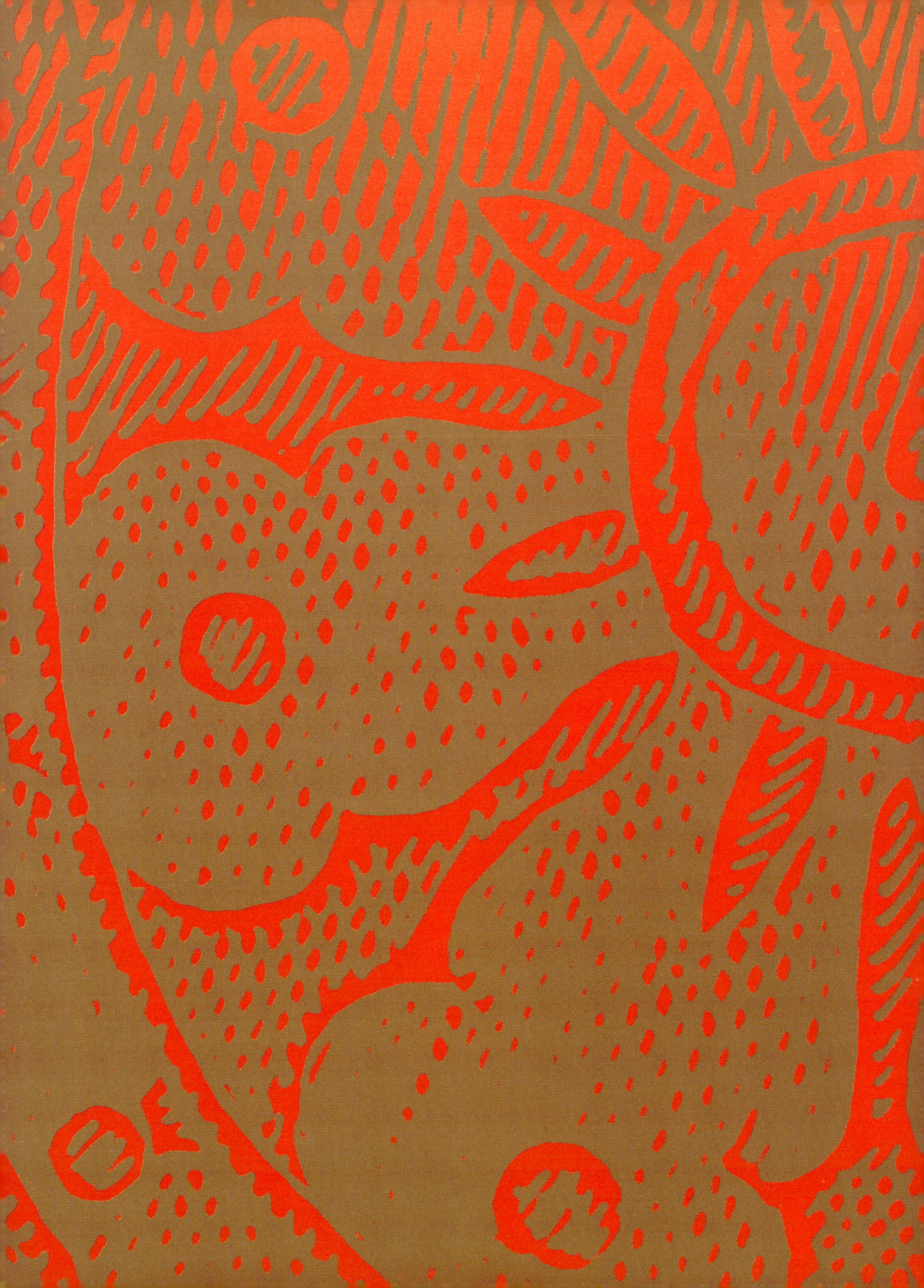

I

Born in the Revolution

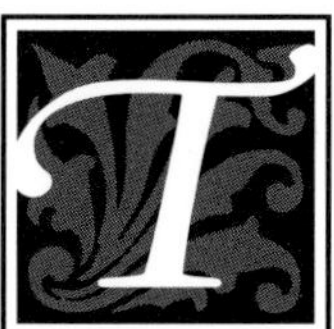

The year 1910 was one of turmoil throughout Mexico. Don Porfirio Díaz, who had been a hero in the expulsion of the French under Maximilian and Carlota, had turned into a dictator who favored foreign investors and their good opinions. The lowly Mexican who wore *huaraches* (cowhide sandals) was barred from places in Mexico City where the foreigners might be offended by such an unwashed presence. Politicos were shouting and printing in newspapers "Effective Suffrage and No Reelection" to a country ripe for revolution. A cultured *rico* (rich man), Francisco I. Madero, led the fight for change—and such less cultured ones as Francisco "Pancho" Villa and Emiliano Zapata entered the battle more personally, and more bloodily. The Mexican Revolution had been foretold, some said, by the explosion of the volcano at Colima, in the south of Mexico. The eruption of war dislocated people of all levels of life: the rich fled the country, the poor were often forced out of their familiar surroundings by fighting and political pressures, and the growing middle class was caught up in the struggle that was to devastate Mexico for decades.

The *campesinos* and *vaqueros* (farmhands and cowboys) of the state of Durango were among the people who probably had the most to gain by the impending revolution. Kept down for decades by poverty and lack of education, they could only profit by the breakup of the peonage system which kept them in virtual slavery. But the little village of Villa Ocampo in northern Durango was reasonably prosperous in those early days of the war. Many, like the Cisneros family, were descended from early Spanish settlers in the area—propertied people, closely related to each other, living in peace and harmony. Fair skin was very common, as were green and blue eyes, like many of their Spanish forebears. Both the Cisneros family and the Barragán family had more to lose from the coming revolution than to gain from it. Artist José Cisneros recalls:

> My father claimed that his family descended from the original Spanish settlers of the colonial town of Río Florido, one of the oldest

> settlements in Southern Chihuahua. My mother's side, the Barragán family, had a lot of Tarahumara blood like natives of Villa Ocampo, which was originally founded as a Tarahumara mission.

The political situation soon to become so volatile was the scene, and April 18, 1910, the date when José Cisneros was born into this year of change. Historic times they were, and it is fitting that a person who has devoted so much of his life to the study and depiction of history came into the world at this particular time and place. Within half a year the nation was in turmoil and the Mexican world turned upside down; soon after José was thirteen months old, Don Porfirio yielded to political pressure and resigned the presidency, later to flee the country for self-exile in Paris, leaving chaos behind for people of all levels of life.

* * *

Don Fernando Cisneros was a hard-working man of many talents—a master carpenter and cabinet maker, musician, barber, stagecoach driver. He had even worked for a time helping to build the Atcheson, Topeka, and Santa Fe railroad on its transcontinental route, long before the Revolution. He was a proud property owner, a self-sufficient man, a supporter of the Porfirian regime that had brought peace and prosperity (*tiempos normales*—normal times, he called those days) to such lower-middle class citizens as himself. Señor Cisneros's carpentry tools were of the finest quality, and his skills matched them. He did outstanding work on a hand-powered wood lathe, the artist recalls, and his wooden chests, held together with dove-tailing or wooden pegs, in the old Spanish style, were frequently requested by the townsfolk. He created decorative moldings with a planer, and generally made his products beautiful as well as useful. In earlier days he had driven the stagecoach from Chihuahua to the prosperous mining town of Cusihuiriachic, and had made thrice-yearly trips with wagon trains to Mexico City, hauling wheat, hides, and other local products to the capital.

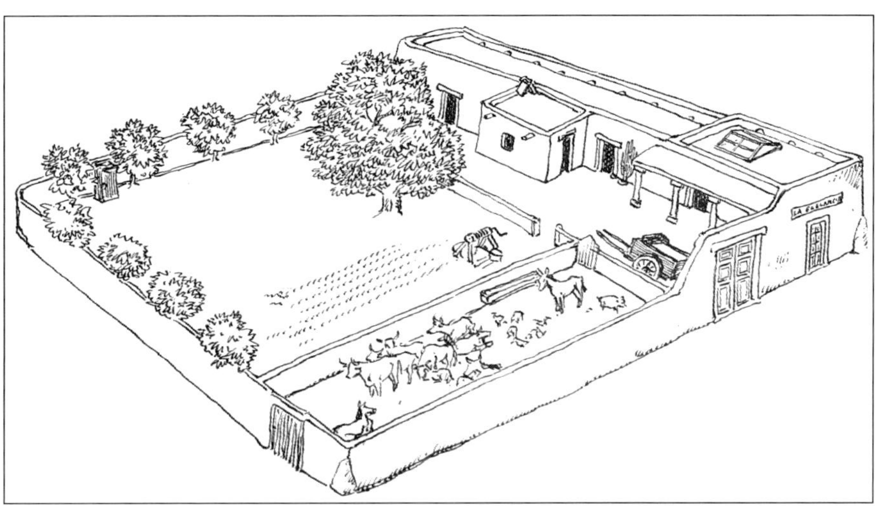

The Cisneros ranchito, *the artist's childhood home in Villa Ocampo, where he attempted his first drawing, a cow, in a tumble-down room (top). His father's barber shop (side).*

Now he was content to live and work at home with Juanita, his wife. The house and garden were surrounded by a high adobe wall, recalling days when Indians raided the area—and the absence of exterior windows reflected the same perilous times. The Cisneros acreage was spacious, a plot measuring 816 meters square, approximately twenty-seven acres. The man Don Fernando bought the property from had purchased it from the family who had settled it initially, about 1630. The enclosed space held a number of *membrillo* (quince) trees, as well as a huge Mexican elder in the center. A garden plot, irrigated by hand from the dug well, produced corn and beans, chile and squash under the care of the owner. One corner room, facing the street, had an outside entrance and a sign proclaiming proudly *La Elegancia Barbería* (the elegant barbershop), where Don Fernando did barbering for the men of Villa Ocampo. He even worked at blacksmithing. The son recalls watching while his father shrank an iron tire onto a wagon wheel, a process requiring great skill. A ring of cow chips lay on the ground, surrounding and covering the iron rim; set on fire, they heated the rim red hot, after which the wooden spokes and wheel would be put into the rim. Then water was doused on the whole thing, putting out the fire and shrinking the tire to fit the wheel. The father made a *carretón* (a big-wheeled cart, larger than the common *carreta*) with iron-tired wheels of his own making. Yet, the son remembers, despite the fact that Don Fernando had so much work to do with his hands, he took time to read widely as well, and kept up with what was going on in Mexico.

* * *

For several years the Revolution had bypassed small towns like Villa Ocampo. Life went on pretty much as usual, although more important places like Chihuahua and Ciudad Juárez were often the scenes of battles and destruction. But times were changing rapidly, and toward the end of 1917, Cisneros remembers, government troops under General Murguía drove everyone out of Villa Ocampo, thinking that they were supporters of the Revolution. Don Fernando lost everything of value that he had—six or eight cows, two mules and a burro, the houseful of furniture, and his carpentry tools. Everything had been carried off or destroyed by raiding revolutionaries or government troops (both sides lived by looting, having no regular pay). As the boy—then seven-and-a-half years old—and his family left town on foot, bereft of any belongings, headed for Parral, they saw the body of his maternal grandfather, Evaristo Barragán, hanging from an oak tree as a warning to would-be revolutionaries.

The family never reached Parral. Rosalio Hernández, one of Pancho Villa's lieutenants, drafted Don Fernando and two other Villa Ocampo musicians to join Villa's army, and the family was stranded in the hamlet of Rosario for about three months, eating acorns from the trees that grew profusely thereabouts. Cisneros recalls:

> They were not too bad, sort of bittersweet. But we survived. After a time my father escaped, rejoined the family, and we fled in the night to Parral, where my eldest brother was working. From Parral we

moved to the little railroad station of Baca. My father never went back to Villa Ocampo, nor tried to reclaim his property. He was never the same after that.

About 1919, while the family was in Baca, the nearby mines of Almoloya began operating, and Don Fernando was offered work in construction there. Meanwhile his brother, whose mining supply store and grocery business in Dorado had been hard hit by revolutionaries, fled to Juárez and asked Fernando to look after the large house he had left vacant. The Cisneros family, their world destroyed and with little more than the clothes on their backs, took up residence in Dorado, in a house furnished only with a few broken chairs and wrecked tables. The Revolution had come to their area with a vengeance.

* * *

The urge to draw had come early to young José. Among his first memories, at the age of five or six, is his attempt at drawing a cow, using a burnt stick on a whitewashed adobe wall of the family home. It was in a room no one used any more, and the roof was coming down, so he was free to indulge his childish whims. He had other ambitions as well: little by little he taught himself to read, using a book entitled *Silabario Metódico*. Familiarly called *Silabario de San Miguel*, it was an elementary textbook with the words divided into syllables for the young reader, employing a method of reading that had been developed and used in Mexico since colonial times. This was the means by which he unlocked the printed page, which was to prove so vital in his life. The determination to learn which drove him then has been with him all his life. Cisneros came by his artistic interest naturally, it seems, since his father had set a good example with his own creations, adding beauty to their utility.

Finally the Revolution was beginning to slow down. The artist recalls quite well the next few years:

> Estación Dorado, a railroad station between Jiménez and Parral [in Chihuahua], was the place my parents finally settled after the Mexican Revolution. We lived there from 1918 to 1925 when we headed north to Ciudad Juárez. It was late in 1921 that an important event occurred. My father's brother-in-law from the town of El Valle de Allende came to visit us. My mother had never learned to read, and I used to read to her stories from five-cent children's books, little twelve or fifteen page pamphlets, very common in those days. I enjoyed them mostly for their illustrations. In the course of the conversation someone mentioned the fact that I read to my mother, and my uncle became curious as to how I had learned to read. My father told him that with a little help I had managed to join words from the *Silabario de San Miguel*. My uncle was impressed, and he thought—since there was no school in Dorado—I was already too big to be wasting time. He convinced my parents to allow me to go with him and enter school. They put me in a little group comparable to kindergarten, but by the end of the week I was promoted to second grade on account of my reading ability.

Allende was a historic place. From there (back when it was known as El Valle de San Bartolomé) it had served as the gathering point for the sixteenth century expeditions of Don Antonio de Espejo and Don Juan de Oñate, heading northward to explore and to settle the area now called the Spanish Southwest, the scene and subject of many of the artist's illustrative labors. And here he found a teacher to put a spark in his soul. He says that Profesor Don Manuel Villaraus was the *director* (principal) of the Escuela Primaria No. 190 in Valle de Allende.

> When I was in the fourth grade, three times a week he would come to our classroom and give us an hour class on Mexican history. It was customary for the rest of the teachers to write their lessons on the blackboard; we all had to copy them and memorize them. Prof. Villaraus was different. He didn't use a text, but talked in the most

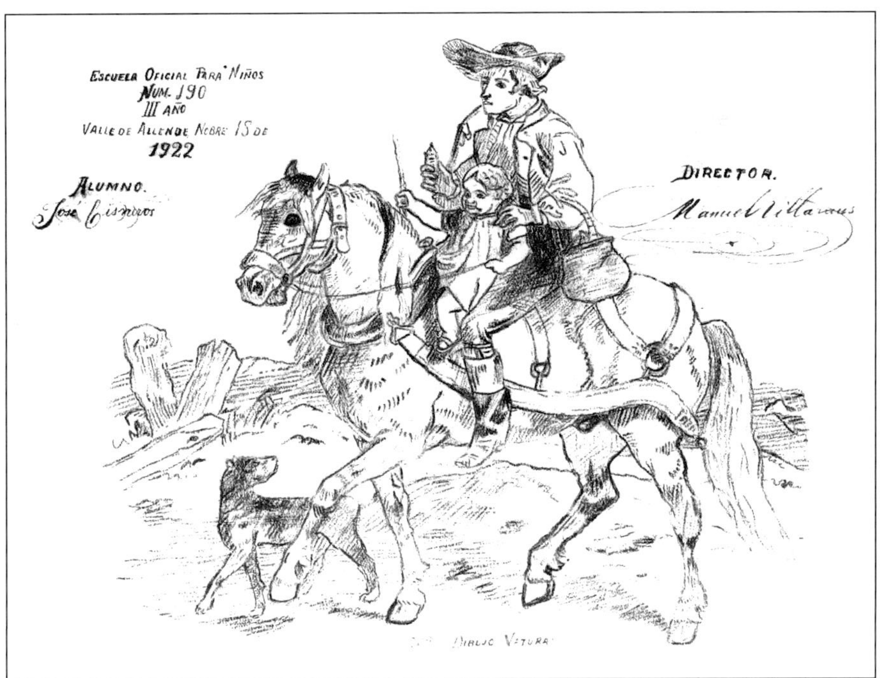

Cisneros's first horseman drawn for his mentor, Profesor *Don Manuel Villaraus of Escuela Primaria No. 190. The teacher signed and returned the drawing to the twelve-year-old artist.* (*Artist's collection*)

agreeable manner, making history come alive as if he had been a witness to the happenings. We were free to ask all kinds of questions, and he was very tolerant with those who couldn't grasp his ideas. Since then I became entangled in the intricacies of the past.

One of Cisneros's earliest treasures is a drawing he made as an exercise for that teacher, Don Manuel. The boy imitated a drawing the teacher provided, but he added details, things he knew from the life around him: a farmer on a plowhorse, harness accurate in every detail, giving his daughter a ride in front of him with a curious dog trotting alongside. Dated November 18, 1922, the picture shows the artist's budding skill at the age of twelve, and the equestrian subject matter—as well as the occasional dog—that would absorb his talent for many of the following seventy years.

Pictures became his life:

Ever since I can remember I have been fascinated with pictures in books, even more than those you see on walls, probably because those in books I can enjoy at leisure and as long as I like to see them.

Don Salvador Luján was the owner and pharmacist of the only drugstore in Valle de Allende where I acquired my academic background–three or so years of elementary school. Before the Mexican Revolution it was a very prosperous town with a very impressive Spanish colonial history and traditions. Señor Luján's drugstore was a very delightful place to visit—ample, airy, very Victorian, surgically clean with a peculiar pungent odor, tile floor, and lots of white wrought iron chairs. It was a meeting place for older citizens where they discussed religion, politics, the price of corn. Also it was the place where they could get newspapers and magazines from Mexico City.

One day I went there and one of the customers was reading *Revista de Revistas*, at that time the most important magazine in Mexico. I took a glance at the cover, and I was so impressed with it that I took courage and asked the gentleman who was reading it to allow me to see it. He graciously allowed me to look it over at leisure, and I thanked him. The cover was a beautiful picture of a charro on horseback, holding a Mexican flag. It was done by the then very famous Mexican illustrator Ernesto García Cabral. (Coming from school in El Paso one day, years later, and browsing in an old magazine stand on South Stanton Street, I found that issue which had attracted my attention when I was twelve years old. I still have it, and treasure it very much.) Several years later, while still living in Juárez, I submitted a batch of my pictures to *Revista de Revistas*. They used five of my drawings on their covers. Although I didn't get any compensation in money, it was thrilling and a great satisfaction to see my work reproduced in the same place where one of Mexico's favorite artists had been before.

But that was not the first time the budding artist's work had appeared in print.

While living in Allende the young student became friends with another man—much older, and middle class, Cisneros says—who had been to the United States but came home again without accomplishing very much. "He wasn't used to working," Cisneros recalls. Frustrated because he didn't achieve anything in the States, he had become something of a recluse, following his whims. Among them he was studying Morse code, as was his young friend. The two of them strung up wires between two rooms in the man's house and sent messages back and forth for practice. The man was also interested in pen and ink drawing, but there were no stationer's shops in Allende, so he had to order ink from Mexico City. Since he was terribly shy, and hated to go to the post office, he put the boy's name on the order, without telling him. When the order arrived, the puzzled youngster took the ink home and tried it out. He tried it so much that when the friend brought the subject up, the boy had to add water to the ink to make up the original volume.

The friend had another fascination—Don Quixote, of whom the boy had never heard. The young student was infected with the story of this Spanish dreamer, and as a result of this interest began a new venture. At the age of fourteen Cisneros dared to send off a story and a self-portrait to a Mexico City family magazine, *El Hogar* (The Home), and his first publication was a reality. Published in a section for children's writings, the essay describes a child's *viaje* (journey) for the first time to school—naturally it was Escuela No. 190. A second essay, *"La Primavera"* (Springtime), came out early the next year, along with a note to the editor of *El Hogar* expressing the author/artist's pleasure and surprise at seeing his work published. A line drawing of a Springtime scene, with clouds, mountains and trees, illustrated his poetic outburst of praise for Spring, the "goddess of pleasure."

The young artist was determined to learn more about art, and he studied the work of others. He was fascinated with all the pictures he could lay hands on—especially those with historical subject matter. The

Sunday rotogravure sections in the newspapers were particularly fascinating to him, and he collected them avidly. One such collection—he had taken it home during the summer vacation—was sold for wrapping paper by his mother, who had no idea what treasures they were to her son. (The family was not impressed with his artistic efforts, he remembers. They called his drawing *haciendo monos* (making monkeys—"doodling"). Undaunted by the loss of his treasures, he began his collection again, feeding his latent artistic soul on these printed records of life.

Other pieces of the past linger in his memories of those days:

> When I was attending school at Valle de Allende, we had only one month vacation. I anxiously waited for the end of school to join my parents, because I was very much attached to them and loved them very much. I looked forward with great expectation to the departure date, because that gave me a chance to ride a mule wagon that made the trip to the railroad station. This wagon made two trips daily, carrying freight, mail, and passengers. The ride took about an hour and a half and cost fifty centavos; the fare on the train to my destination was seventy-five centavos.
>
> On one occasion the riders on the wagon included Don Manuel Machado, who had a private school in El Valle, and two or three other gentlemen. Don Manuel was a very talkative sort of person, and he monopolized the conversation. While riding beside him I felt awkward, comparing my bare feet with his shiny black shoes decorated with bunion bumps. As we rode, he ignored my presence, probably thinking that I could not understand what he was talking about. As I remember, he was telling his audience that he was writing a book that he intended to call "Adventures of Lupercio," and one episode that he was describing dealt with a great scare his hero received from a band of thieves. As Don Manuel put it, Lupercio's "ejected fecal matter was enough to make him a monument." He was roaring with laughter as he delivered this punch line, but he suddenly

> stopped short and looked at me. I am sure I appeared impassive and unimpressed. That was my first encounter with a literary man.
>
> After the month's vacation was over my father would rent or borrow a couple of burros from Don Tiburcio, a neighbor, to take me back to school. The journey would take us about five hours at the slow but steady pace of the beasts. My father was very witty, and I greatly enjoyed his company. He would relate his own adventures along the way. For myself, this was the longest equitation experience I ever had.

This admission, from a man whose life has for so many years been intertwined with horses and horsemen, proves that imagination can be more compelling than experience.

By 1925 the Cisneros family had reached Ciudad Juárez, Chihuahua, across the Rio Grande from El Paso, Texas. To help out family finances young Cisneros worked at a variety of jobs, including delivering papers, morning and afternoon. A student visa enabled him to cross the river daily to study at Lydia Patterson Institute, a Methodist school that specialized in teaching English to Spanish-speakers. His report cards show steady improvement, in subjects such as English, history, and manual training—but *dibujo* (drawing) was not in the curriculum. Perhaps the omission was unimportant, considering his first—and last—experience with an art teacher.

About 1927, he remembers,

> I was attending school at Lydia Patterson Institute in El Paso; while passing through South Stanton Street, I had noticed an itinerant painter working in a little shack. He had a sign outside advertising painting lessons for twenty-five cents an hour. One day I decided to sacrifice my lunch money and enrolled for one of his lessons. After a few preliminary preparations he began to discuss the beauty and the magic of colors and how by blending the three primaries we could get an infinite array of new colors and shades. He asked me to do

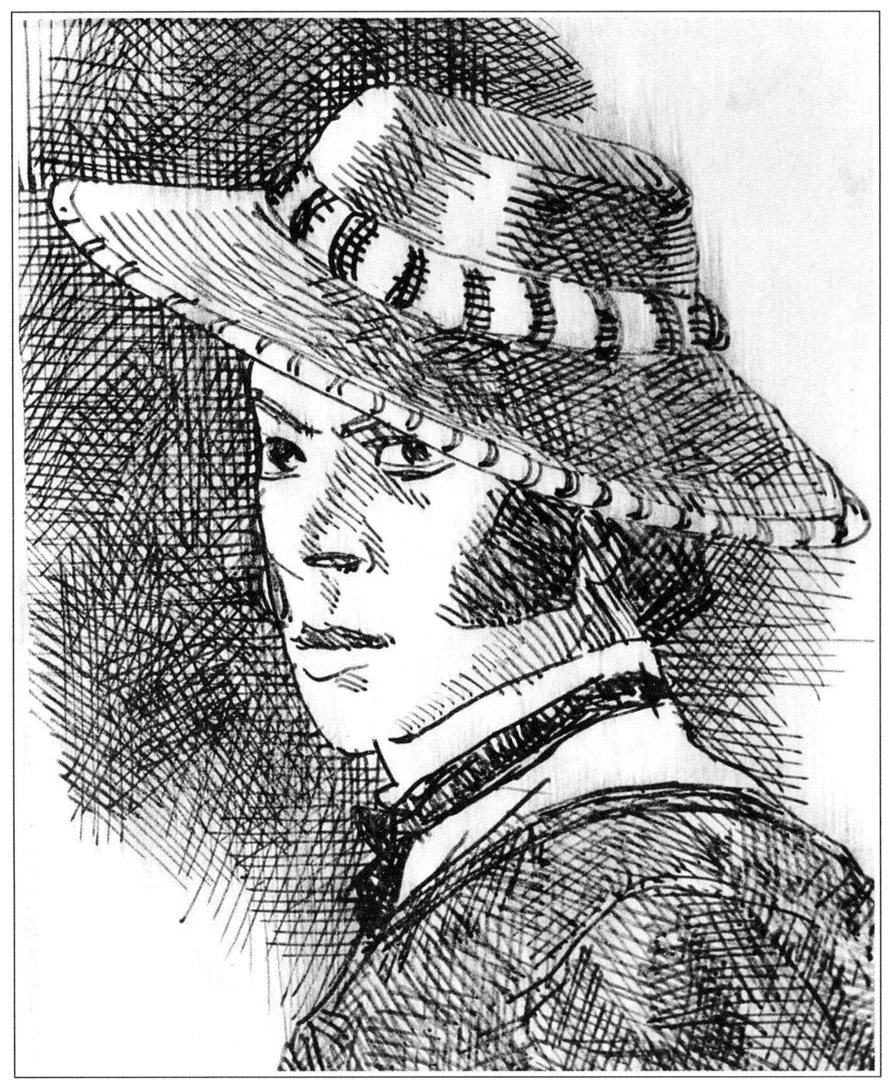

An early effort by the artist, about 1925, is his study of a young Mexican. Never before reproduced. (Author's collection)

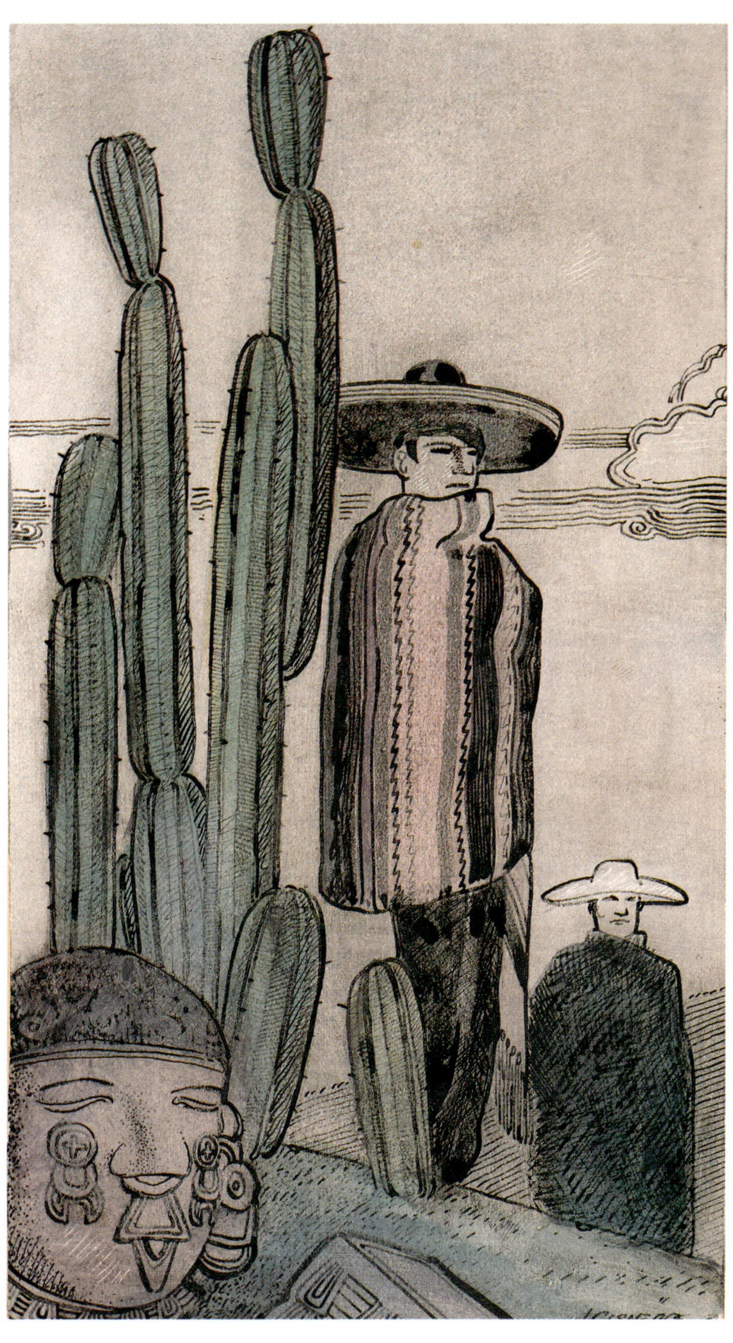

A very early desert scene, drawn about 1927, shows some of Cisneros's favorite subject matter.
(Author's collection)

> some blending myself, and I got so confused that I had to quit right there and then. He had discovered that I was color blind. His advice was that I would never make it in the art world, but that I would probably be an outstanding bricklayer. In spite of that, sad and disappointed as I was, I went home, taking refuge in my reliable pen and inks. That experience added to my shyness, my inferiority complex, and my introversion.

True to the determination that drove the artist onward, the matter of being color blind has never held him back. His pencils have the names of the colors they bear, written on the sides, and his wife Vicenta advises him when he adds color to the basically black-and-white drawings for which he has become famous.

Those trips to and fro across the border brought other humiliations to young Cisneros.

> It must have been in 1930. I was forced to leave school by financial circumstances. After working at odd jobs I finally got a steady one with the Canton Grocery Company on South Stanton, delivering groceries for the meager sum of five dollars a week. Things were cheap then, though. I used to cross the Santa Fe bridge from Juárez about 7:30 in the morning. Sometimes on Saturday evening (the international bridge closed at midnight) I had to remain in El Paso and sleep wherever I could, because people from Smeltertown, East El Paso, Sambrano Addition, and the Quarry, ordered their groceries on Saturday evening and they had to be delivered early Sunday morning. We started at 6 a.m.
>
> In those days people crossing from Juárez—especially those on foot—were likely to be sent to the steam baths installed in the basement of the immigration offices. Those detained there were ordered to undress and their clothes, shoes, and everything they had on were made into a bundle and fumigated with steam, while the owner was showering in scalding hot water. Probably because of my working clothes and my poor countenance I was subjected to this

humiliating process a couple of times. On the first occasion, when I arrived at work one of my fellow workers began to make fun of me. "What happened," he said, "did you sleep in jail or were you tramping?" It was no wonder that he taunted me; my clothes were wrinkled and shrunk, and so were my shoes and my spirit. The next time the border officials did that to me, I had to go back to Juárez and change clothes.

Even so, those trips across the border were sometimes exciting—and humorous too, Cisneros recalls:

> There used to be several second-hand clothing stores along South El Paso Street, and many of the owners would hang samples of the clothes outside. One time a tramp passing by grabbed a pair of pants and ran with them. Sam, the storekeeper, ran after him, yelling "Police! Police!" There was a policeman at the corner, and to scare the thief he pulled out his gun. Seeing that, Sam began to yell "Don't shoot him in the pants! They're mine!"

South El Paso had a very positive effect on the young man:

> My daily contact with South El Paso in my early years chiseled in my memory the sounds, the smells, the familiar characters—typical, indigenous to that part of town. There was a retarded youngster who made the rounds in a one-horse wagon collecting bottles in exchange for a gummy sort of candy that he carried in paper cones. He rang a bell at the same time that he shouted in a shrill tone *"Pirulii de goma!"* There was always someone coming out from the alleys and tenements with two or three bottles exchanging them for the peculiar candy. It was customary for a lot of kids, when he yelled, to mimic him in a sort of rhyme: *"El que la coma se atorzona"*—He who eats it gets cramps!
>
> And then there was Panchito *"el shinero,"* a shoe shiner stationed across the street from the Colon Theater. Dressed in a very shabby

> old suit spotted with drippings of food, bearing tattered sleeves and pant cuffs, but sporting a red tie and a rose on the lapel of the coat, he was always smiling and talking nonsense to the passersby.
>
> One old man whom I never knew by name struggled every morning with a huge basket through the neighborhood offering sweet breads; his monotonous and familiar cry was *"Ya llegó, ya esta aquí, el famoso Pan de San Luis Potosí"*—Here it comes, here it is, the famous bread from San Luis Potosí. Another character was *Simón el camotero*—Simon the sweet potato man—who by six in the morning was selling his sweet potatoes, cooked in brown sugar. He was funny, outspoken, and aggressive. He would say *"Ya estoy aquí; Abranme la puerta; levánten al marido."* Roughly translated, he was saying "I'm here. Open the door for me, and send your husband out." One morning in answer to his demands an alluded-to husband, annoyed with his insinuations, came out in his red flannels and pushed him down the steps of the tenement, with sweet potatoes and tray flying all over. Trying to get up, his clothes dripping with molasses, and flies buzzing around, he exclaimed—in a most nonchalant manner—*"Hasta que un día acabé temprano"*—This is the first time I ever finished early!

South El Paso was a sort of second home to many people who came to the United States from Mexico, and even today street signs, advertising, and conversations mingle English and Spanish. Stores cater to Mexican tastes and appetites, and tourists marvel at the flavor of Mexico that surrounds them. The area continues to hold many memories for Cisneros; as he points out:

> By a strange coincidence, many events in my life took place in and around South El Paso during my early years in the city. On the corner of Fifth and El Paso streets, on the northern side, there was a five-and ten-cent movie house called *Teatro Edén*. It had a stairway on the side that led to an upstairs row of tenement apartments with a wide balcony over the entrance to the theater. This balcony was very important to me because when I started working downtown I came

> through El Paso Street and turned to the right to visit Sacred Heart Church; from the corner I had a full view of the balcony. In those apartments there lived a very attractive girl named Vicenta, who many years later became my wife. Of course I was unaware of it then, but she maintains that one day when I was rounding the corner, she was on the balcony with her girl cousins, saying to them "You see that fellow with the very white shirt? I like him very much." Weeks later, she said, I smiled at her and she reciprocated. That pair of smiles tied us for life, and we have succeeded in remaining together ever since.

The marriage of José and Vicenta, however, was far in the future. Times were hard, and the artist had a long way to go before he could think of taking a wife. In the meantime, an event took place that was to have a lasting effect on the life of José Cisneros:

> Still in school and living in Juárez, I searched for a job during vacation time. There was a book store on South El Paso Street—*La Mexicana*—where after I had tried several other places the owner agreed to use me as an errand boy and cleaning and sweeping administrator. The job was tiring and boring on account of the long hours, from nine to nine. It was my first job, but it lasted less than two weeks, because one day while I was crossing the bridge from Juárez the immigration inspectors discovered that I was working on a school passport. The event became a blessing in disguise, because when I notified the principal at Lydia Patterson Institute, Mr. Herbert Marshall, of the incident, he set in motion the proceedings for my legal residence in the United States—and personally attended to the whole business.

The artist's journey was beginning in earnest, with the encouragement of his history teacher in El Valle de Allende, near the point of origin of the pilgrimages of two Cisneros heroes—Don Antonio de Espejo and especially Don Juan de Oñate. Young José Cisneros was on his way.

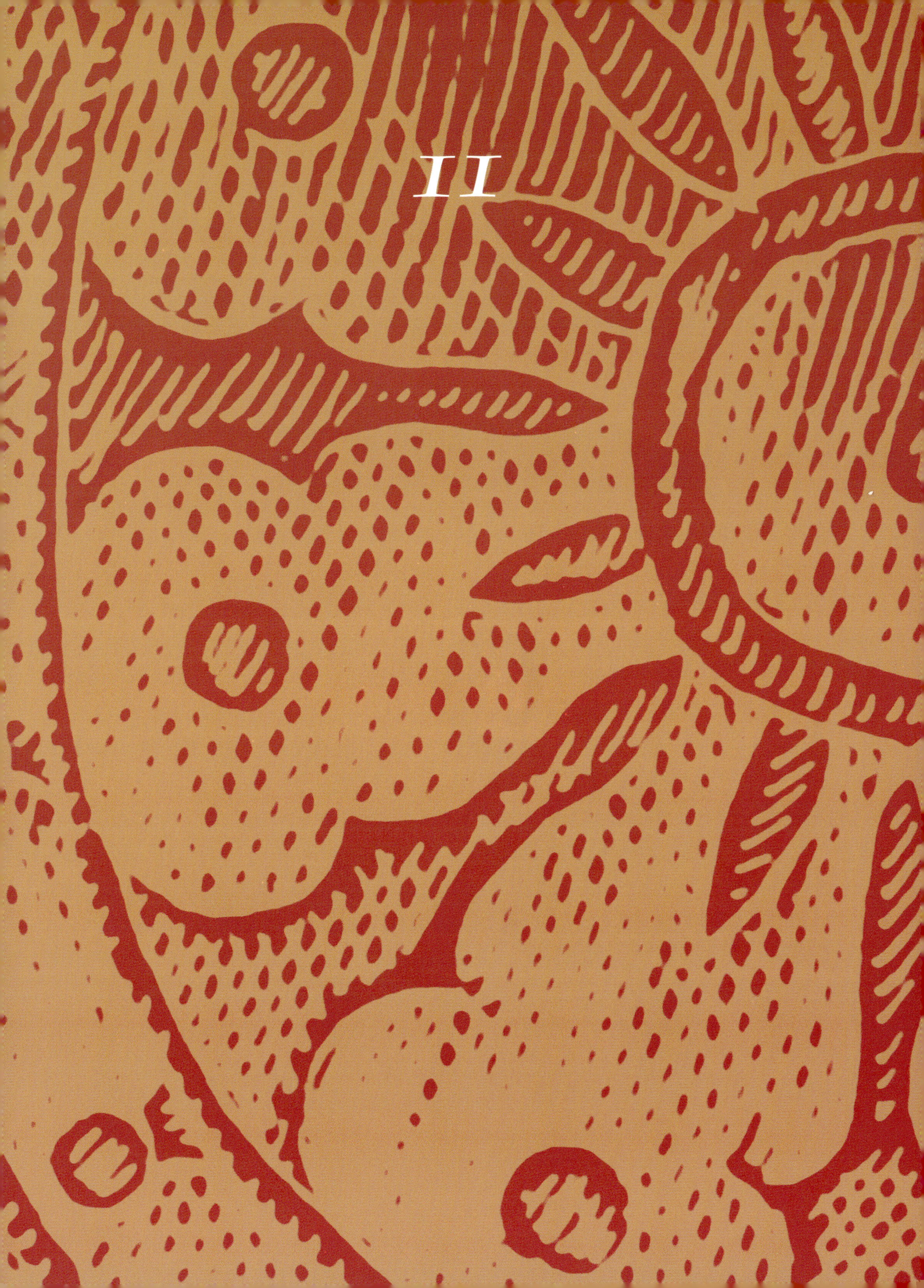

II

II

Carl Hertzog, Tom Lea

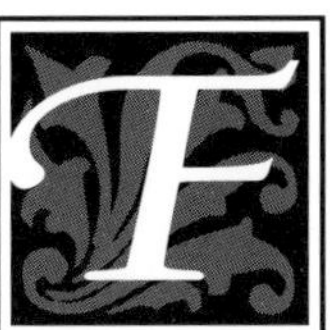

For several years after José Cisneros's schooling at Lydia Patterson Institute, he continued to explore the artistic possibilities in Ciudad Juárez. During the 1930s a strong supporter, Armando B. Chávez, encouraged the young artist, and brought him into groups of people with literary and artistic interests, notably the Ateneo Fronterizo (the border Atheneum) as well as the local Lions club, long a promoter of things cultural in the Mexican border city. When a Cisneros cover (the first of five) appeared on the popular Mexico City magazine *Revista de Revistas*, notice was taken in the local papers, and Cisneros was feted during a special evening at the Ateneo Fronterizo; there were speeches and entertainment celebrating the emancipation of women, but the occasion was centered upon a showing of Cisneros work, "received with well deserved applause" by the members and their guests. Poet Heriberto García-Rivas (a fellow member with the artist in the Ateneo) wrote approvingly of Cisneros's talent, and another member, Federal District Judge Miguel López Schoeffeger, offered to send the artist to the Instituto de Bellas Artes in Mexico City to study. His mother feared that she would never see her son again if he went so far away. Ever family oriented, he listened to his mother's pleas and stayed in the area, continuing to illustrate poems and articles written by his fellow association members and others who became aware of his talent.

After Cisneros left school to support his family, he took a job with the White House, a prominent El Paso department store. Working on the window displays, he discovered a gold mine of material, a veritable treasure for one with limited funds: the showcards displayed in the windows were used on only one side, and the posterboard was then discarded. Cisneros asked for and received permission to keep the material, which he began to employ for his artistic experiments. One technique he developed involved scratching the surface of the posterboard with his pen, an action, he recalls, that allowed the ink and any watercolors he used in his early years to spread in varying degrees of intensity, creating an unusual effect. One such drawing was published in the

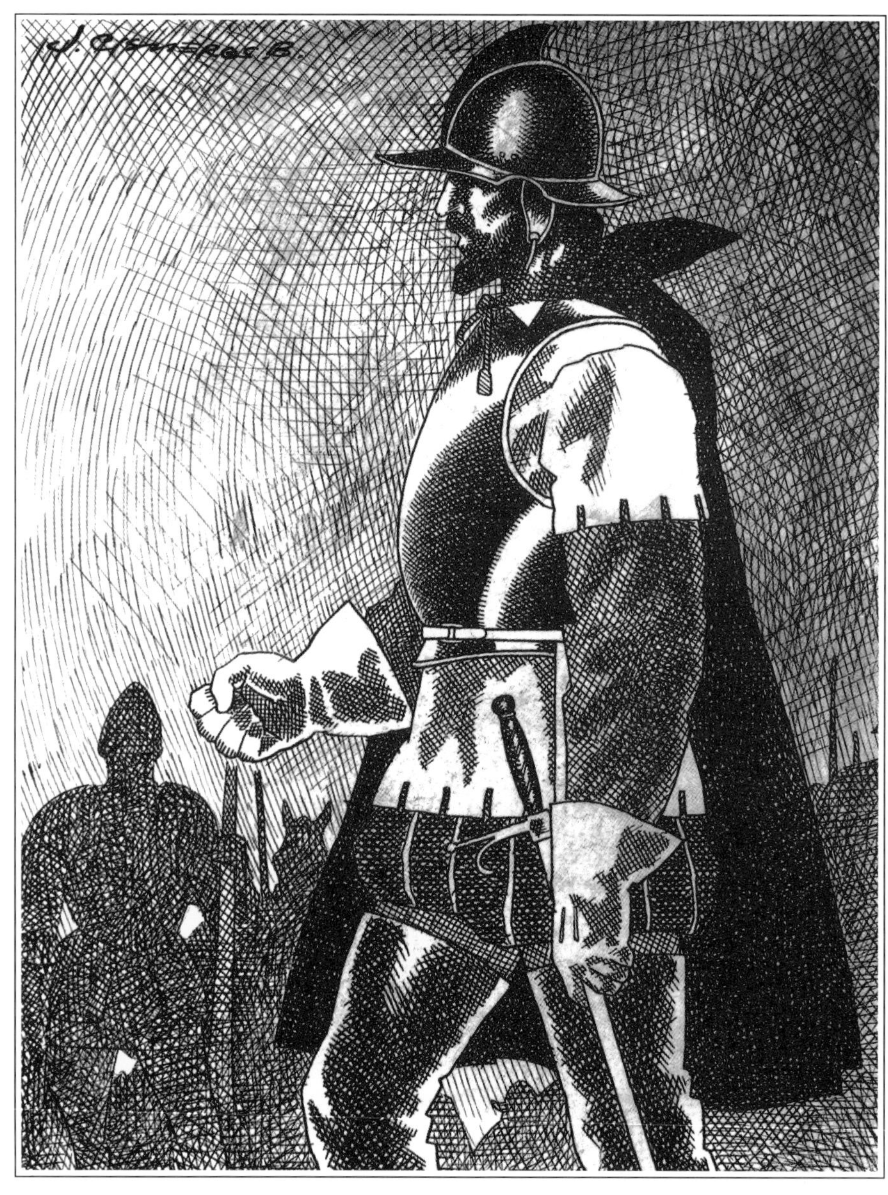

This drawing of explorer Francisco Vasquez de Coronado was among the works Cisneros showed to artist Tom Lea at the Federal Courthouse, where the latter was painting a mural. (Author's collection)

Mexico City magazine *Hoy*, and others were sold or given to friends. (Years later, he discovered that someone had developed a material called "scratchboard" for just such a use.) Even now, some sixty years later, posterboard continues to be his favorite drawing surface.

The Juárez Lions Club took pride in the budding artist, and printed several of his drawings illustrating the works of local writers in their publication, *El León Juarense*. His reputation was growing, especially in Juárez, but in 1937 an event of great importance opened doors for him in El Paso as well. Muralist and artist Tom Lea, a man of established reputation, was completing a mural at the federal courthouse in El Paso. His subject was historical—the people who had come to the Pass of the North throughout its history. Naturally interested in both the subject and the technique, Cisneros watched the creation take shape, and then took courage and came to see Lea with a portfolio of his own work. Lea's response was immediately enthusiastic, and he wrote a note to Maude Sullivan, librarian at the El Paso Public Library, recommending the young artist to her. Mrs. Sullivan arranged for an exhibit of forty of Cisneros's drawings in the library, and a broader audience was thus made available to him. The showing produced excellent reviews, as well as positive comments from Tom Lea, who had helped to bring it about.

Insistent on boosting the young artist's reputation and opportunities, Señor Chávez arranged for the continuation of the library exhibit in Juárez in an important showing of his art in an evening that must have been a gala event.

The scene was the March, 1938, opening of a *salón* (auditorium) at a new school in Juárez, Centro Escolar Benito Juárez, named for the city's historical patron. Professor Chávez started the evening off with a discussion of the work of the young artist, pointing out that this was a momentous occasion. The art showed a perfection of execution, original in conception, "a symphony of lines and colors," he said, in a virtual flood of compliments about Cisneros's work. Then came a dazzling presentation of music and dance by the city's most renowned teachers and performers. The memory of that evening remains strong with the

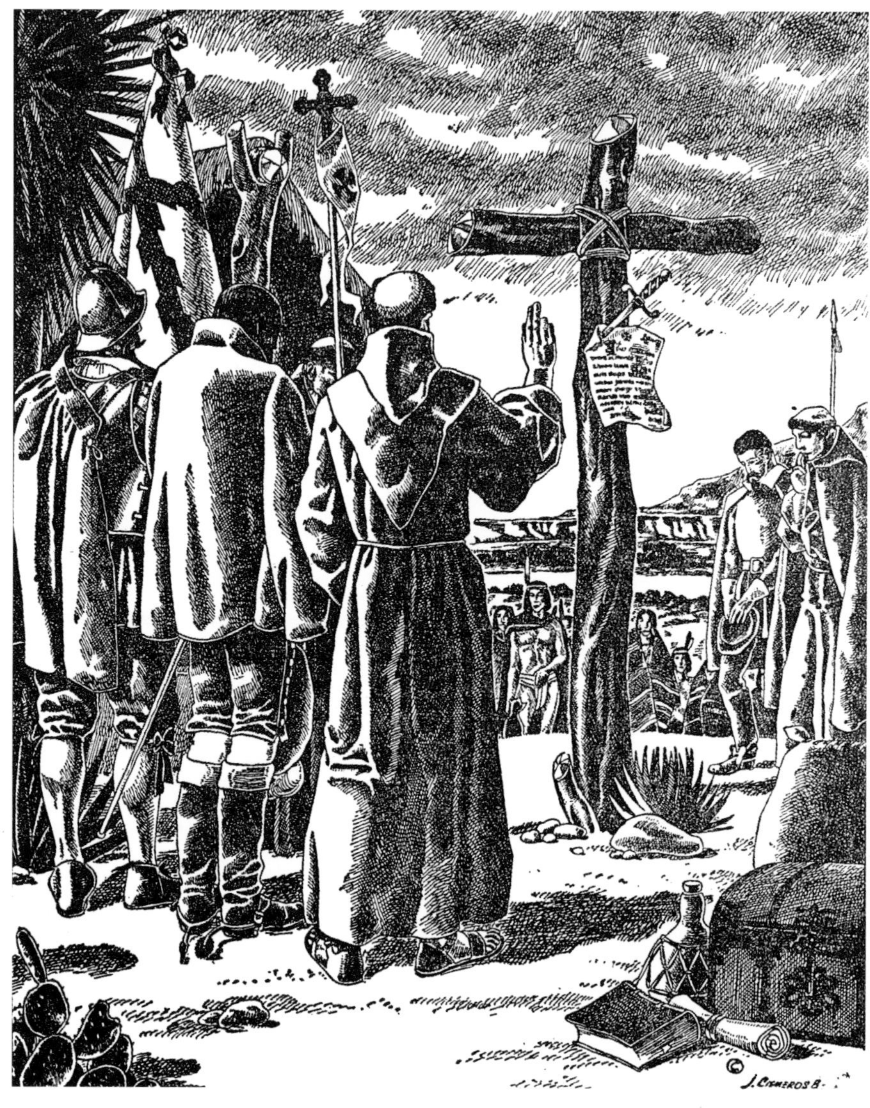

Taking Possession of New Spain, *an early illustration, appeared in* El León Juarense. *It was among Carl Hertzog's first uses of Cisneros's work, and served as the cover for one of the first* Academic Reprints *of Texas Western Press, Herbert E. Bolton's* The Mission as a Frontier Institution *(1960).*
It also appeared in W.H. Timmons' El Paso: A Borderlands History *(1990).*

artist, well over half a century later.

Soon after came an expansion of the young artist's talent: he had been illustrating a wide variety of stories and poems for *El León Juarense*, experimenting with a wide variety of styles of ornamentation and capturing dramatic moments in the stories printed there, but now he began writing and illustrating his own articles. Called *Apuntes Históricos* (historical sketches), they were of a regional and historical nature: "The First Europeans in This Region"; "The Expedition of Rodríguez-'Chamuscado' "; "Expedition of Don Antonio de Espejo"; and "The Entrada of Don Juan de Oñate," the latter one being of a subject most firmly established in the pantheon of Cisneros heroes. He recorded, in words and pictures, the founding of the city of Juárez; the construction of the first mission in the area, *La Misión de Nuestra Señora de Guadalupe*; and the growth of Paso del Norte (present-day Juárez, Chihuahua), to cite only a few of his ten productions in the Lions publication. One result of Cisneros's association with teacher/entrepreneur Chávez was a contest the latter conjured up: a competition for the design of a coat of arms for Ciudad Juárez. Chávez and Cisneros had talked about the project, and Cisneros's entry was already done by the time the contest was announced. No record exists at this late date of who the other competitors were (if any existed), but the Cisneros entry, the winner, is still the official logo for the border city, carved above the doorway of the *Palacio Municipal* (city hall), and is widely distributed in the form of postcards; curiously, the cards note that the idea was that of Professor Armando Chávez, but they fail to give any credit to the work of the artist.

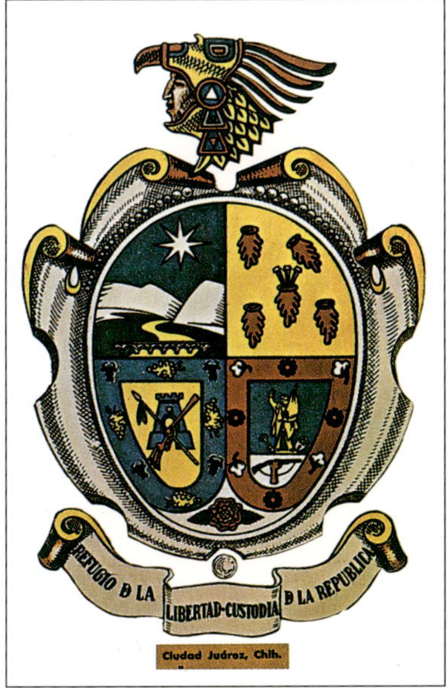

In the Juárez Coat of Arms, *Cisneros combines graphic elements of the border city's early history and areas of importance.*

Another opportunity arose in 1938 and 1939 when Hilda and Lloyd Burlingham, in an innovative publication called *Mexico*, published in both English and Spanish, used some of the Cisneros art, especially in full pages. For the first time he got paid for his work, only four or five dollars per item, but it was no longer published just for the prestige involved. His art was in good company as well, since the cosmopolitan Burlinghams were patrons of a number of artists and writers in the Southwest, even down into Mexico.

The thirties brought both artistic growth and personal change to the life of artist Cisneros. He continued his evening practice of his art, polishing techniques and adding others. But there were changes in his life, as well. Don Fernando died in 1939, leaving Jose's mother totally in his care. Even so, his financial situation had improved to the point that he could marry his long-time sweetheart, Vicenta Madero, that same year. Research at the El Paso Public Library, guided by his mentor Mrs. Sullivan, was used to enrich his knowledge of art and technique. He studied the work of other artists regularly. The covers of the *Saturday Evening Post*, especially when they were illustrated with the work of Norman Rockwell, provided lessons in skillful illustration—and at the five cent price of the magazine during those days, he had a very inexpensive source of models. Other artists, often Hispanic, gave him examples to study, duplicate, and sometimes improve upon. Ernesto García Cabral of Mexico and Alejandro Sírio of Argentina were among his ideals, partly because of his cultural ties, but also because of their outstanding skills at illustration. But war clouds were gathering in Europe, and soon the artist became an artisan, via a course in aircraft metal work. The skills that made him an artist helped make him a craftsman as well, but aircraft factories were far away from El Paso, and there were family responsibilities to consider. He now had his mother to support, and his wife Vicenta did not relish a move to strange surroundings. The compromise Cisneros reached was to have lasting consequences.

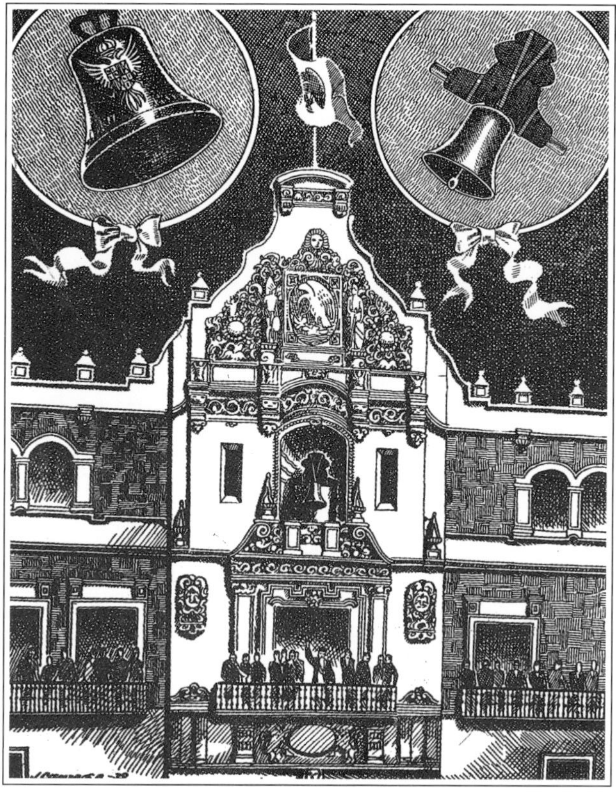

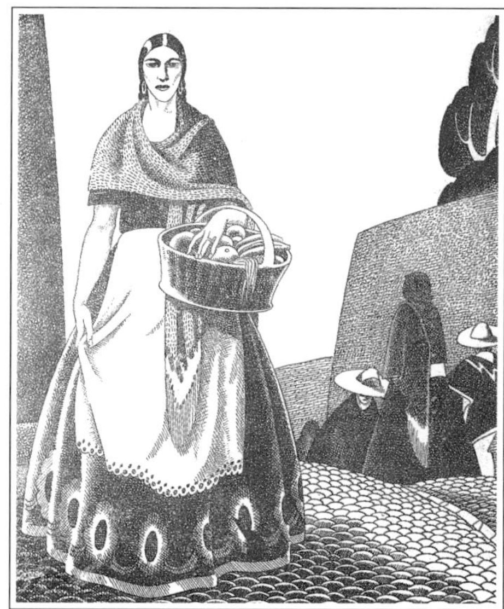

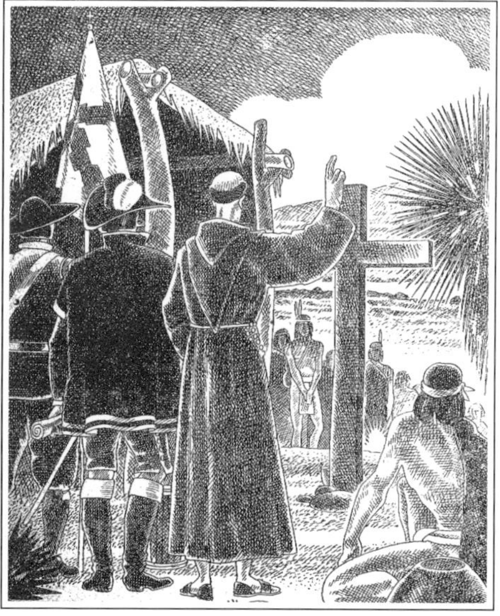

Mexico Magazine *offered an outlet for several of Cisneros' drawings. (Courtesy of Kenneth Burlingame)*
top: Christmas cover featuring a Mexican Palacio Municipal, lower left: Cover with woman at the market, lower right: Foundation of the City of Juárez

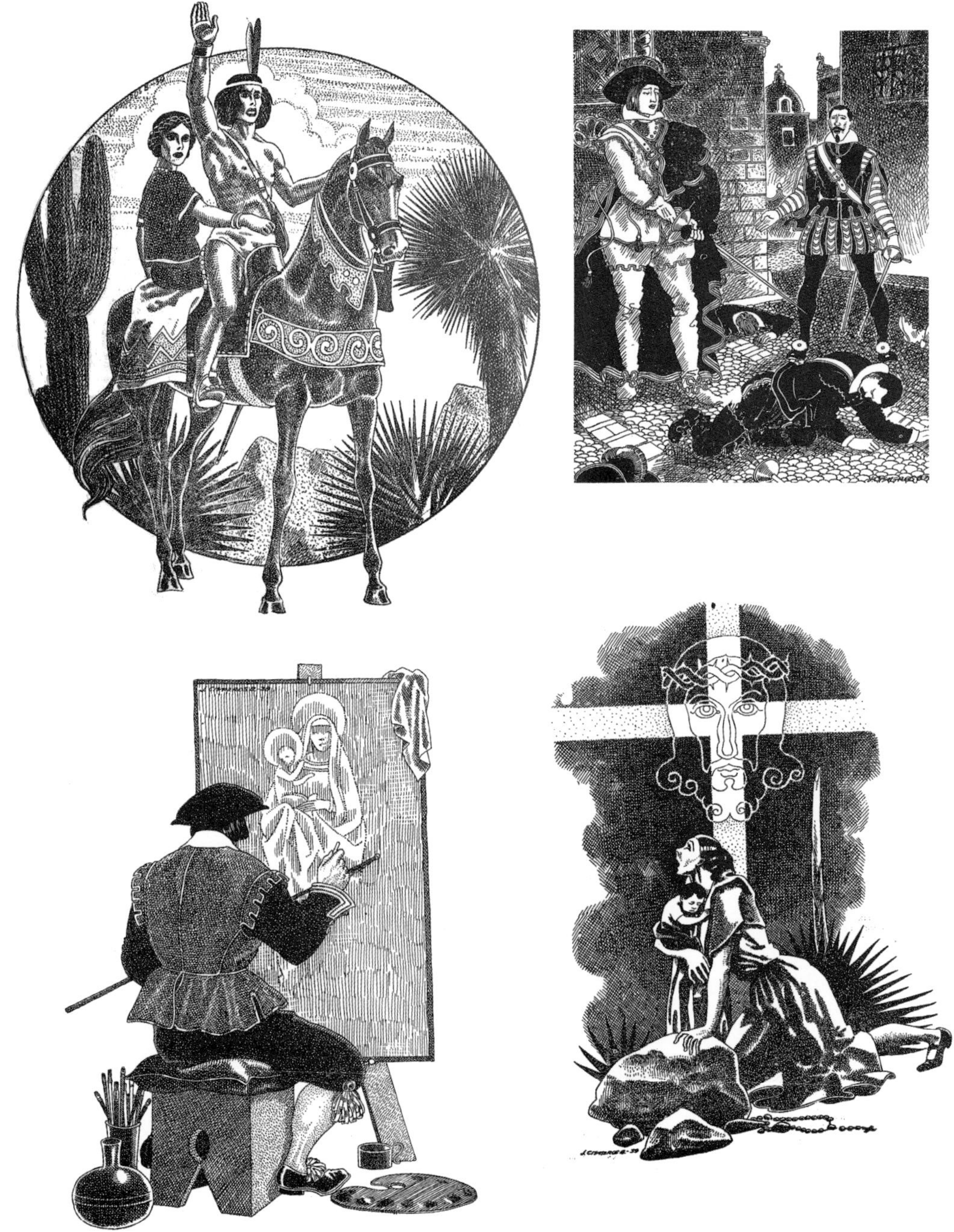

Mexico Magazine *(Courtesy of Kenneth Burlingame)*
upper left: Short story illustration, upper right: Short story illustration,
lower left: An artist at work, lower right: A distraught mother at prayer

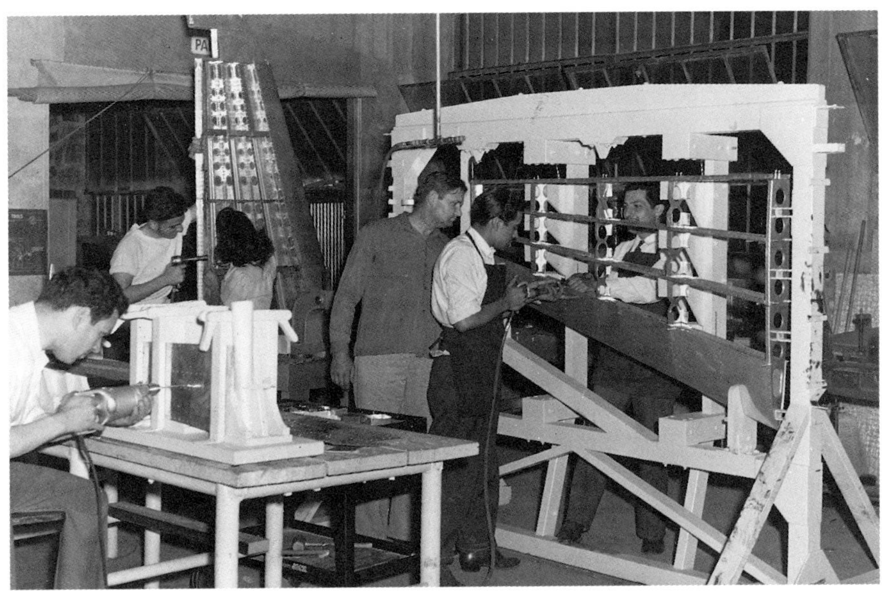

Studying aircraft metalwork offered Cisneros a chance at defense work during World War II. At right the artisan learns a new trade at Western Technical Institute.

El Paso City Lines was an essential industry, providing transportation for soldiers at Fort Bliss, refinery and smelter workers, and other vital war-related concerns. Cisneros obtained a job with that organization, remaining there until his retirement and rising to the position of painting division foreman. An especial delight he recalls from those days involved the international streetcars that crossed the downtown bridges into Juárez. These he decorated with the colorful flags of the states along the United States-Mexico border. He was thus able to express himself artistically in the daytime, and continue his studies and practicing at night. His family was beginning to grow as well, eventually including five daughters: Inéz, Nena, Irene, Patricia, Rita, and a niece, Sylvia. But art remained a consuming passion for Cisneros, and the job decision proved to be a wise one.

The association with Tom Lea also brought Cisneros into contact with Carl Hertzog, printer and book designer of El Paso, who had an immense effect on the artist's career. Cisneros did the illustrations and illuminated letters for a number of Hertzog's printing jobs: memorials to

Englishmen'." Obviously Hertzog was proud of his "find," and had told others about him—but at the age of thirty-seven José Cisneros was hardly a boy. In fact, Hertzog was only about eight years older.

In 1949, in another collaboration, Hertzog designed for Southern Methodist University Press Cleve Hallenbeck's *The Journey of Fray Marcos de Niza* with several full page illustrations by his protegé. Miss Fannie Ratchford, curator of rare books at the University of Texas, wrote Cisneros praising:

> Your illustrations for *Fray Marcos* are dramatically impressive, and delightful in details of execution, but even more I like your exquisitely historiated capitals. They breathe the spirit of Fray Marcos and his day.

And Everett DeGolyer wrote that the artist "has a knowledge of the period and a feeling for his subjects that place him easily first as an illustrator of Sixteenth Century Spanish narrative." Indeed, the illuminated initials that charmed Miss Ratchford are among the finest features of the book, which was listed by both the American Institute of Graphic Arts (out of 500 competitors) and by the American Institute of Arts and Letters as ranking among the Fifty Best Books of the Year. It also earned for the artist an award for the Best Illustrations by a Texas Artist from the Texas Institute of Letters and the Dallas Museum of Fine Arts.

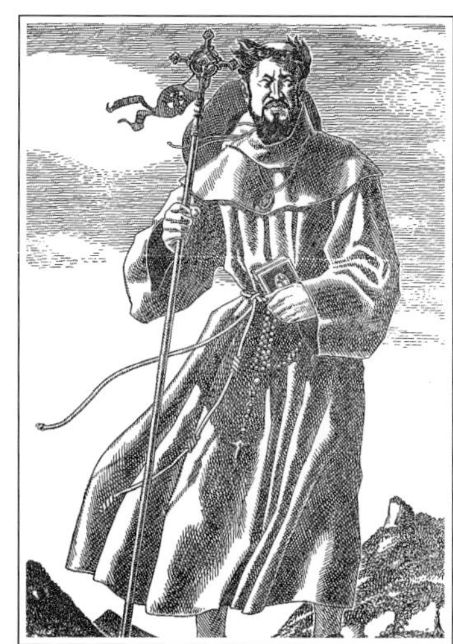

Hertzog himself noted that Cisneros had achieved a special result in depicting the book's central character with a drawing that simulated a woodcut contemporary with the only known process of producing illustrations at the time of the original book's printing. In fact, the volume was intended to resemble closely the books of the six-

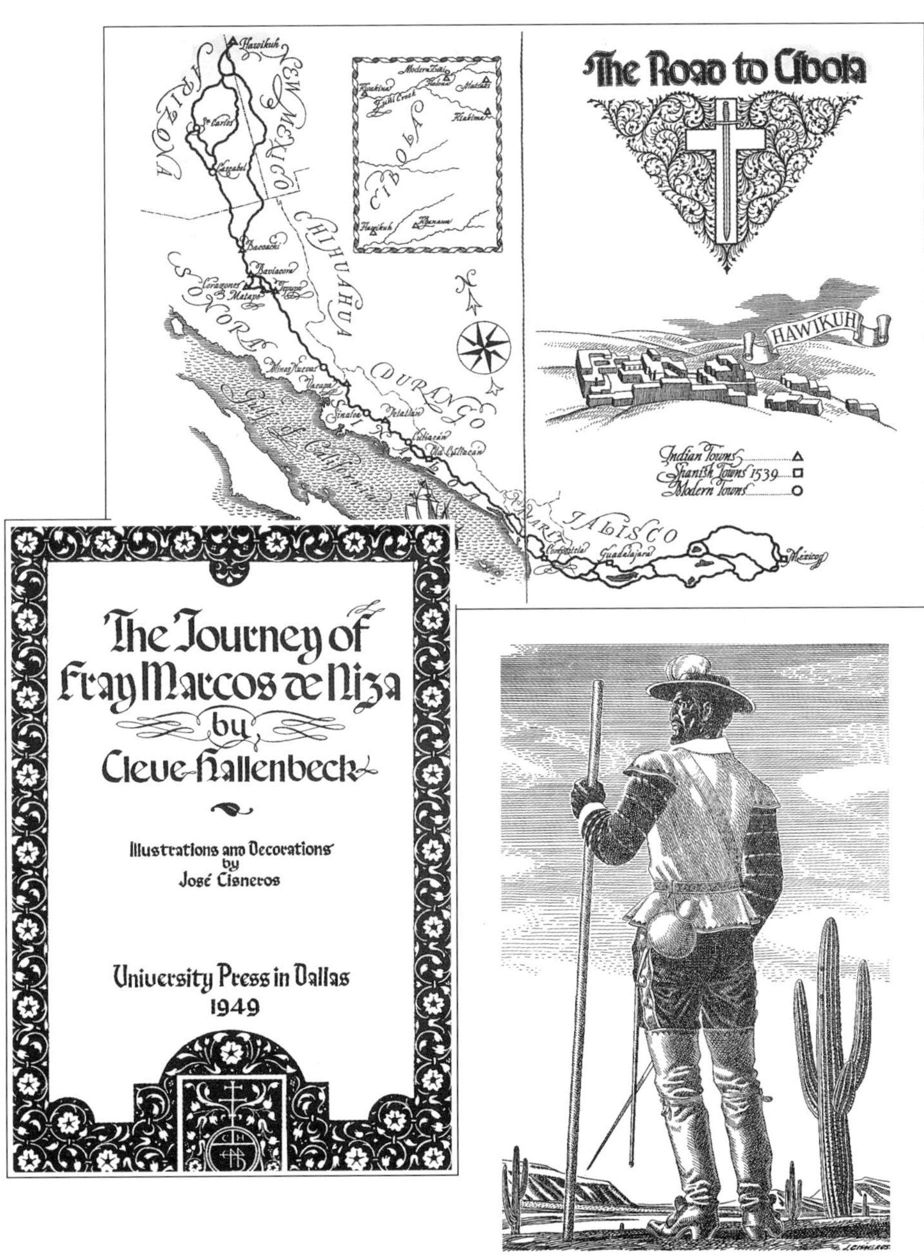

Cleve Hallenbeck's translation of The Journey of Fray Marcos de Niza, *published in 1949, included several Cisneros illustrations, and won a number of awards for Carl Hertzog, the designer, and the artist. Previous page: Fray Marcos; this page, top: endpapers included a map of the area Fray Marcos traveled, as well as a view of Hawikuh, the fabled city, object of the friar's search; bottom, left: the title page with lettering and border illustrations by Cisneros; bottom, right: Esteban de Dorantes, a guide for the friar.*

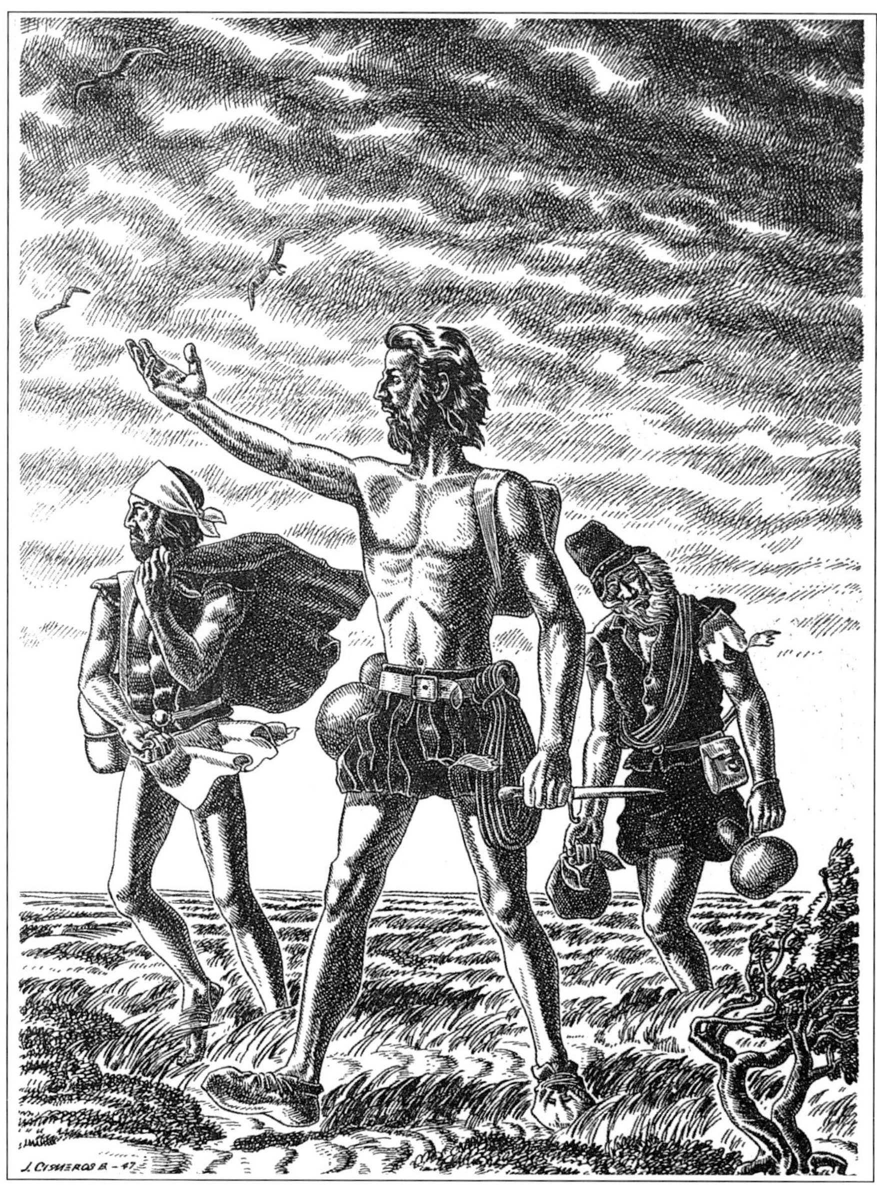

Across Aboriginal America, *the story of three stranded sailors, broke new ground in 1947 for Cisneros in collaboration with Tom Lea and Carl Hertzog, who used this scene for the dust jacket.*

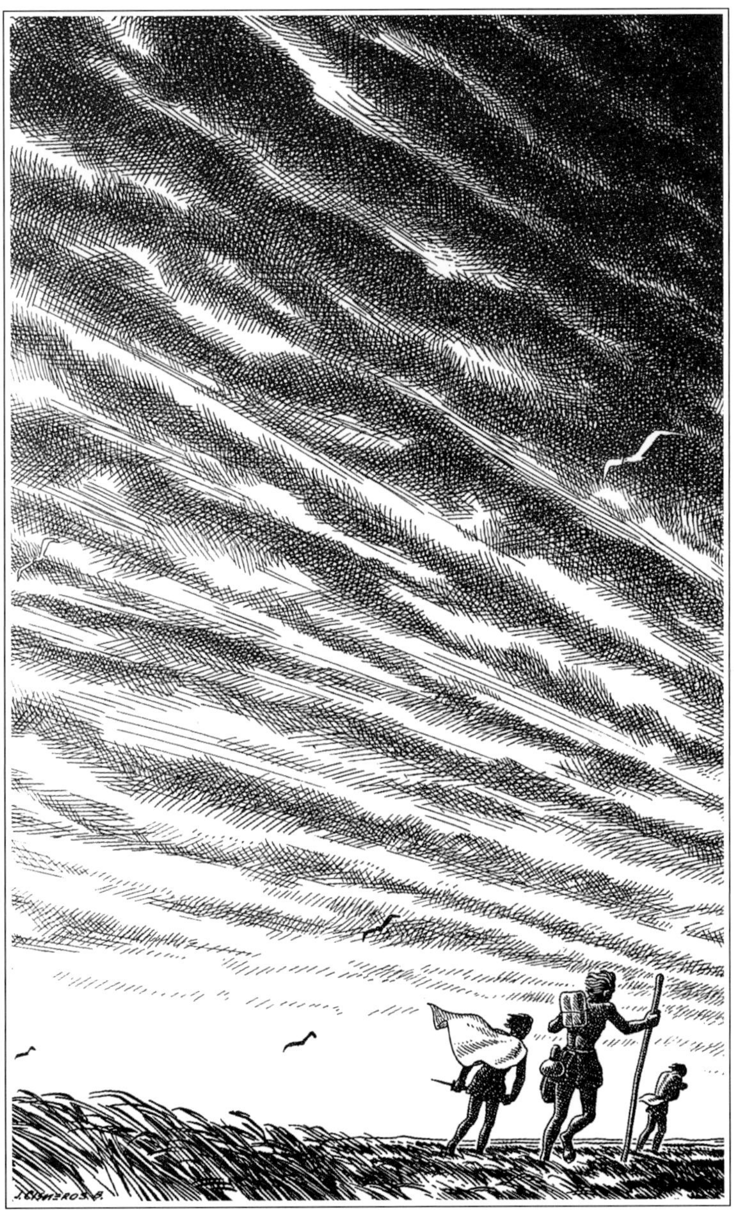

Another view of the stranded sailors served as the book's frontispiece.

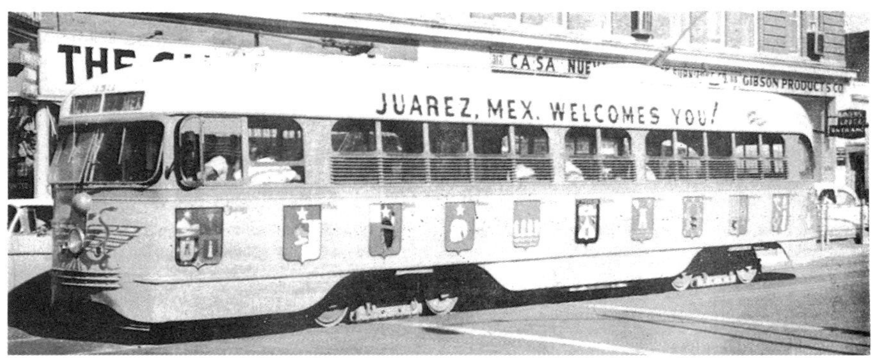

El Paso City Lines, providing transportation for El Pasoans during World War II, gave Cisneros employment within the city. This street car displays his work in the form of flags from all the states on the Texas-Mexico border.

prominent El Pasoans, as well as historical scenes and decorations for a host of proclamations and presentations. One memorable production with Hertzog was a National Music Week program featuring a series of pictures of prominent musical composers by Cisneros. Hertzog could locate only widely differing pictures of the musical greats, and he wanted a top quality production with comparable illustrations (a favorite quotation of his was "Perfection is no trifle, but trifles make perfection"). With such perfection in mind, he hired José Cisneros for the project.

The artist had by this time added calligraphy to the range of his applications of talent, and as usual, had learned the process by himself. In essence, he drew the letters, rather than following the stroke patterns employed by beginning calligraphers who have the advantage of instruction books to follow.

Widely known among art lovers in the Southwest is the story of an outstanding early production that involved Cisneros. Tom Lea and Carl Hertzog were conferring on a book Hertzog was to design and publish, a facsimile reprint of an account of three marooned sailors whose story appeared in Hakluyt's *Voyages*. In 1947, Dallas book collector and oil geologist Everett DeGolyer wanted Carl Hertzog to use his printing and design skills to produce a memorable volume for book lovers. The project, Lea said, called for the sort of illustrations Cisneros had proved himself master of, fine steel pen work. As Lea and Hertzog stood outside the latter's shop discussing the book, Cisneros walked by on his way home to lunch and was drawn into the conference. The resulting work, *Across Aboriginal America: The Journey of Three Englishmen Across Texas in 1568*, featured dust jacket, map, and frontispiece by Cisneros. It is a classic, and is widely acknowledged as being among the best books ever published in Texas. Cisneros recognizes the book as one of his most significant productions.

Hertzog wrote DeGolyer, telling him:

> I found a Mexican artist who does gorgeous pen drawings of old Spanish historical subjects. . . . His technique is good, and his research surprisingly accurate.

Hertzog was given permission to proceed, but Tom Lea did not approve of Cisneros's first draft of the three wandering sailors. They had been set ashore in 1568 near Tampico when English privateer John Hawkins met a near-disaster that reduced his formidable fleet to one overloaded vessel. Lea suggested a new illustration, with vast Texas plains and an immense empty sky dwarfing the men, and Cisneros's version following that suggestion became the frontispiece. Hertzog liked the original picture, so it was used as the dust jacket. Cisneros also redrew the original map from Hakluyt's volume, in a memorable style appropriate to the 16th century, complete with monsters in the deeps. Published in a limited edition of 700 copies, the book sold for five dollars; in 1977 a bookseller's catalog listed a copy at $70, and in 1983 it was offered for $195. Recently it was advertised for $500.

Of related interest is the 1948 invitation Hertzog received to address museum staff and journalism students at Texas Technological College on the subject of fine printing and book design and their value to lovers of the past. Dr. William Curry Holden, who tendered the invitation, insisted that Hertzog include in his presentation "an account of your discovery of the Mexican boy who did the illustrations for 'The Three

teenth century; Hertzog had followed a book printed in Spain in 1537 to get the "feel" of the era. Author Hallenbeck had drawn a series of maps for the volume, but when he saw Cisneros's versions he approved the artist's cartography and lettering without hesitation, recognizing the superior period design therein. In sending a copy of the book for review by *Time*, Hertzog wrote "I am glad to send you the book because it shows the work of José Cisneros, a Mexican artist of unusual accomplishment, entirely self-taught." The drawing of Esteban drew some comments from critics, reflecting a running argument over the slave's ethnicity; some insisted he was a Moor, while others noted that the text called him *El Negro*. Historian F. W. Hodge thought that the slave was too dressed up, thinking he should have been naked or clad in rags—but Cisneros asserts that Hodge was confusing what the slave would have looked like when he was a fugitive with Cabeza de Vaca with what he would have been as a guide to Fray Marcos' expedition several years later.

In 1990 a new edition of the classic was issued by Southern Methodist University Press, a facsimile-plus, with both the original and new Cisneros illustrations of the central figures in the story and a new introduction by Dr. David Weber, a historian who praises the accuracy and skill of Cisneros's historical art at every opportunity.

In many ways the joint work of José Cisneros and Carl Hertzog begun in the year 1950 was the most important project the two ever developed. The *Flowsheet*, the yearbook for the (then) Texas Western College, was being planned by faculty member Hertzog for Dean of Student Life Judson Williams, who asked Hertzog to supply a theme for David Cohen, the student editor. As Betty Ligon, longtime El Paso journalist and book reviewer, tells the story,

> The result was an outstanding piece of artistic and historical work. The theme, "Our Spanish Heritage," was selected for reasons which Hertzog delineated: "First, we had it; second, half the names on the campus were Spanish; and third, I knew a guy who could

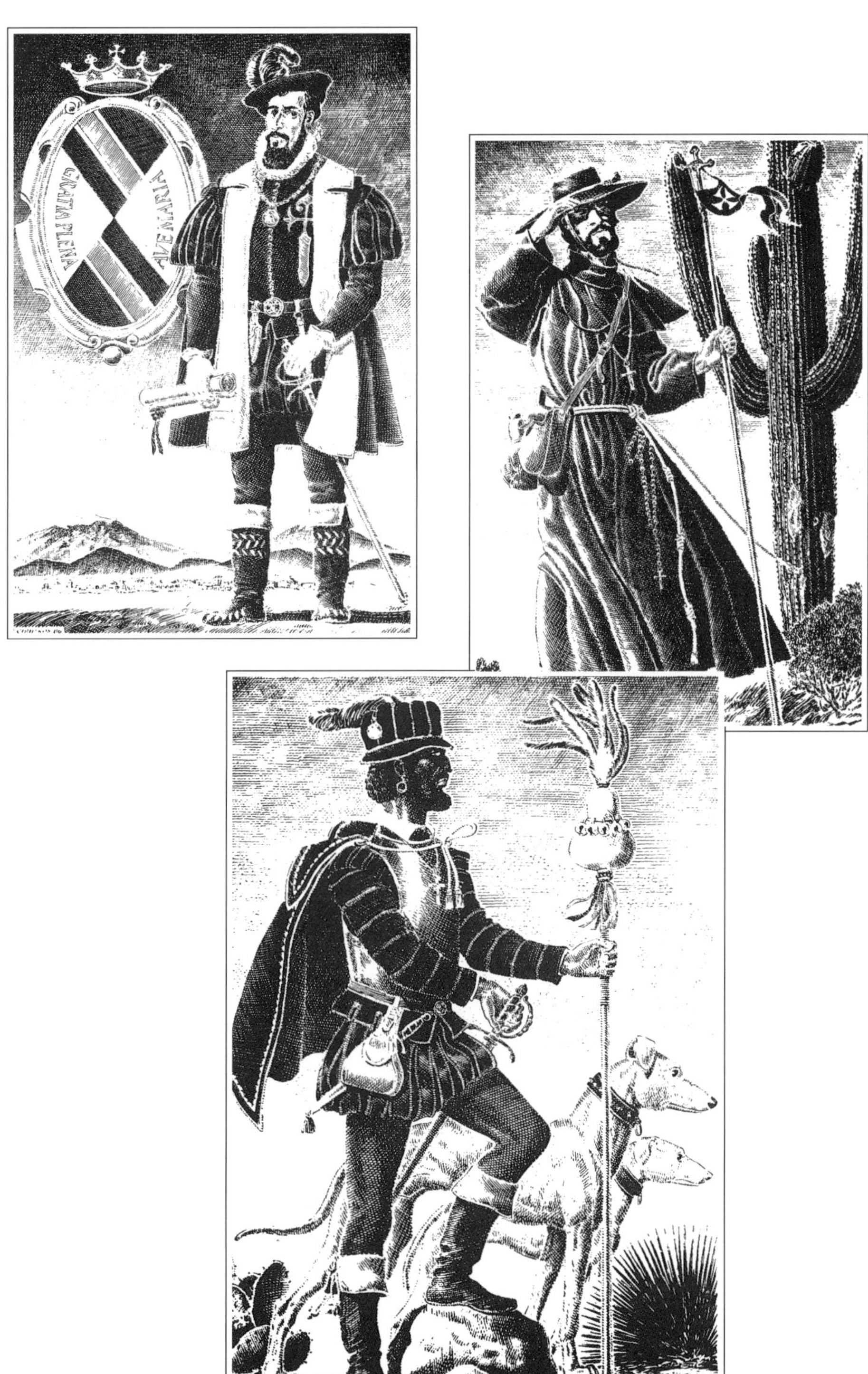

David Weber's reissue of The Journey of Fray Marcos de Niza *(1987) included all the old art work plus a new set. (Courtesy of the editor) Top left: Viceroy Antonio de Mendoza, who sent the friar on his search for the Seven Cities of Gold; top right: Fray Marcos; bottom: Esteban the Moor.*

> make the drawings."
>
> The "guy" turned out to be José Cisneros, who had been discovered and had been encouraged by Hertzog for several years and was fast becoming one of the Southwest's most popular illustrators.
>
> Cisneros quickly was charmed with the theme, and soon presented a series of drawings for the book's division pages—but he had changed his style:
>
> "I expected his usual pen and ink style, but was surprised that his first pictures were done in light pencil which wouldn't reproduce well," recalls Hertzog. "He then went to see Tom Lea who showed José how to bear down to make stronger lines."

Nonetheless, Hertzog noted that Cisneros's trying a new style was indicative of his desire to grow as an artist.

Hertzog wrote a few lines to go with each drawing in the *Flowsheet*, but was astounded when the annual was dedicated to him—with complimentary text written by colleague Tom Lea. The annual, unusual for a college yearbook, soon became a collector's item of great value, and the illustrations (with the addition of a Cisneros map of the Southwest) served as the catalyst for the first-ever publication of what was to become Texas Western Press. With extended text by Francis Fugate, illustrations by José Cisneros, and artful book design and printing by Carl Hertzog, *The Spanish Heritage of the Southwest* (1952) is among the most distinguished productions ever to come out of the area.

Hertzog employed an unusual method in creating the cover, smoothing an adobe block with a carpenter's plane and then varnishing the surface; with the application of an ink roller, he was able to produce a lithograph-like surface print. He enjoyed relating that a curious configuration on the cover print was discovered to be from a lump of horse manure in the adobe—he first time, he asserted, that such matter was to be found on the *outside* of a book!

After this beginning of the fledgling press, the Cisneros association with designer/printer Hertzog led quite naturally to a long series of

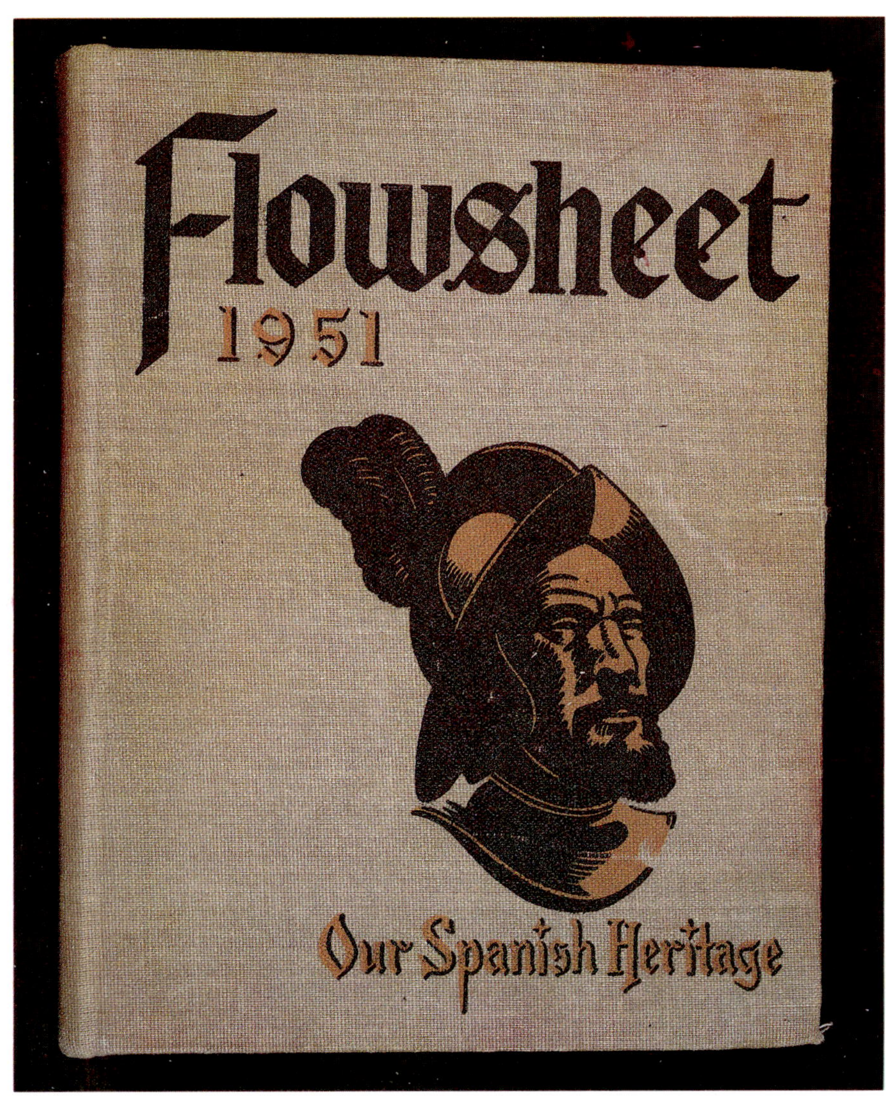

This cover, from the 1951 Texas Western College yearbook, was one of the most important items produced by the collaboration of Carl Hertzog, Tom Lea, and José Cisneros.

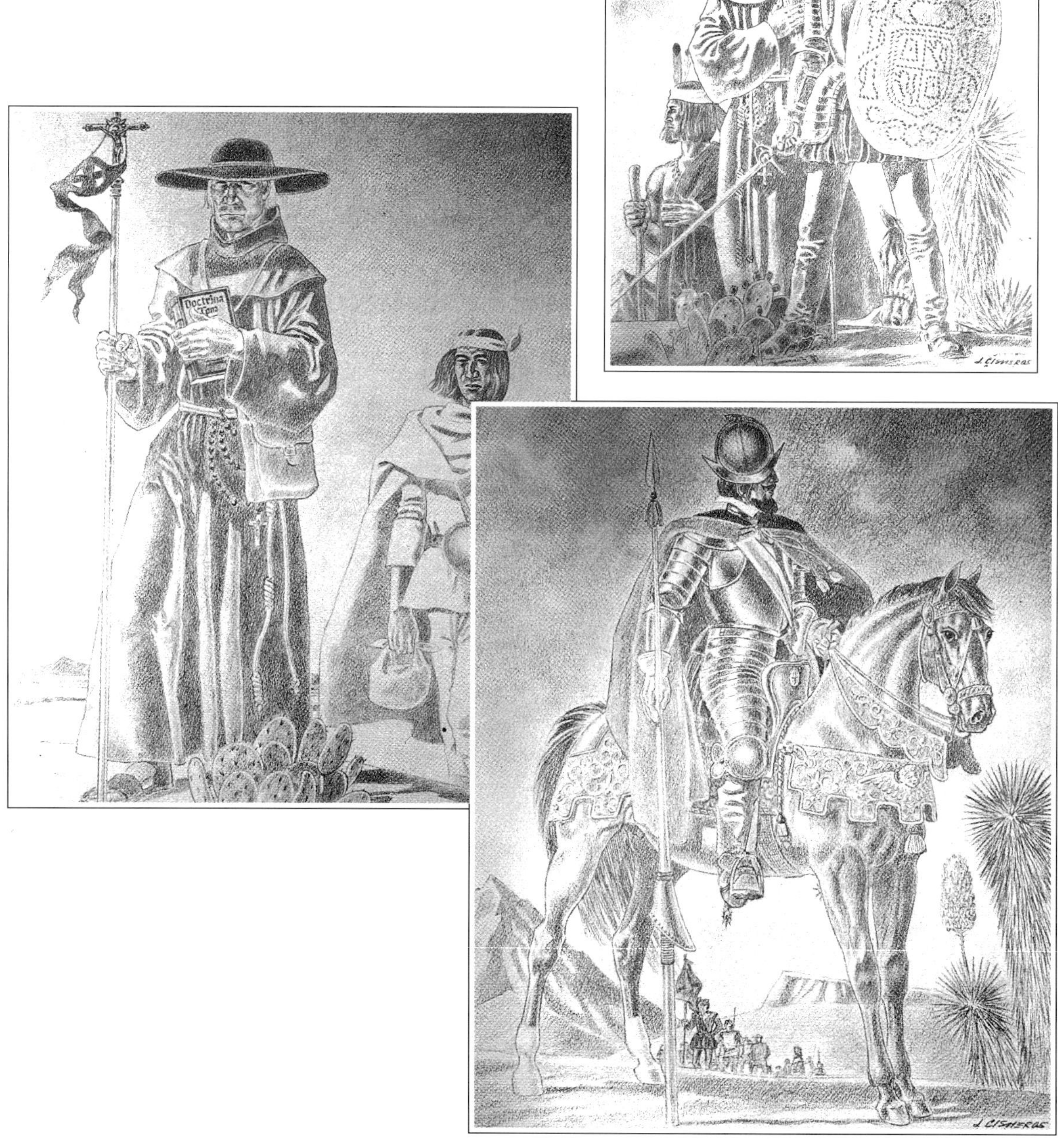

The 1950 Flowsheet, *the yearbook for Texas Western College, reflected a wide range of Spanish culture and history; the illustrations were later made into the first publication of Texas Western Press,* The Spanish Heritage of the Southwest. *Top right:* Elements of the Conquest, *left:* the Seeds of Christianity, *bottom right:* The Beginnings of Government.

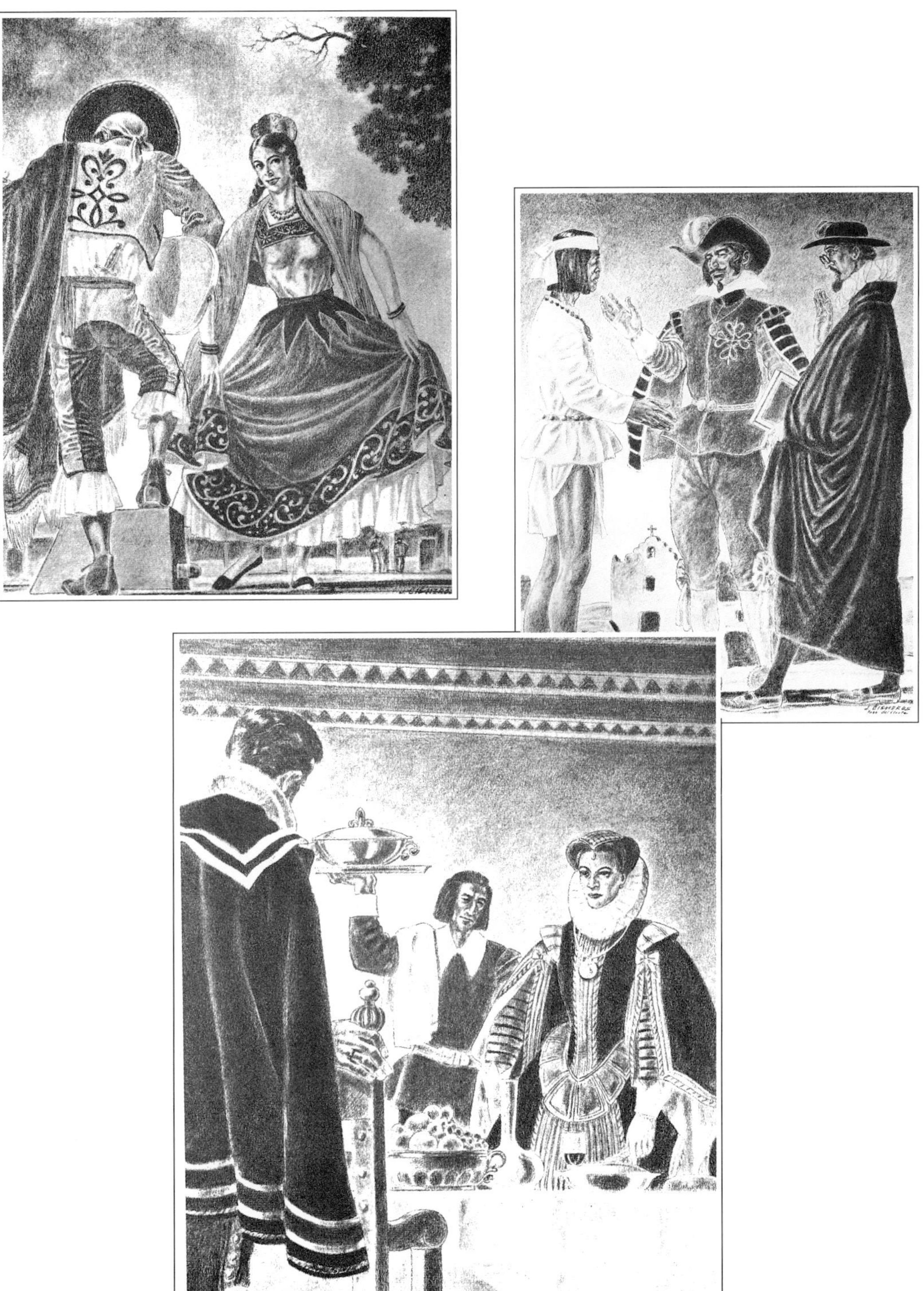

The 1950 Flowsheet
Top left: The Victory of the Fiesta; *right:* The Aftermath of Conquest; *bottom:* The Flavor of the Food.

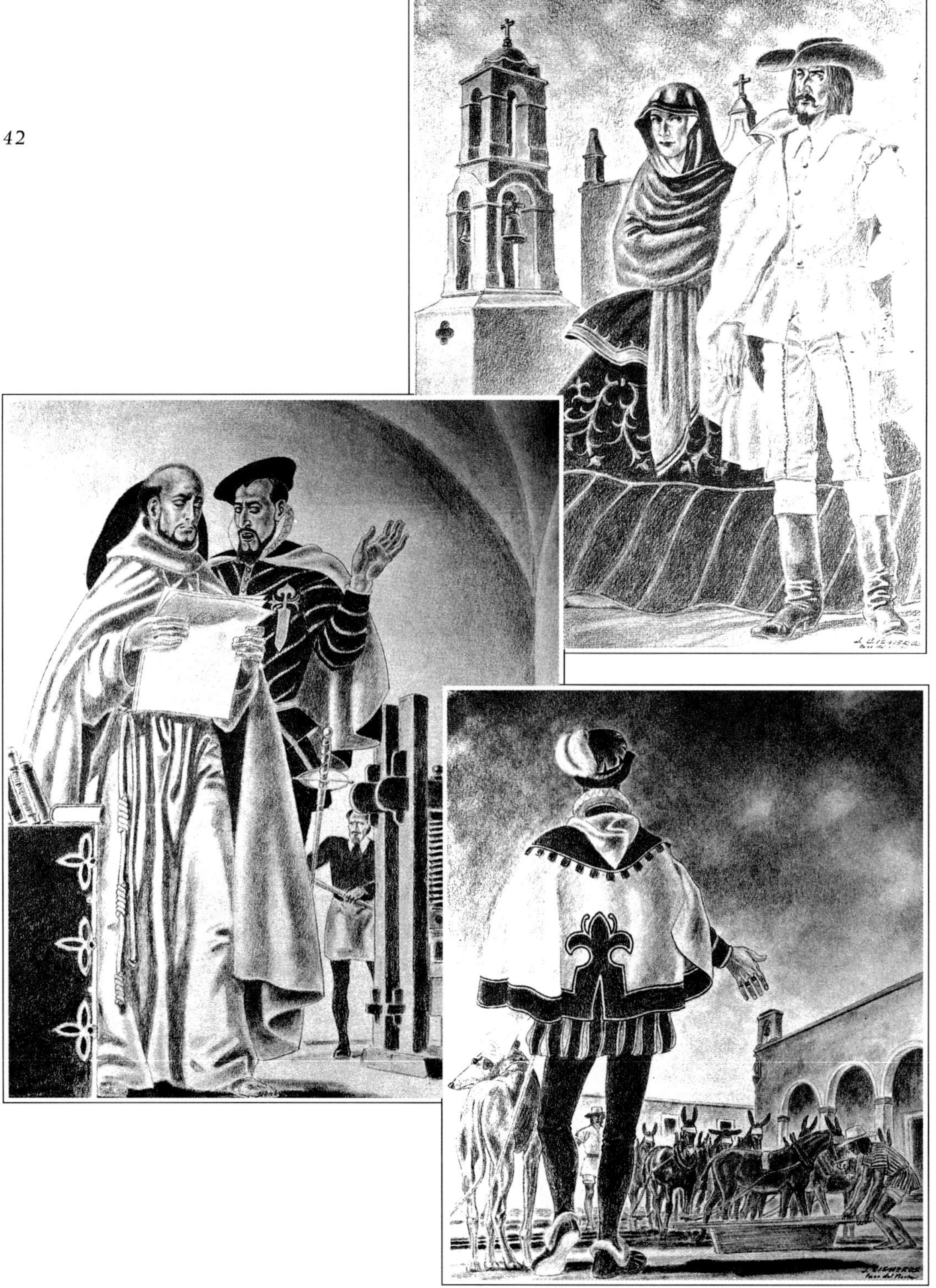

The 1950 Flowsheet
Top right: Building the Churches; *left:* Telling the Adventures; *bottom right:* The Glitter of Gold

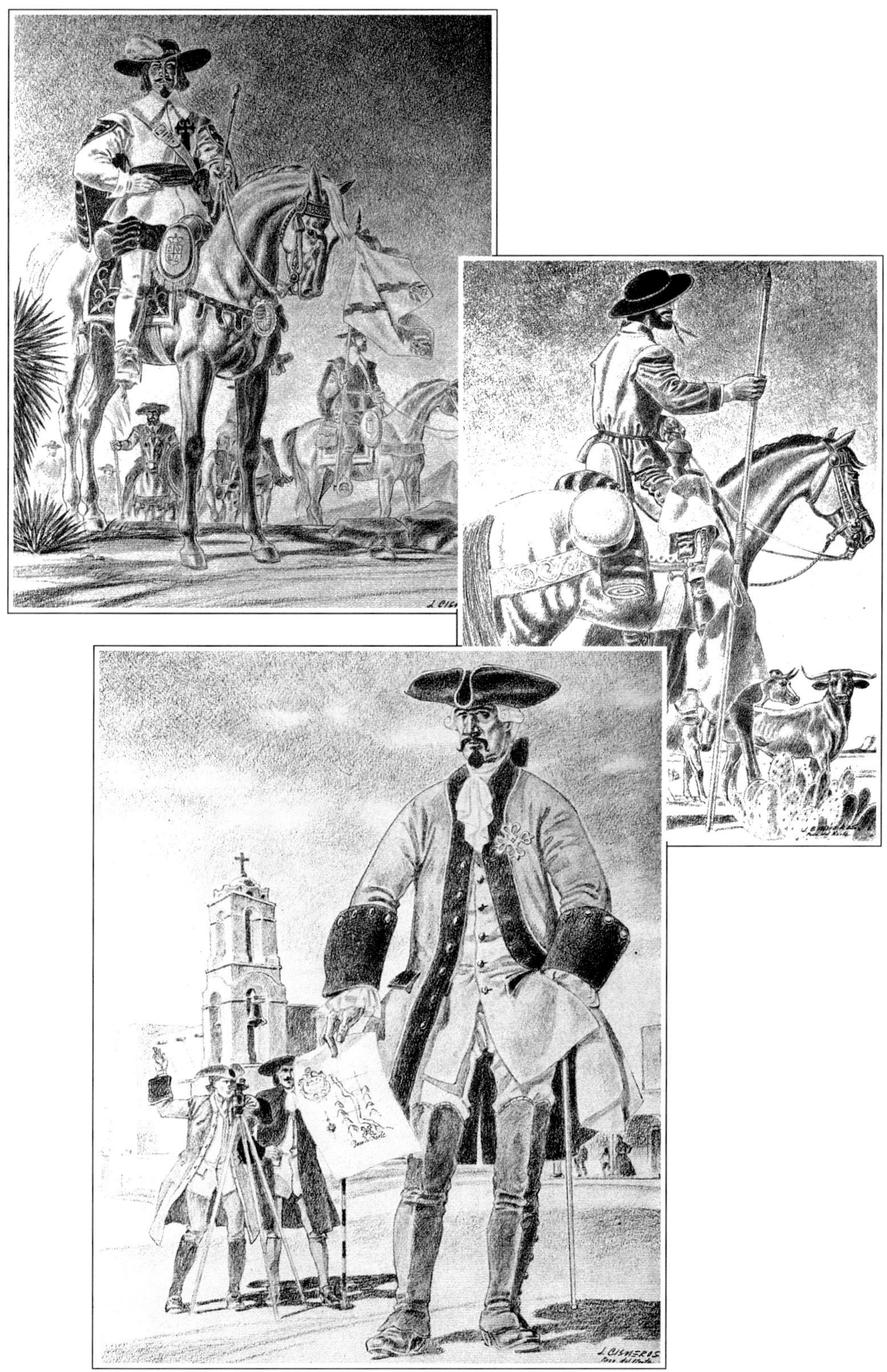

The 1950 Flowsheet
Top left: The Point of the Sword; *center:* The Coming of Cattle; *bottom:* Naming the Land

collaborations, especially with the productions of Texas Western Press. The first was *Bells Over Texas* by Bessie Lee Fitzhugh, winner of the 1955 Summerfield G. Roberts Award for the best book published on the Republic of Texas, as well as the Dallas Museum of Fine Arts award as best designed book of the year. *El Sal del Rey* by Wallace Hawkins came soon after, with *Frontier Newspaper: The El Paso Times* by John Judy Middagh in 1958. Repeatedly the artist's skills were called into action with the wide variety of books Hertzog designed, particularly since the focus of the Press was upon materials related to the El Paso Southwest, so dear to Cisneros's heart. And even after Hertzog retired officially in 1978, the close association of Cisneros with the Press and with the University of Texas at El Paso has continued unabated.

The Southwestern Studies series, which for years carried a cover map of the region from the pen of Cisneros, also devoted two books to his work: No. 30, *Riders of the Border: A Selection of Thirty Drawings*, celebrating the twenty-fifth anniversary of Texas Western Press which had begun with Cisneros art, and No. 52, *Faces of the Borderlands: Twenty-One Drawings*. Several classics published by the Press have been illustrated by Cisneros, including C. L. Sonnichsen's *El Paso Salt War* (1961) and his two-volume *Pass of the North* (1968, 1980), and of course Cisneros's own *Riders Across the Centuries: Horsemen of the Spanish Borderlands* (1984), winner of several prestigious awards, including the Western Heritage Award from the National Cowboy Hall of Fame. Incidentally, because of a binder's error, 200 collector's items of this work exist: an ancient Spanish spur stamped on the cover was printed upside down, on a work created by an artist known for being a perfectionist.

But Cisneros has become far more than a "house illustrator" for Texas Western Press. His historical accuracy and skill at illustration have brought commissions from a wide field of publishers and authors. Just as Carl Hertzog designed publications for other publishers and presses, José Cisneros illustrated literally hundreds of items, often in association with Hertzog. Bibliographer Jeff Dykes in his 1975 *Fifty Great Western Illustrators: A Bibliographic Checklist* lists 197 items, chiefly books, illustrated

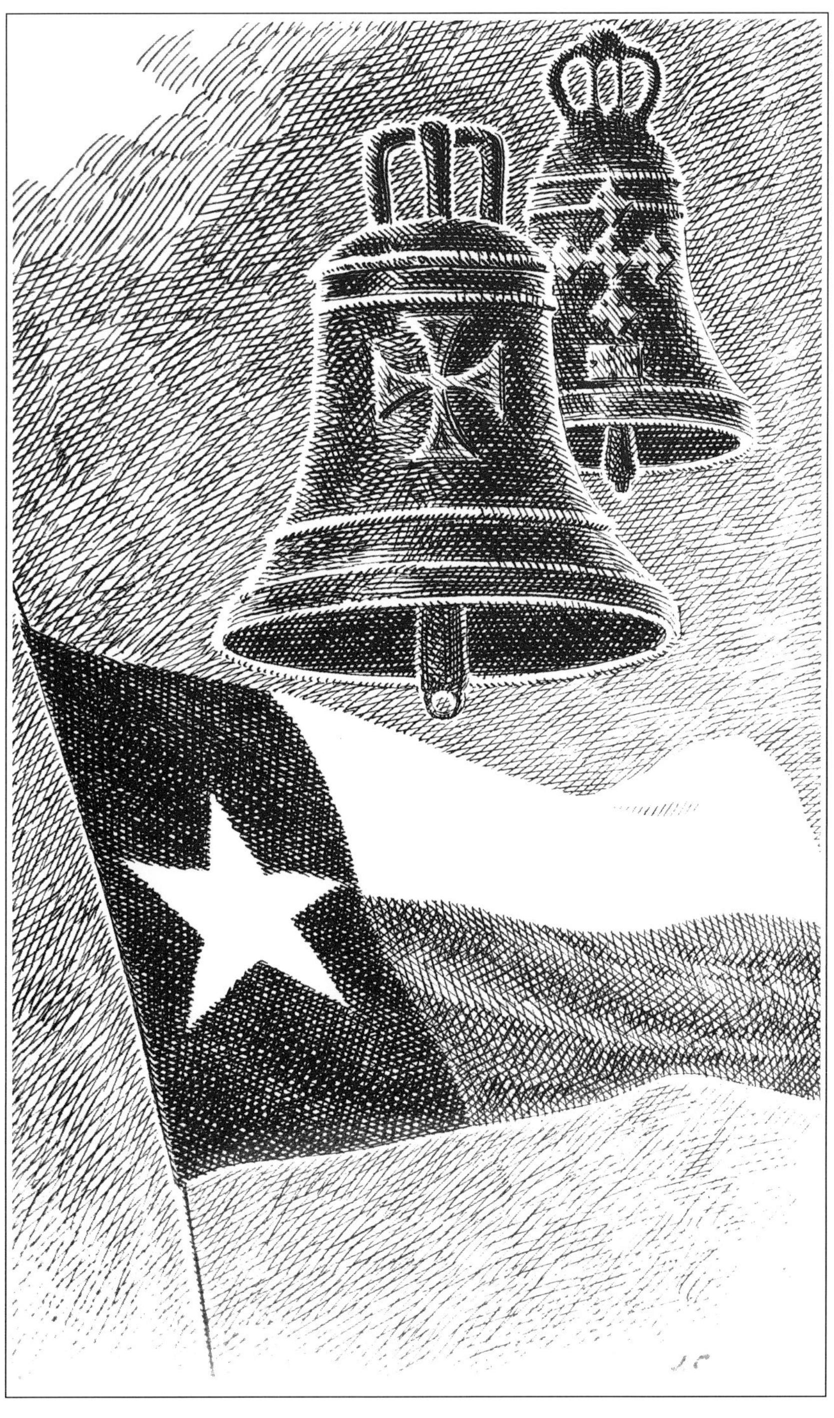

Bells Over Texas *(1955) was an early publication by Carl Hertzog with book jacket by Cisneros.*

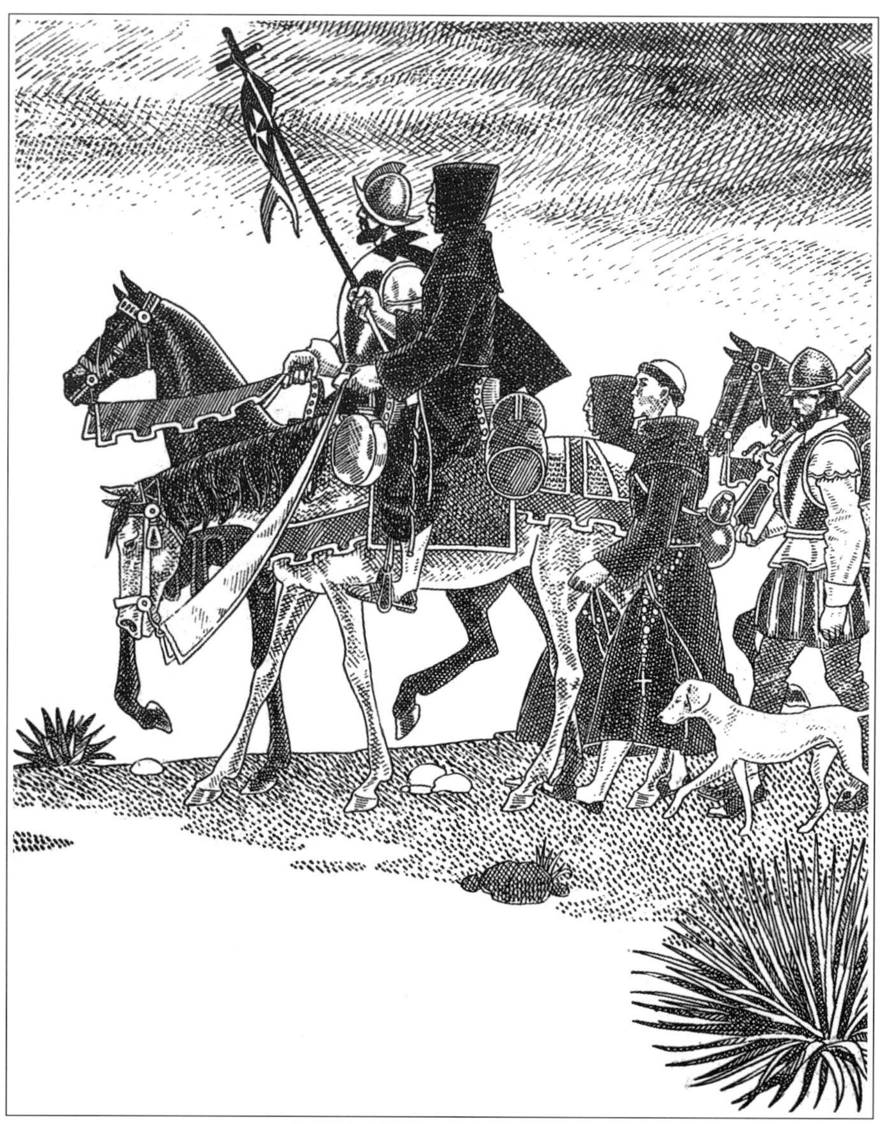

First published in El León Juarense *about 1940, this scene is one of Cisneros's favorite subjects, the coming of the Spanish to the Southwest. Here Francis Vasquez de Coronado leads missionaries into the area in 1540.*

in whole or in part by Cisneros, including twenty-eight Southwestern Studies. Such a checklist if prepared in 1993 would doubtless be double that number, with Texas Western Press publications adding considerably to the total.

El Pasoan Francis Fugate (who augmented the text for *The Spanish Heritage of the Southwest*) told a tale of an unusual collaboration between Cisneros and Hertzog. The famed book designer was producing J. Evetts Haley's *Fort Concho* for the San Angelo *Standard-Times* when a problem arose. Fugate had made up the pages for the first sixteen-page signature of the work and pulled proofs when he noticed that the illustrator, Harold Bugbee, had committed an anachronism. The artist was drawing a view of the building of the fort, and the copy required a soldier pushing a wheelbarrow, so Bugbee looked out the window and copied such a vehicle from life, a steel, riveted, balloon-tired modern wheelbarrow that did not exist back in the nineteenth century when the fort's construction actually took place. "That ain't gonna make it," Fugate told Hertzog, and so Cisneros was called into the breach. He drew a substitute barrow modeled after one from the correct period, which was then inserted into the Bugbee picture and all was under control. "José saved our lives," Fugate said. Incidentally, two proofs of the wrong wheelbarrow had been made, so Hertzog (who loved to collect printing rarities) bound them into two copies of the book, "The Wheelbarrow Edition," to add to his collection, and to the Fugate collection as well.

Another Hertzog/Cisneros joint production came about in 1948 when the North Texas Publishing Company of Paris, Texas, wanted to honor the long-time editor of *The Paris News*, A. W. Neville, on his eighty-fourth birthday with a collection of his writings in that paper over the previous sixty years. Cisneros was commissioned to do the endpapers—a historic scene recalling the days when the Red River was blocked for many miles by a huge log jam. And each of the twenty-six chapters was to begin with a unique Cisneros illustration, in the form of a triangle, as Hertzog specified, "high on the left side." Years later Hertzog recalled, his mischievous eyes twinkling, that he had anticipated Cisneros's running into problems sticking to that format, especially when the subject of the chapter was the coming of the railroads. But Cisneros was equal to the task, and every chapter heading fits the demand Hertzog laid on him. *The Red River Valley, Then and Now* is a treasure, especially for those who know the story of the Hertzog challenge. The book had another significance, as Hertzog once pointed out: it was Cisneros's first true experience as an illustrator, in a non-Western, non-Hispanic book.

As planned, the book was presented to Neville on his birthday, in a gala affair attended by hundreds of well-wishers, including Carl Hertzog and José Cisneros. According to Hertzog, who was obviously proud of his illustrator, it was a new and almost overwhelming experience for the artist:

> The remarkable fact is how he could continue to read and study when he has no one to talk to—no companionship along the cultural lines he pursues. . . . Cisneros illustrated this book without seeing the country or the people, except for a few poor photos and clippings. He got his ideas from the manuscript. . . . I went to Paris (Texas) for Neville's birthday on which the book was published, and 100 newsmen gathered to pay tribute. I took Cisneros with me and both he and I were amazed. As he met people in Dallas and Austin who could appreciate his plans for historical research and know the references and books he had studied, he opened up and expressed himself beautifully in English. He didn't know he could do it. He'd never had a chance before.
>
> In the Dallas Art Museum . . . José saw the work of painters he knew through his own books but never expected to see their work. Standing before a Goya the tears streamed. He couldn't eat any lunch.

After Dallas and Paris, the pair went to Austin, with Hertzog introducing Cisneros to book lovers, librarians, writers, and others who were impressed with the budding artist. Hertzog continues:

> In Austin at the Library we had an elegant exhibit of our work in glass cases [in the Stark Library of the Rare Books Collection] and José got to talk with eminent historians who were as impressed as he was. He picked up some missing links in his research on the costume of the horseman (Cortez to Cowboys) which may get done in the next five years.

Among those Cisneros met in Austin was historian Carlos Castañeda, and commissions for illustration came for two of Dr. Castañeda's series on the history of the Catholic Church in the New World: *Our Catholic Heritage in Texas*, and *The Church in Texas Since Independence, 1836-1950* (vols 6, 1950, and 7, 1958).

Another result of Cisneros's visit to Austin with Hertzog was a connection with J. Frank Dobie, editor of the publications of the Texas Folklore Society. Cisneros drawings were standard features in such annual publications for several years. In 1951, volume 24, *The Healer of Los Olmos*, had a Cisneros drawing on the title page, plus four other illustrations of Mexican folk themes. The 1954, volume 26, was a special edition reprinting the best from the first quarter century of publications, including six drawings by Cisneros. And when James Bratcher brought out his *Analytical Index to Publications of the Texas Folklore Society, Volumes 1-36*, he reprinted several of Cisneros's best drawings for the society, besides commissioning an endpaper map of the Southwest with forty-eight scenes of familiar folk characters and tales ranging from Arizona to Louisiana and reflecting several cultural groups.

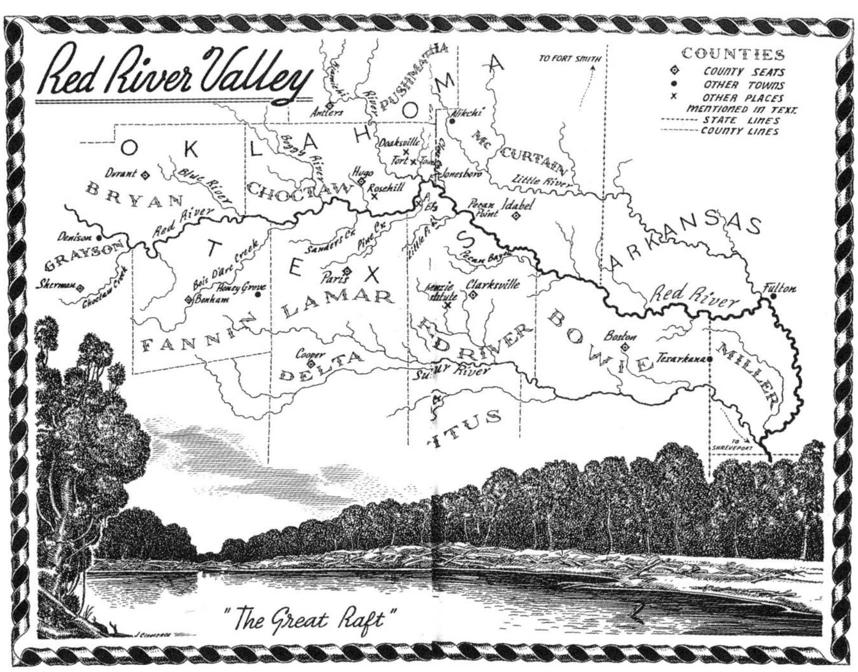

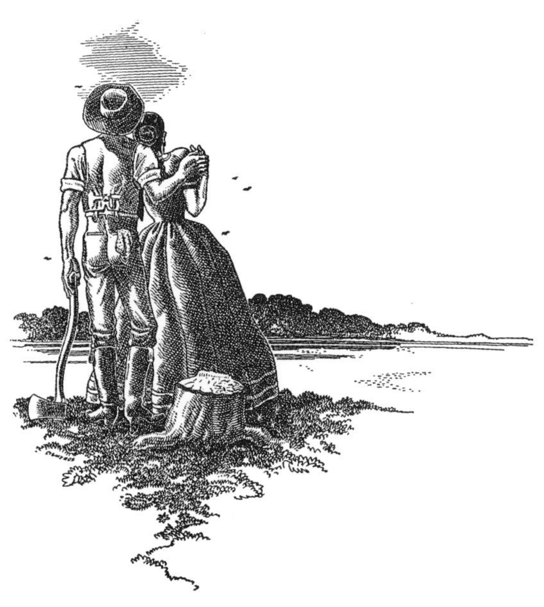

The Red River Valley, Then and Now (1948) *took Cisneros's skills outside the Spanish Southwest for the first time, with a map of the Red River area and chapter headings to Carl Hertzog's specification. Top: Map of the Red River Valley; bottom: Settlers in the rich farmland.*

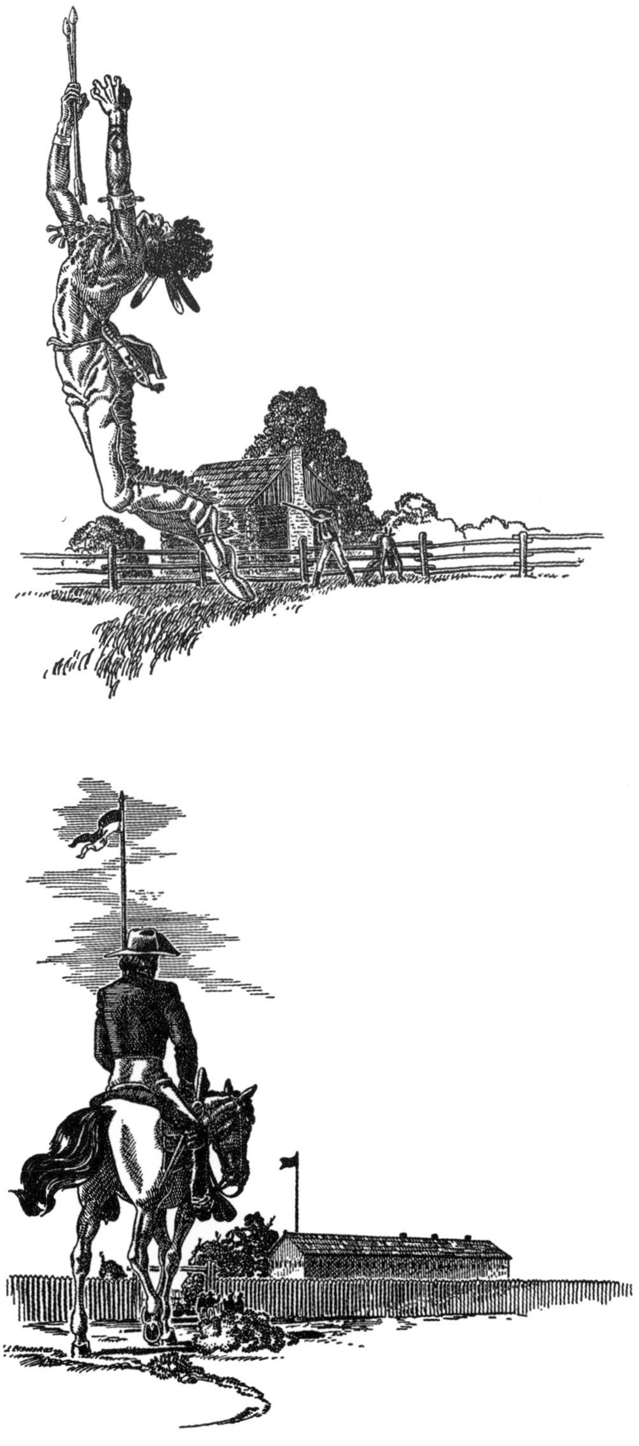

The Red River Valley, Then and Now
Top: Indian troubles; bottom: Fort Towson, bulwark against the Indians,

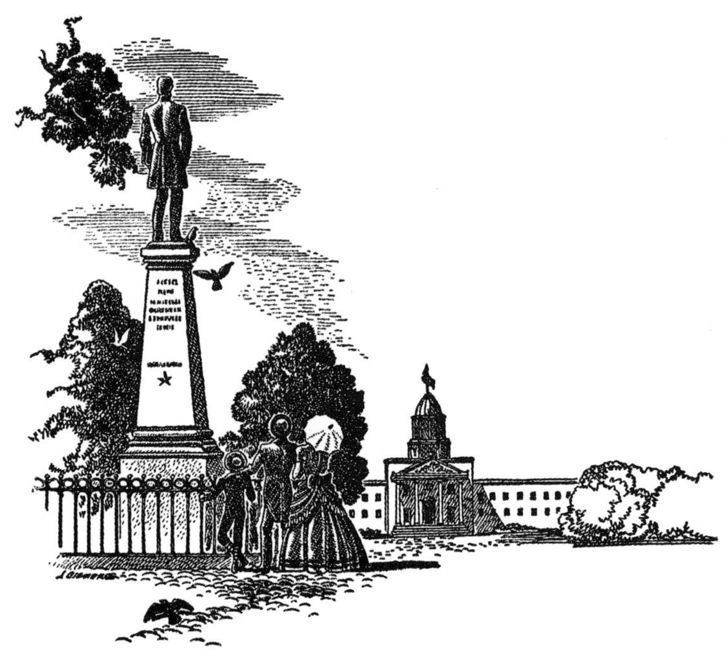

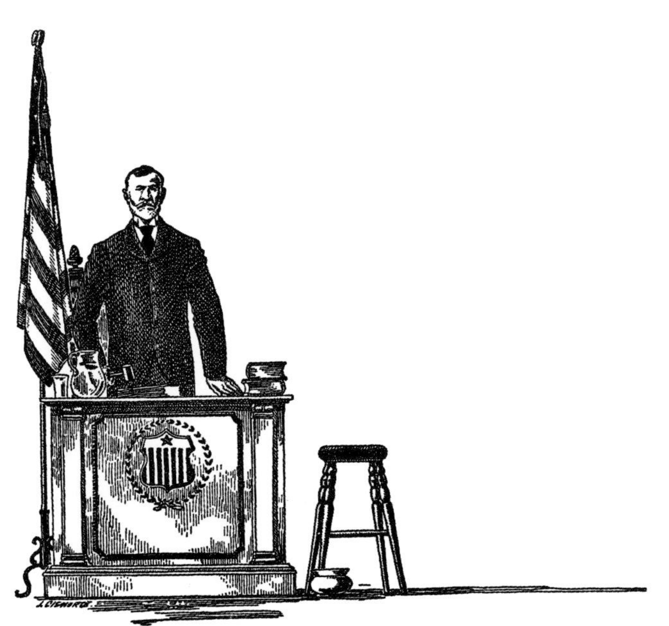

The Red River Valley, Then and Now
Top: The Paris Federal Court; *bottom:* Monuments to Eminent Men.

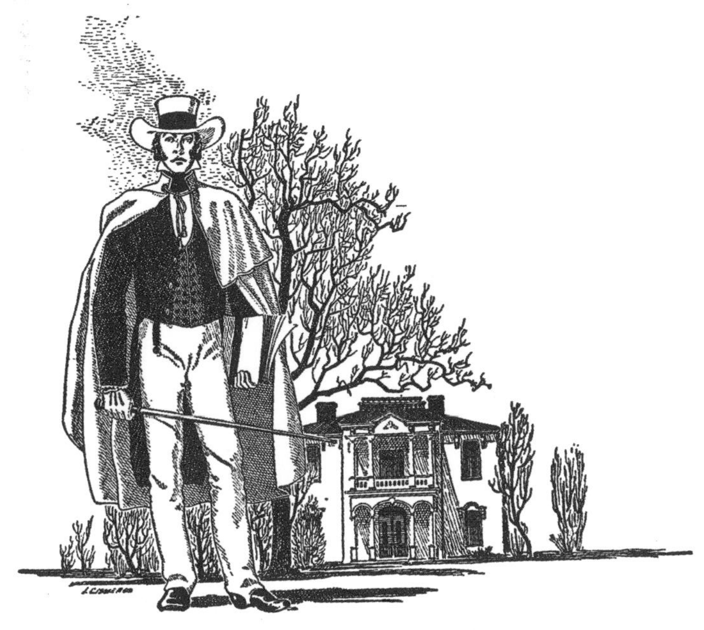

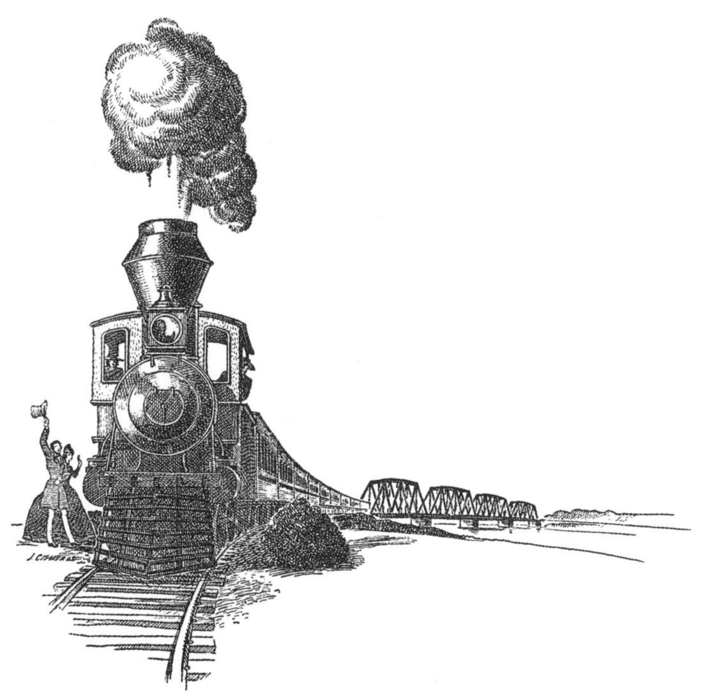

The Red River Valley, Then and Now
Top: Lawyers—a necessity in a new territory; *bottom:* The Coming of the Railroads.

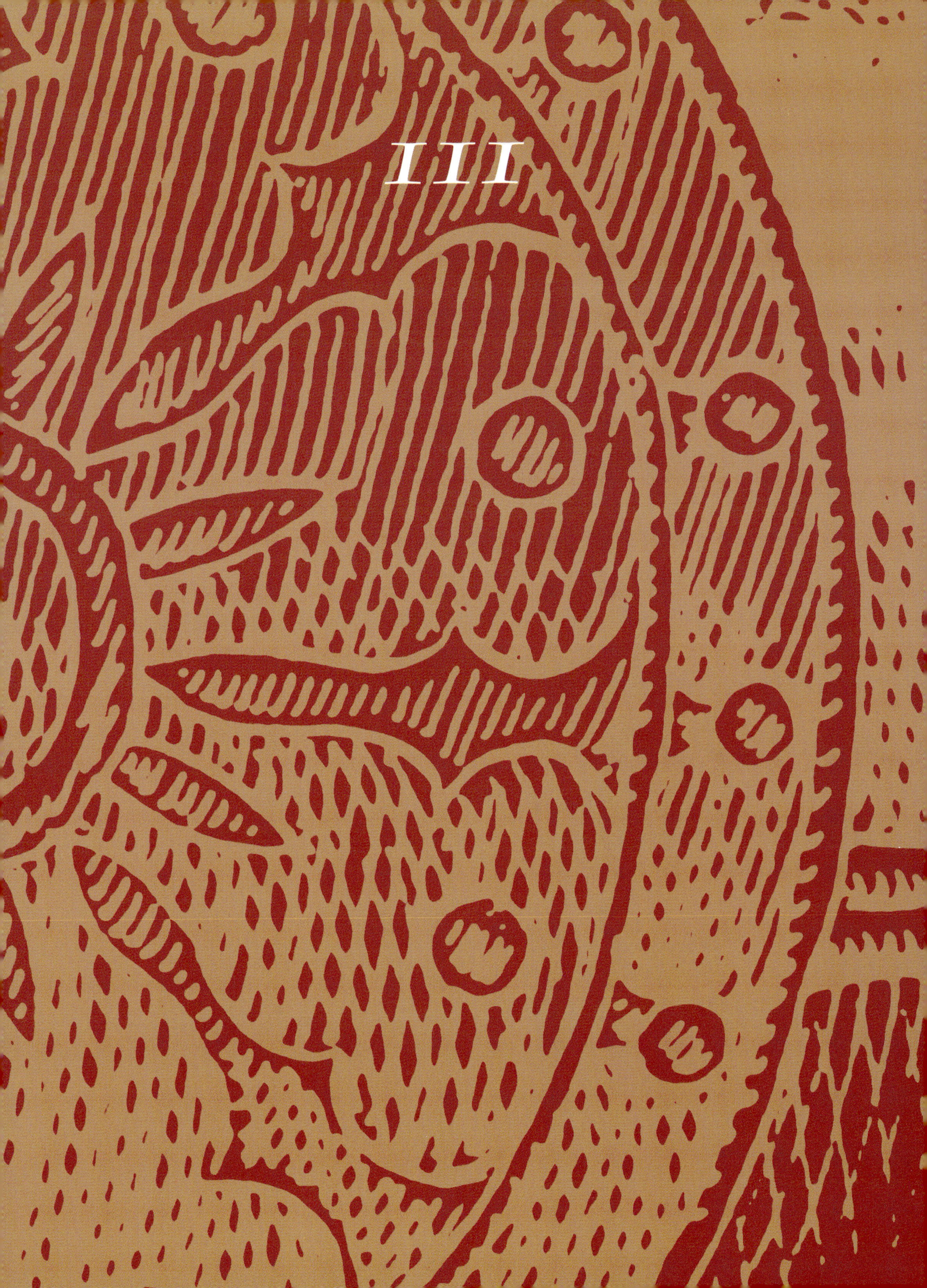

III

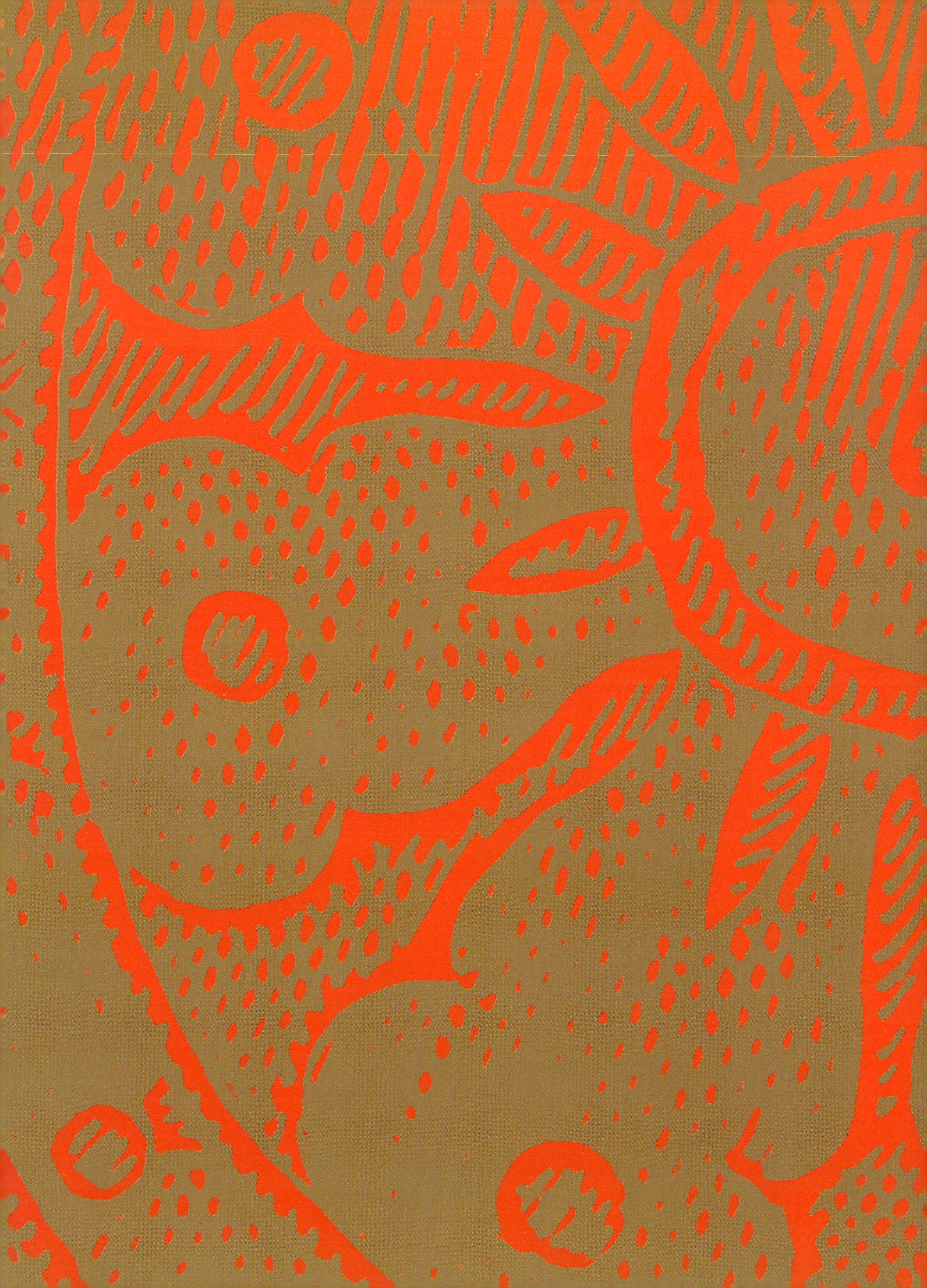

III

Historian With a Pen

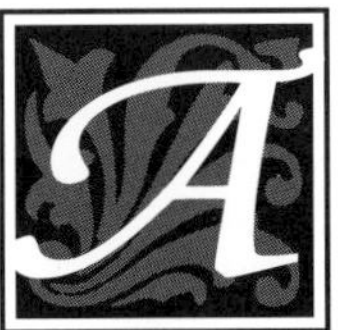

s the reputation of José Cisneros as an illustrator grew, he had a wide number of opportunities to use his talent—in illustrating books and magazines, in creating logos and letterheads for firms and organizations, and in broadening the scope of his artistry generally—often in ways he had not anticipated.

One of the most unusual directions that his talent took him was in the area of wood carving. He had designed religious art, particularly, for artisans to reproduce in wood—designs he drew for his own parish church, for example. But when he designed a pair of plaques for a church in Las Cruces, New Mexico, and the woodworker departed from the design, Cisneros asked the patron to retrieve the wood for him. He bought the tools he needed and taught himself—as might have been expected—to finish the job right. Other woodworking tasks came his way, and he continued employing the new skill occasionally—which he said was almost the same as drawing, except that it took more time because of his initial unfamiliarity with the tools. While he was in the mood to use the medium of wood, he made a wooden plaque that hangs beside the front door of his house with the simple announcement *The Cisneros* carved in antique lettering. One might be inclined to wonder if memories of his artisan-carpenter father, Don Fernando, were not present in his mind as he worked with wood.

Wood carving techniques came to his aid in another project, making a model in plaster of Paris for the casting of a bronze plaque that greets tourists and El Pasoans who stop at Scenic Point on Mount Franklin's Scenic Drive. There, facing the view of El Paso and Juárez, with the Rio Grande meandering between, one can see in bronze the before and after situation of the Chamizal Settlement, the result of more than a century of haggling between the United States and the Republic of Mexico over a piece of real estate—originally an undeveloped area covered with *chamiso*, a native shrub—left in limbo after the river left its banks in one of its many wandering escapades. But this change in the river's course was unlike those back in times of Mexican or Spanish territorial posses-

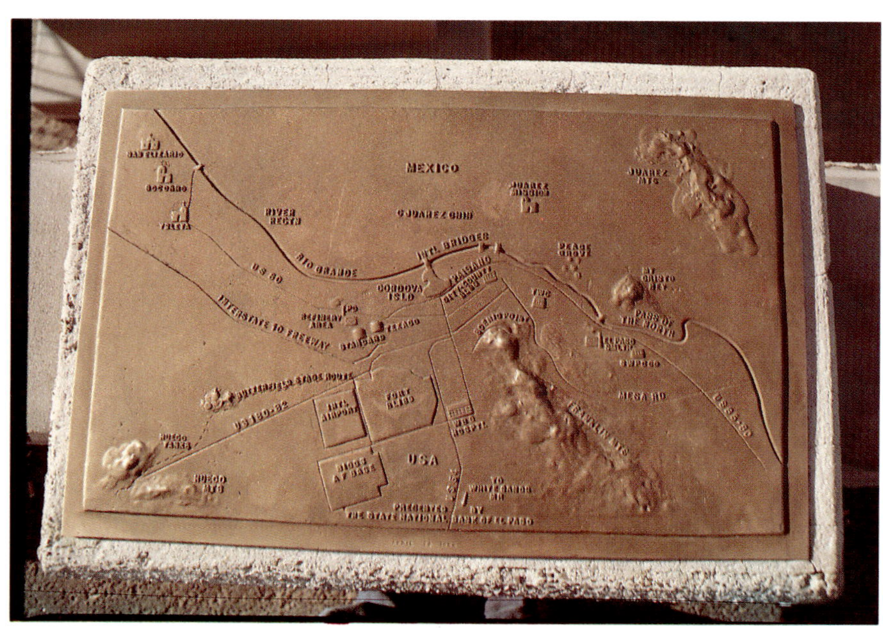

This plaque commemorating the peaceful settlement of the Chamizal dispute was produced from a plaster model by Cisneros and then cast in bronze; it is mounted at Scenic Point on Mount Franklin, in El Paso, Texas.

sion, when it was just another river. After the Treaty of Guadalupe Hidalgo ending the Mexican War, the river became the international boundary between two sovereign nations; but the Rio Bravo del Norte (the wild river of the north, as early explorers sometimes descriptively called it) promptly left its old channel and confused the issue. Finally Presidents John F. Kennedy and Adolfo López Mateos of the two countries worked out a peaceful agreement on the international boundary—and José Cisneros, son of one nation and adopted son of the other, was commissioned to carve out a plaque that showed the results of the settlement.

Another new departure for Cisneros skills came about when El Paso's Episcopal Pro-Cathedral of St. Clement was building an addition, and decided to honor a beloved rector, the Rev. B. M. G. Williams. A two-storied passageway between two areas was to be decorated with leaded glass windows of unusual design: they could be viewed equally well from either side, from the hallway or from the adjoining offices and classrooms. Essentially they were clear glass, united with lead strips, and bearing only occasional touches of color, created from Cisneros designs by El Pasoan Ralph Baker. The twenty-three windows that resulted illustrate New Testament scenes—among them Jesus blessing the little children, healing the sick, and feeding the five thousand, as well as events in the lives of the apostles. Again the challenge of a new task captured the artist's fancy and he worked out stained glass designs for his own front door, suggested by a pattern from a china cabinet in the Cisneros living room. Although the St. Clement windows are among the most outstanding examples of Cisneros's religious art, he has done a wide variety of work for his own and other churches. Saint Joseph's Catholic Church, which he and his wife attend (down the street from their home), is graced by Cisneros-designed Stations of the Cross and other pieces of his design. Churches from a number of different denominations have examples of Cisneros's work, both in El Paso and in neighboring Las Cruces. Perhaps in the same category of religious art are the illustrations he provided (without charge) for Cleofas Calleros' impressive history of Juarez's Church of Our Lady of Guadalupe, the oldest mission in the area (dating from 1659) and now the cathedral of the diocese.

Another challenge to the Cisneros imagination came in 1967 when his friend Francis Fugate wanted a mural painted on the wall of his garage, overlooking a backyard pool and patio. Again, Cisneros experimented, relying upon his instinct, and created a masterpiece that still, many years later, provides a lively scene of Spanish dancers, from the same historical period that inspired the work he and Fugate had done together years before, *The Spanish Heritage of the Southwest*. The figures still dance beside the patio, now faded by time and sun. A local newspaper reporter wrote that as the light changes at sunset the colors change, giving an ever varying effect. It was Cisneros's first experience painting with oil, he recalls. The technique he had used was learned by watching his friend and mentor Tom Lea at work on the courthouse mural.

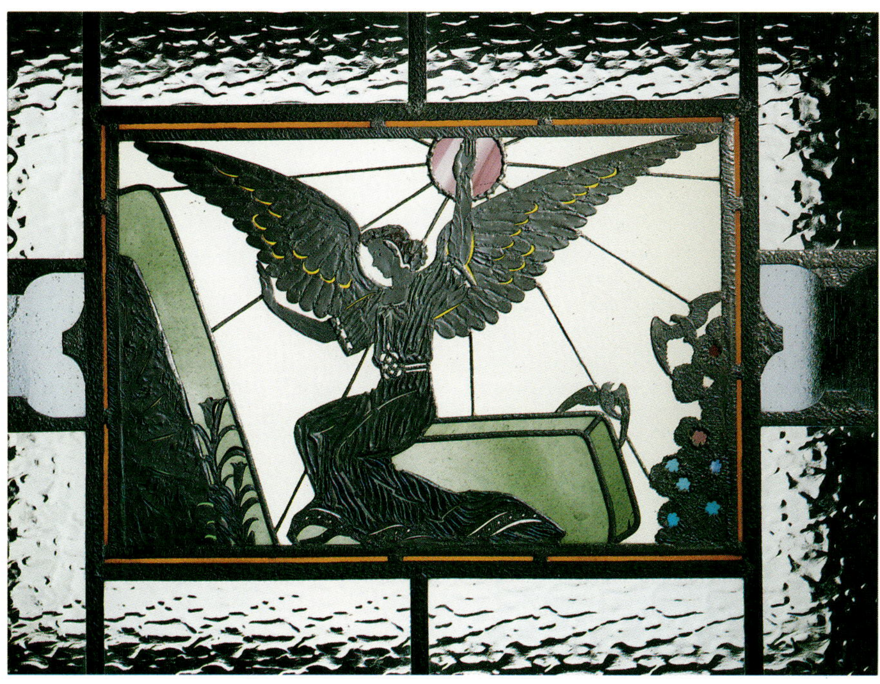

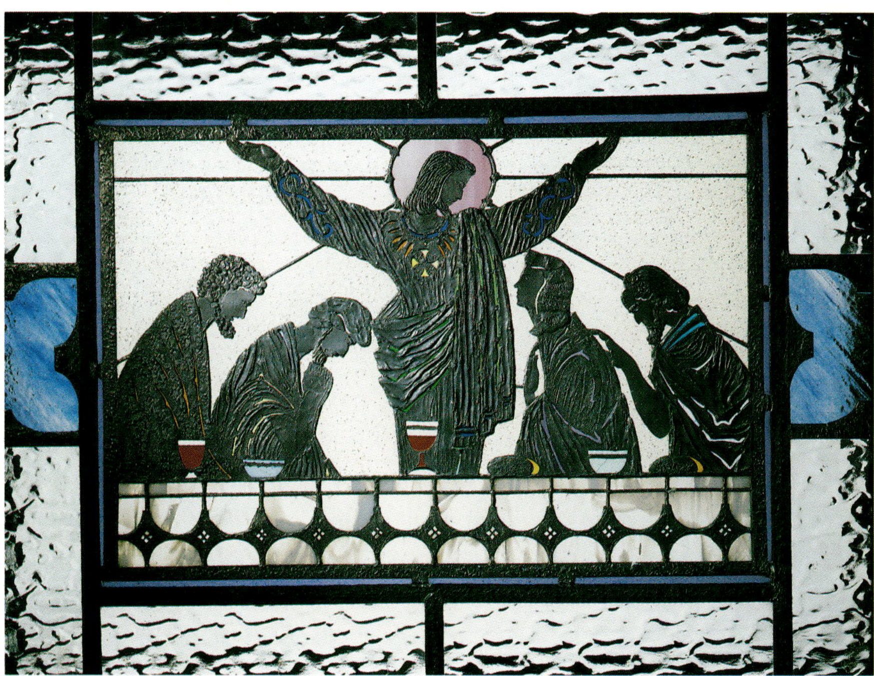

Top: an angel at Christ's tomb, depicted in stained glass, St. Clement's Pro-Cathedral, El Paso, Texas; bottom: the Last Supper is among the glass windows in St. Clement's Hall.

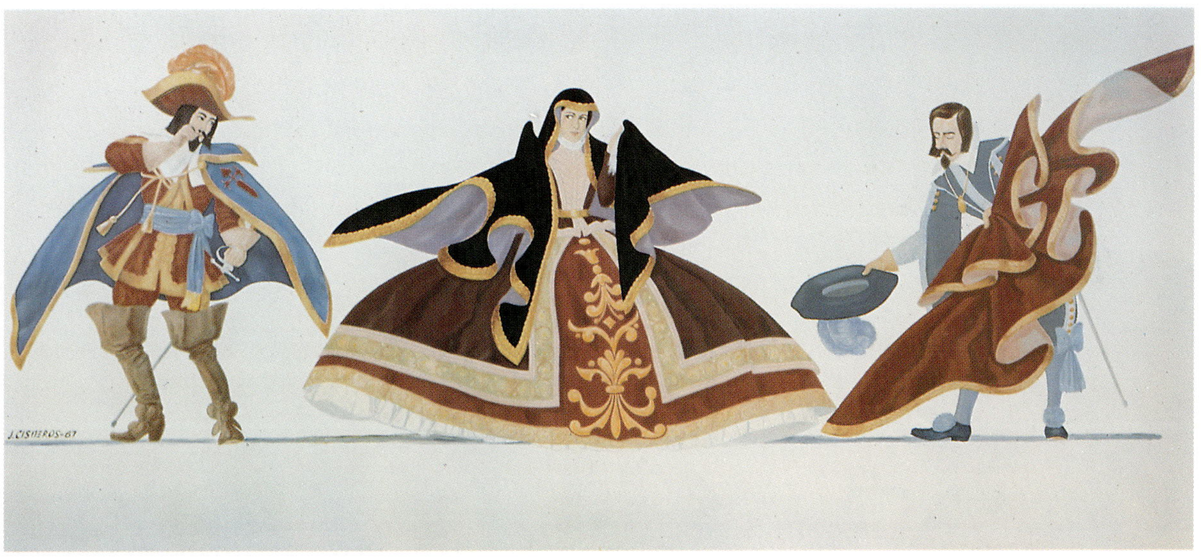

One of the earliest privately commissioned murals in El Paso, this trio of Spanish dancers was painted in 1967 on the patio wall at the home of Francis Fugate, Cisneros's collaborator on The Spanish Heritage of the Southwest. *(Photo courtesy of Roberta Fugate Treece)*

Although he is innovative and self-reliant, José Cisneros is not above borrowing from himself. The dust jacket he provided for Joseph Leach's *The Typical Texan* (Southern Methodist University Press, 1952) had an arrangement of four faces around a dominating central figure, a pattern that lent itself to interesting variations. The El Paso County Historical Society letterhead and emblem has a similar arrangement, with six historic heads in an oval around an El Paso mountain and a Texas star. Other logos have seen similar patterns coming from Cisneros's pen, including the Southwestern American Literature Association publication cover, and a memorable creation commissioned for a Texas Sesquicentennial library celebration entitled "Texas Voices." Each symbol is different, of course, and each shows the imagination, the historical accuracy, and the skilled touch with the steel pen that have been so long identified with the work of José Cisneros, but also showing his continued efforts toward artistic growth and improvement. And, perhaps to show he is not a slave to habit, the letterhead he designed for the Mission Trail Association of El Paso used a circle of the organization's name, with a small parade of an Indian, a padre, a mother and child atop a mule, and a conquistador in the center, almost a reverse of his more usual pattern for such pieces.

Among Cisneros's many talents, but one he swears he does not really enjoy, is the creation of maps. He feels cramped by the factual aspects of the task, he says, which infringe on his imagination. Even so, each map he creates has a special touch, and there is always evidence of the Cisneros imagination at work. Just as he let his fancy run free with the map for *Across Aboriginal America*, he allows cattle to range through his creation of a map of a cattle trail, or sets missionaries to trudge across the barren wastes of the area where real live Franciscans once went looking for Indian souls to save. The map he added to the 1951 *Flowsheet* illustrations to provide geographic orientation for *The Spanish Heritage of the Southwest* is sprinkled with cactus, conquistadores, clusters of pueblos and other buildings, Indians in hot pursuit of their prey, ox-drawn *carretas*, buffalo, and of course the missionary. All this is superimposed upon a

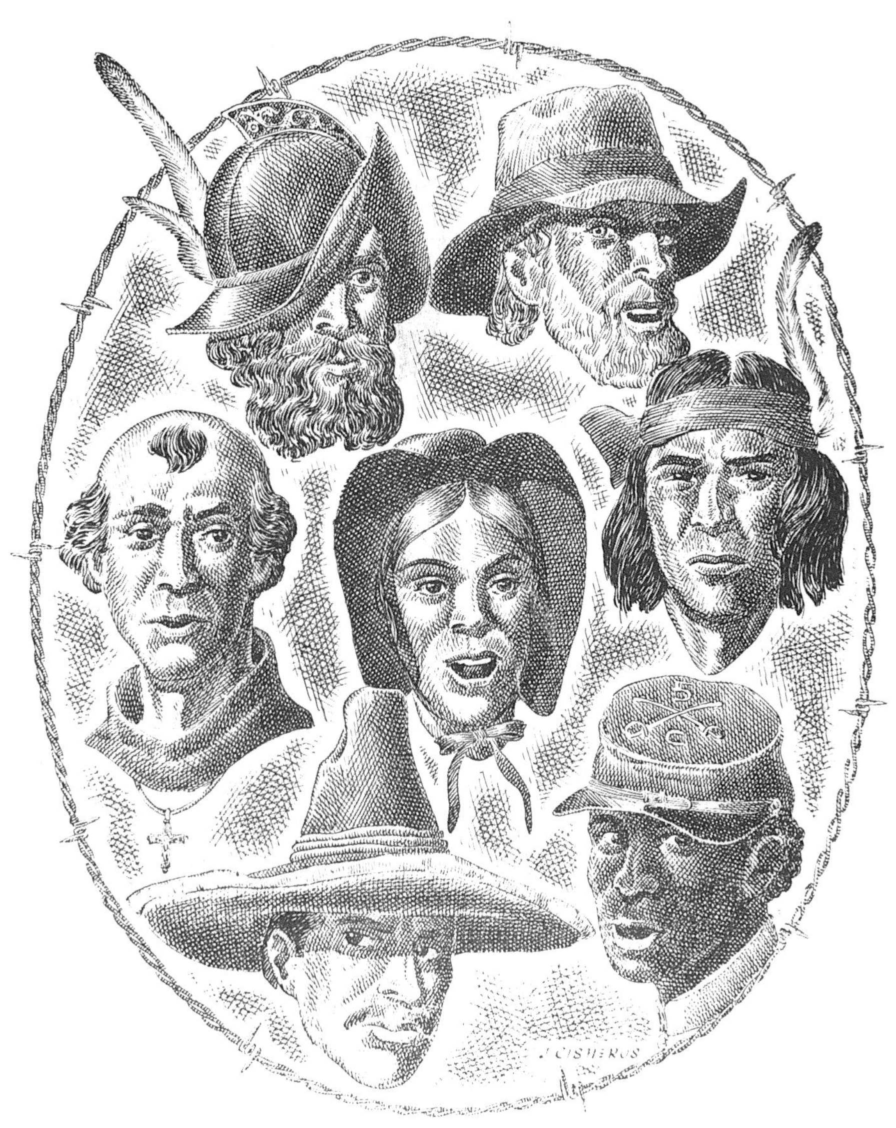

Cisneros has illustrated a variety of publications:
The Southwestern American Literature Association publication featured an assortment of regional faces.

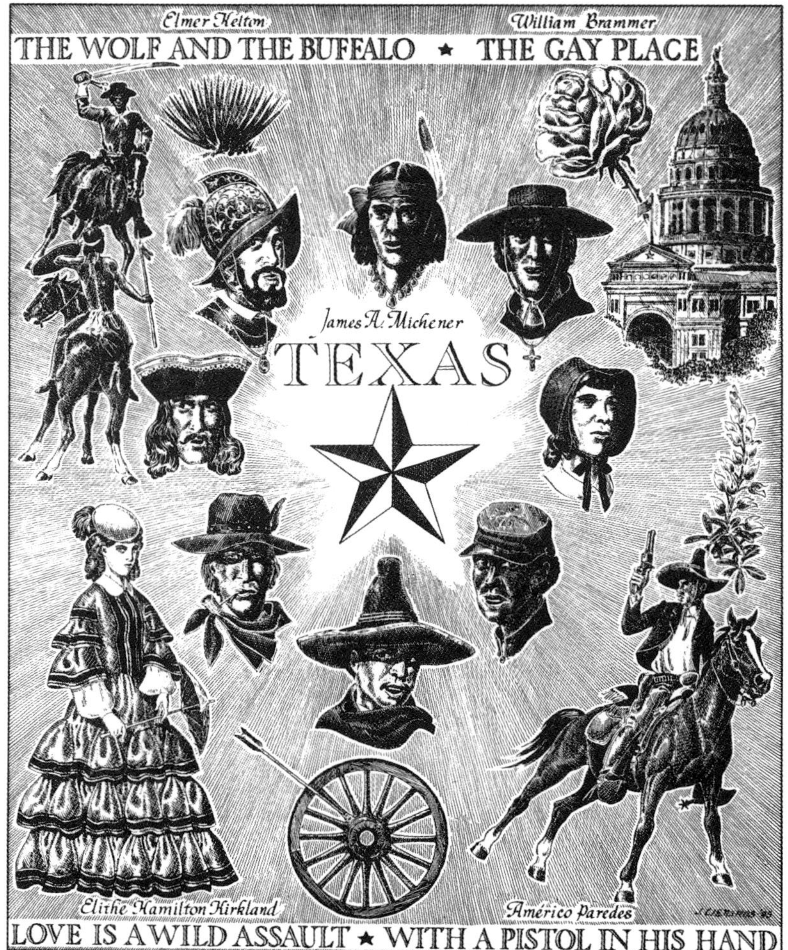

Texas Voices

Celebrate Texas In Books
At Your Public Library
With Book Discussion Programs

A Sesquicentennial project, "Texas Voices," encouraged reading of works by Texas Writers.

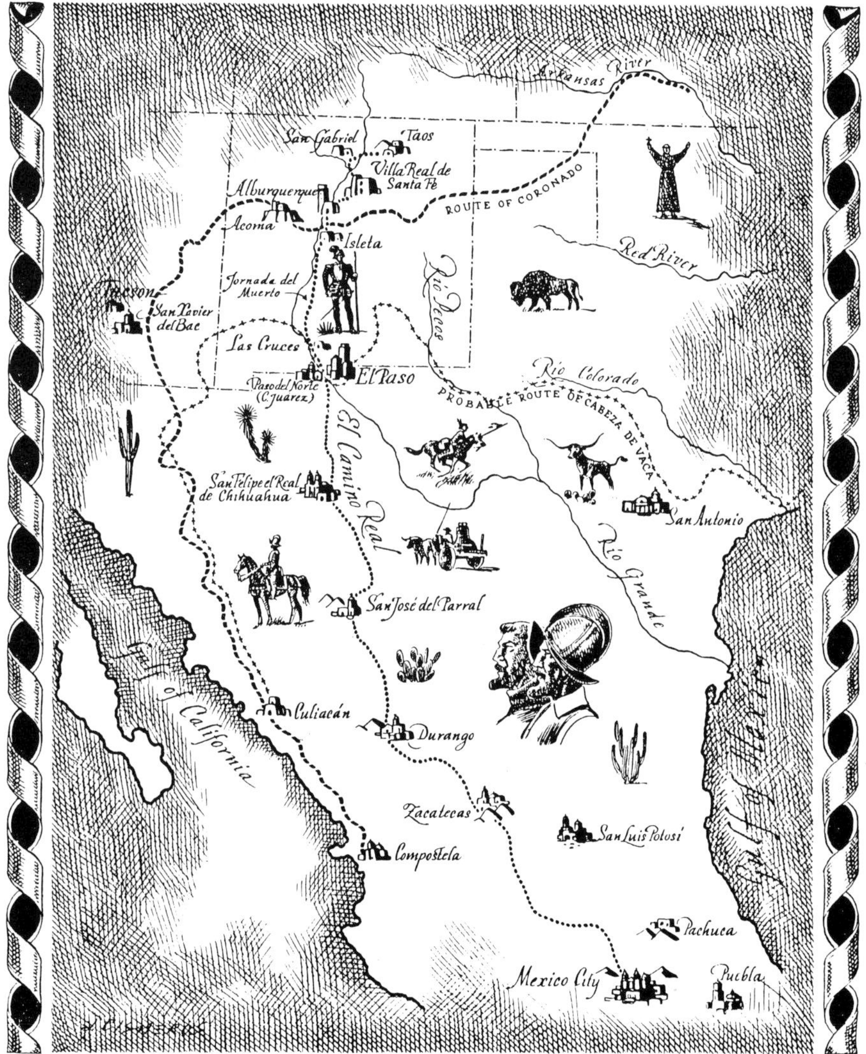

Map from the 1951 Flowsheet

map with the factual state boundaries of the present, together with the routes of early day explorers and the Camino Real, the royal highway from Mexico City to Santa Fe and Taos. Cisneros does admit, on occasion, his pride in some of his maps, like the one on the endpapers of a work he illustrated for the Academy of American Franciscan History—*Life of Fray Antonio Margil, O. F. M.* The subject of the biography, who served as a missionary in New Spain for forty-three years and was a co-founder of the San Antonio, Texas, missions, strides across western Mexico, and the whole map is bordered with a cord like the rope belts the Franciscans wore about their robes. Another map he enjoys browsing over, created for Fray Angélico Chávez's *Archives of the Archdiocese of Santa Fe, 1678-1900*, was done for the same organization. The endpaper map has Franciscan symbols in each corner, a missionary blessing a group of Indian converts, and a holy day parade of padres, conquistadores, settlers, and Indians following an uplifted statue of La Conquistadora—the representation of the Virgin Mary most closely associated with the missions of New Mexico. Again, the Franciscan rope belt encircles the whole map in a manner that is both symbolic and artistic. But of all the maps he has done, he is most proud of the one in *Captain Cortés Conquers Mexico*, a book he also illustrated profusely. A host of his devotees—including the present author—find his maps to be among his most fascinating productions.

While the work of José Cisneros is often done at little or no cost for religious or charitable organizations, his pen has served the business world as well. Usually his knowledge and feel for history are called into play at such times, not just his artistic ability. For example, his art adorned a twelve-part series of "Signposts of Early El Paso," newspaper advertisements for the State National Bank of El Paso, which for many years has emphasized its founding in 1881, the year the railroads came to the Pass. Historic signs, usually from business establishments of the past, were presented in a bit of historic nostalgia: a meat market had a flag displayed when fresh meat was available; a boot was hung from a shoemaker's signpost; cavalry guidons and flags advertised the army's

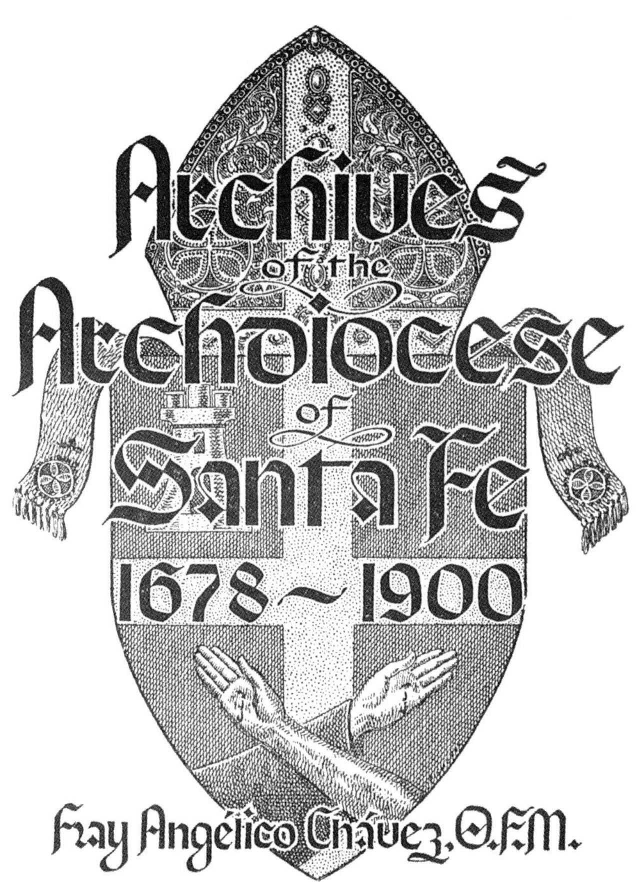

The title page for Fray Angélico Chávez' Archives of the Archdiocese of Santa Fe, 1678-1900 *(1957) reveals Cisneros's love for ornate church symbols.*

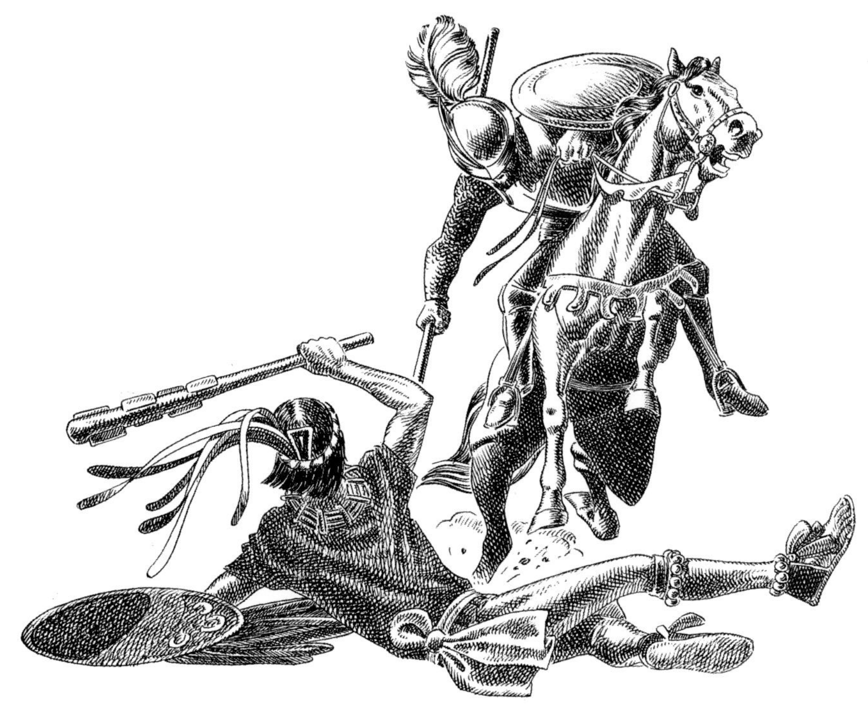

From Captain Cortes Conquers Mexico*: One of Cisneros's favorite subjects is Hernando Cortez. Here, in a 1960 drawing, a clash of cultures ends badly for the native warrior.*

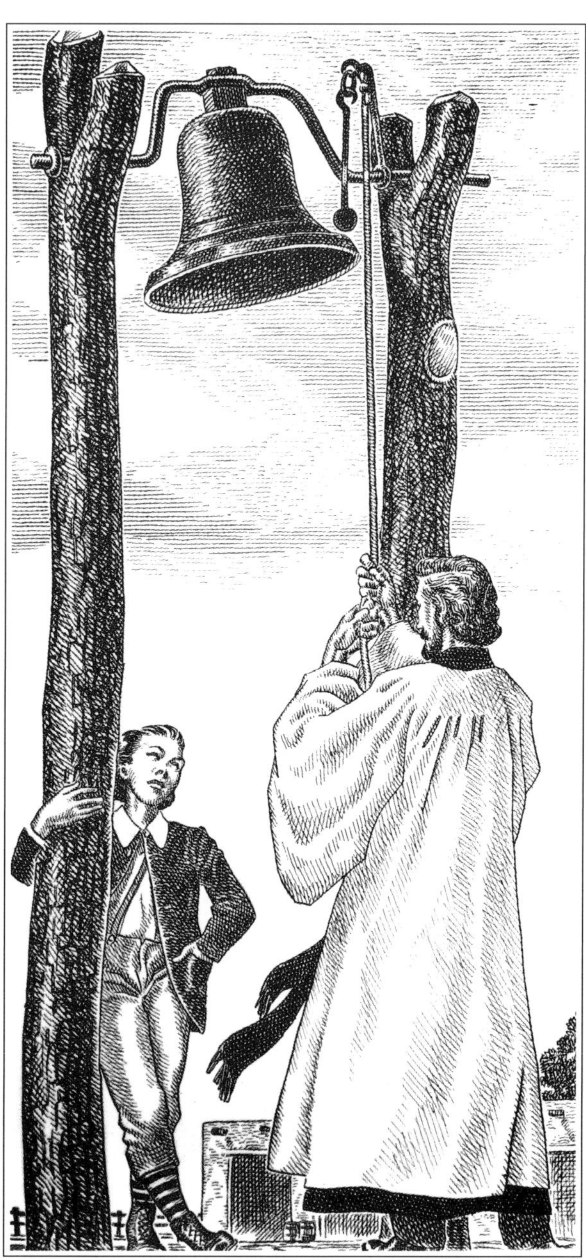

Historical subject matter was featured in the series, "Early El Paso Signposts," showing various scenes from the 1880s. This is one in the series was commissioned by The State National Bank in El Paso, Texas.

presence in the border community; a barber's striped post and a newspaper tree where challenges to duels and other matters of public interest were posted shared their places in the series, along with a bell being rung as a sign of church services about to begin. Period costumes and other historic details made the series more than just advertisements, largely because of the knowledge and skill of the artist. Less historic but still reflecting the Hispanic flavor of the region was a series of ads for Straight American whiskey, distilled by a Kentucky firm that moved to Juárez during Prohibition. The ads featured a typical *mariachi* singer in one, a señorita doing the Mexican Hat Dance in another, a bullfighter, and other figures, each one a part of "The Spirit of Old Mexico," and each one done with detailed skill. Mayo Seamon, the advertising director of the local papers, in remitting a check for Cisneros's participation in a 1946 series commemorating the 289th anniversary of the founding of Ciudad Juárez, wrote the artist: "I would like to say also, that your work is splendid, and was the outstanding feature of the entire series. We have received many compliments on your illustrations, and I am delighted to have had the privilege of using them in our papers."

Another anniversary, the seventy-fifth of the "real" beginning of El Paso, when the railroads came to the Pass of the North, was celebrated by the State National Bank in 1956 with advertisements, most of them featuring Cisneros art: twenty-eight double columns, alternating one day in English, the next in Spanish, were brought to the attention of El Pasoans. The first pair with Cisneros illustrations depicted, of course, the arrival of the first Southern Pacific train, with attendant crowds of celebrating people. The coming of law to "Sin City" was another event from 1881, showing a badge-toting lawman gunning down a "bad guy." Interestingly, the first Catholic church in the growing town was described in an ad, but was not shown in an illustration although the first Protestant one was. Mandy, the mule that pulled El Paso's first trolley, was also commemorated in style, as were the coming of a waterworks, and of course the State National Bank. The historical copy for the series (in English) was written by Cisneros's colleague and supporter, Carl

Hertzog. Two newspaper seventy-fifth anniversaries, those for El Paso and Corpus Christi, Texas, featured Cisneros section pages reflecting the varied activities of three quarters of a century for the two cities.

Branching out almost into the political arena, José Cisneros's art was called upon in the late 1950s when the State of Texas was challenging the federal government over ownership of the tidelands oil rights. Texas Attorney General Will Wilson was involved deeply (and successfully) in the controversy, and his experiences led him to explore the varied boundary difficulties the state had wrestled with from the time it was an independent nation. A twelve-part series entitled "The Shape of Texas" was produced, with illustrations by Cisneros to attract attention; the articles and stereotype mats were sent out free to some seven hundred weeklies. Wilson estimates that at least one hundred of them printed the stories and the drawings accompanying them, but copies are rare indeed today, because of the tendency of small newspapers to disregard the value of back issues and "morgues" preserving the news of yesterday. Indeed, most of the original drawings are missing, although Wilson managed to preserve three of them; Cisneros lacks even a preliminary sketch of a single one.

The artist has often been called upon to create Christmas cards for people who wanted to send something distinctive, among them Carl Hertzog, local contractor Robert E. McKee, Stanley Marcus of department store fame, and Hugh Gray, an official with the Southern Pacific railroad in El Paso. For the latter in 1947 Cisneros produced a very antique-looking manger scene, with the star beaming down upon the Holy Babe, following the general style of a life-size manger scene that was for years erected in a rock grotto each Christmas by one of the sisters who taught at Loretto Academy in El Paso. Printed by Carl Hertzog, the item was very striking. Six years later, the same drawing was pressed into service on the cover of a program for a Southwestern Sun Carnival Association Christmas pageant, "The Finding of the King," performed by the El Paso Civic Chorus and the El Paso Players.

Bookplates have come often from the Cisneros pen: Stanley Marcus and Dr. Félix Almaráz, Jr., historian whose works have benefitted from Cisneros art, have bookplates that resemble medieval woodcuts. For others (including the present author), historian Leon Metz, the late meatpacking magnate Joseph C. Peyton—among scores of others—Cisneros created bookplates that reflect the work interests of the owners; the artist's own bookplate is in this category. The El Paso Public Library, where his art was first exhibited, and Sul Ross State University are among many library organizations that have used his bookplates.

But the most significant utilization of the art of José Cisneros and the area that has brought him the most fame is in the field of book illustration. For many years he has been literally besieged by writers, especially historians, who want their publications to be embellished artistically and accurately with the skills of this self-taught master. A complete bibliography of such works is far beyond the intent of this present volume, but even a sample list is impressive enough. Here follows a representative collection of books and pamphlets he has illustrated, or provided dustjackets, frontispieces or made maps personally, with emphasis upon those works that José Cisneros himself recalls as significant.

Everett DeGolyer, *Across Aboriginal America: The Journey of Three Englishmen Across Texas in 1568* (1947).

Wallace Hawkins, *El Sal del Rey* (1947).

A. W. Neville, *The Red River Valley, Then and Now* (1948).

Cleve Hallenbeck, *The Journey of Fray Marcos de Niza* (1949, 1990).

Carlos Castañeda, *Our Catholic Heritage in Texas* Vol 6 (1950).

Cleofas Calleros, *El Paso's Missions and Indians* (1951).

Wilson M. Hudson, ed., *The Healer of Los Olmos* (1951).

Francis Fugate, *The Spanish Heritage of the Southwest* (1952).

Joseph Leach, *The Typical Texan* (1952).

J. Evetts Haley, *Fort Concho on the Texas Frontier* (1952).

Bessie Lee Fitzhugh, *Bells Over Texas* (1955).

Fray Angélico Chávez, *Archives of the Archdiocese of Santa Fe, 1678-1900* (1957).

John J. Middagh, *Frontier Newspaper: The El Paso Times* (1958).

Carlos Castañeda, *The Church in Texas Since Independence, 1836-1950* Vol. 7 (1958).

Eduardo F. Ríos, *Life of Fray Antonio Margil, O. F. M.* (1959).

William W. Johnson, *Captain Cortés Conquers Mexico* (1960).

Herbert E. Bolton, *The Mission as a Frontier Institution in the Spanish American Colonies* (reprint, 1960).

C. L. Sonnichsen, *The El Paso Salt War of 1877* (1961).

Thomas of Celano, trans. by Placid Hermann, O. F. M. *Francis of Assisi* (1963).

W. H. Timmons, *Morelos of Mexico: Priest, Soldier, Statesman* (1963).

Haldeen Braddy, *Pershing's Mission in Mexico* (1966).

O. W. Williams, *Pioneer Surveyor-Frontier Lawyer* (1966).

C. L. Sonnichsen, *Pass of the North* 2 vols. (1968, 1980).

José Cisneros, *Riders of the Border* (1971).

Myles Dillon, *There Was a King in Ireland* (1971).

Marc Simmons, *The Little Lion of the Southwest: The Life of Manuel Antonio Chávez* (1971).

John M. Carroll, *The Black Military Experience in the American West* (1971).

_______, *Buffalo Soldiers West* (1971).

James T. Bratcher, *Analytical Index to the Publications of the Texas Folklore Society* (1976).

Emilio Echevarría and José Otero, *Hispanic Colorado* (1976).

W. C. Holden, *A Ranching Saga* 2 vols. (1976).

Donald E. Everett, *San Antonio Legacy* (1979).

José Cisneros, *Riders of the Borderlands* (1981).

Paul Horgan, *Conquistadors in North American History* (1982).

F. W. Hodge and T. W. Lewis, *Spanish Explorers in the Southern United States* (reprint, 1984).

José Cisneros, *Riders Across the Centuries* (1984).

Brian Robertson, *Wild Horse Desert* (1985).

Katherine H. White, *The Pueblo de Socorro Grant* (1987).

John O. West, *Mexican-American Folklore* (1988).

Leon C. Metz, *Desert Army* (1988).
John O. West, *Cowboy Folk Humor* (1990).
W. H. Timmons, *El Paso: A Borderlands History* (1990).
Félix Almaráz, Jr., *Tragic Cavalier* (2d ed. 1991).
Marc Simmons, *The Last Conquistador* (1991).

With the recognition of the breadth of his work, plus these representative few books illustrated by José Cisneros, should come the awareness that his art adorns at least two hundred other books, plus magazines like *The Southwesterner* and *Western Horsemen* and *New Mexico Magazine*; covers for dozens of *Southwestern Studies* for Texas Western Press; programs for business, scholarly and library meetings; certificates of honor or recognition; as well as posters and fliers for a variety of purposes. Such a list should indicate the richness and depth of the artistic contribution this dedicated man has made in his chosen profession.

A pair of recent examples of his significance (and his generosity) have to do with helping other artists. Dave McGary, in competition for a sculpture of Don Pedro de Peralta, who followed Don Juan de Oñate as governor of New Mexico, asked Cisneros for ideas and pointers, which were freely given; McGary won the competition and received his commission; his statue now stands in Santa Fe, and his gratitude to Cisneros is considerable. Another sculpture, one of Oñate for a Hispanic Visitor and Cultural Center to be built north of Española, New Mexico, was based upon a poster commissioned from José Cisneros by Dr. Bob McGeagh, director of the project. The sculptor, Reynaldo Rivera, says he fashioned his Oñate from the sketches of Cisneros, the "foremost authority of authentic historic figures on horseback."

Another example of Cisneros's reputation as a historian with the pen was less flattering: a sculptor who claimed he studied *Riders Across the Centuries* in preparation for a commissioned equestrian statue did not succeed in pleasing his source, who points out that the sculptor gave the horse too much tail, and the muscles on the horse's left hip are too deep (although the right side is all right). Cisneros notes that the stirrups on the statue are not military, nor was the usual pistol holster on the front of the saddle. "After all," Cisneros says, "since he *was* a general, the statue should have had those military details included!"

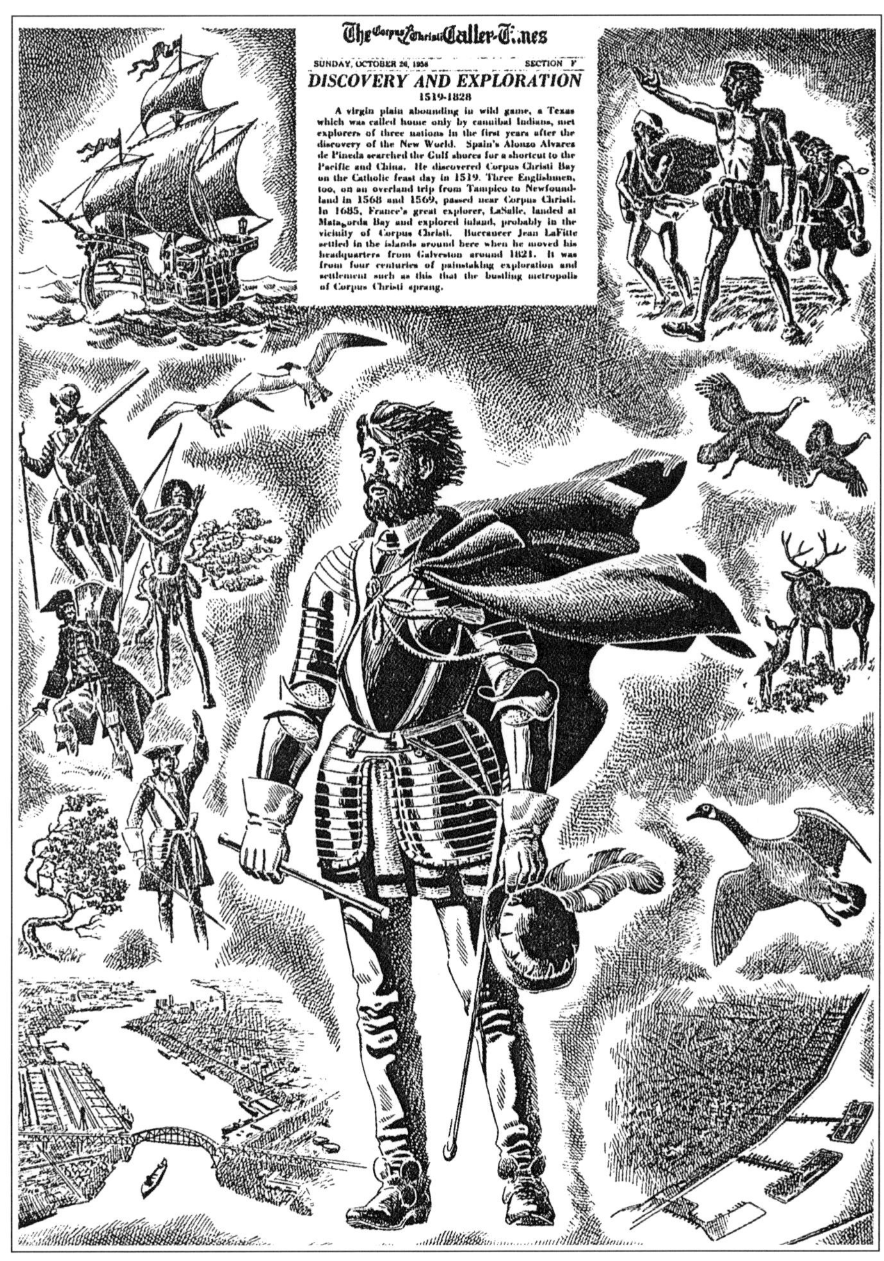

The Corpus Christi Caller-Times

SUNDAY, OCTOBER 28, 1956 SECTION F

DISCOVERY AND EXPLORATION

1519-1828

A virgin plain abounding in wild game, a Texas which was called home only by cannibal Indians, met explorers of three nations in the first years after the discovery of the New World. Spain's Alonzo Alvarez de Pineda searched the Gulf shores for a shortcut to the Pacific and China. He discovered Corpus Christi Bay on the Catholic feast day in 1519. Three Englishmen, too, on an overland trip from Tampico to Newfoundland in 1568 and 1569, passed near Corpus Christi. In 1685, France's great explorer, LaSalle, landed at Matagorda Bay and explored inland, probably in the vicinity of Corpus Christi. Buccaneer Jean LaFitte settled in the islands around here when he moved his headquarters from Galveston around 1821. It was from four centuries of painstaking exploration and settlement such as this that the bustling metropolis of Corpus Christi sprang.

Two Texas newspapers issued 75th anniversary editions featuring Cisneros art. In 1956, The El Paso Times *depicted various areas of the city's development.*

The Corpus Christi Caller-Times *special went back to earliest times for some of its materials above,* Discovery and Exploration

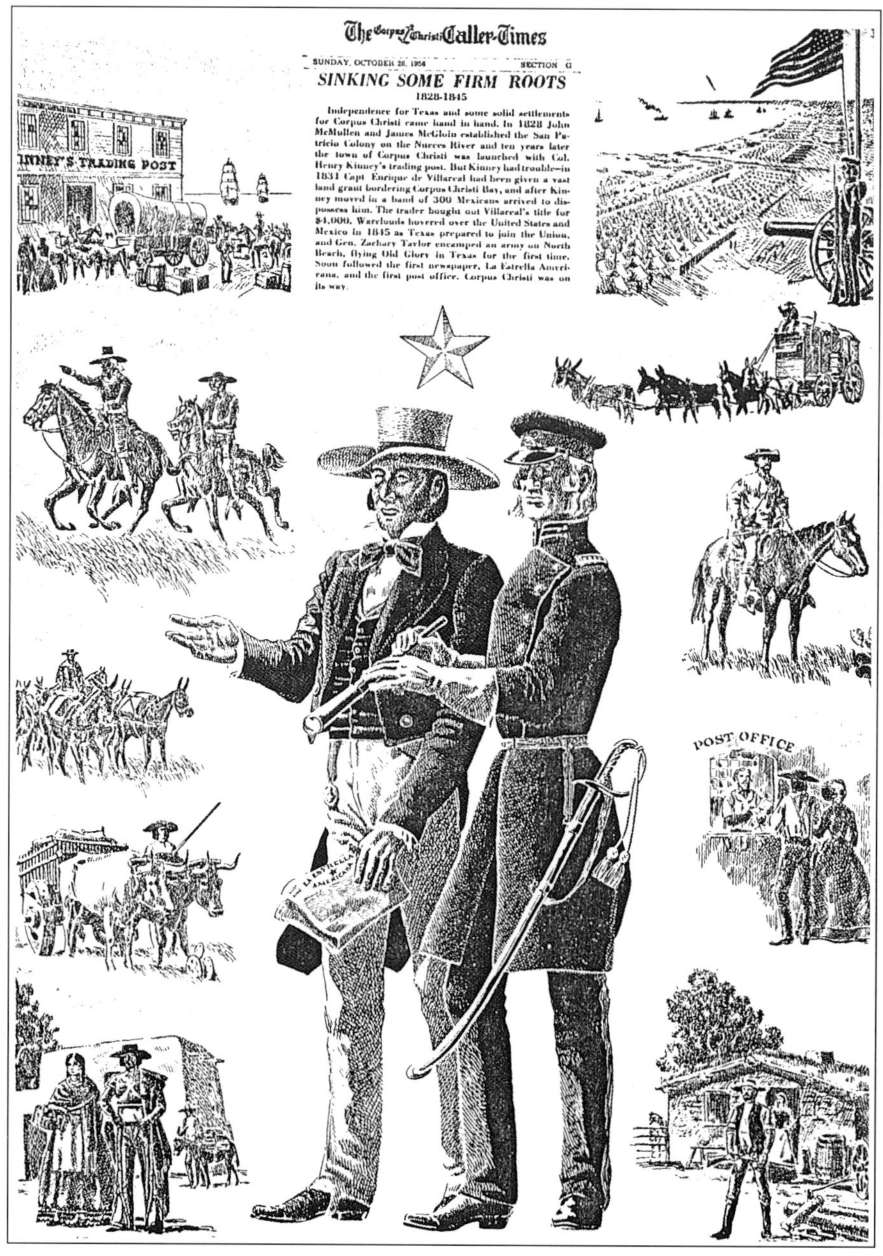

The Corpus Christi Caller-Times

SUNDAY, OCTOBER 26, 1958 — SECTION G

SINKING SOME FIRM ROOTS

1828-1845

Independence for Texas and some solid settlements for Corpus Christi came hand in hand. In 1828 John McMullen and James McGloin established the San Patricio Colony on the Nueces River and ten years later the town of Corpus Christi was launched with Col. Henry Kinney's trading post. But Kinney had trouble—in 1831 Capt. Enrique de Villareal had been given a vast land grant bordering Corpus Christi Bay, and after Kinney moved in a band of 300 Mexicans arrived to dispossess him. The trader bought out Villareal's title for $4,000. Warclouds hovered over the United States and Mexico in 1845 as Texas prepared to join the Union, and Gen. Zachary Taylor encamped an army on North Beach, flying Old Glory in Texas for the first time. Soon followed the first newspaper, La Estrella Americana, and the first post office. Corpus Christi was on its way.

The Corpus Christi Caller Times: Sinking Some Firm Roots

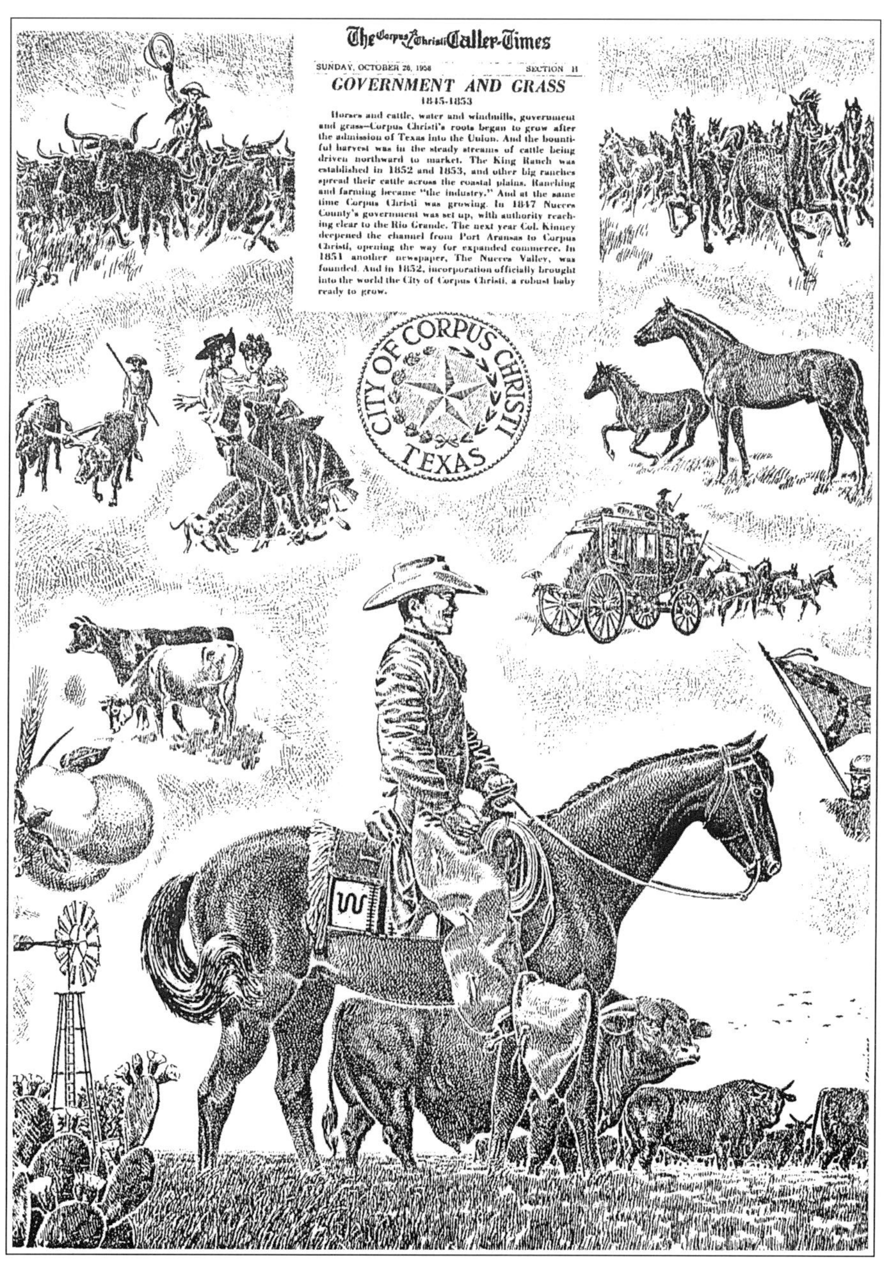

The Corpus Christi Caller-Times

SUNDAY, OCTOBER 26, 1958 SECTION B

GOVERNMENT AND GRASS

1845-1853

Horses and cattle, water and windmills, government and grass—Corpus Christi's roots began to grow after the admission of Texas into the Union. And the bountiful harvest was in the steady streams of cattle being driven northward to market. The King Ranch was established in 1852 and 1853, and other big ranches spread their cattle across the coastal plains. Ranching and farming became "the industry." And at the same time Corpus Christi was growing. In 1847 Nueces County's government was set up, with authority reaching clear to the Rio Grande. The next year Col. Kinney deepened the channel from Port Aransas to Corpus Christi, opening the way for expanded commerce. In 1851 another newspaper, The Nueces Valley, was founded. And in 1852, incorporation officially brought into the world the City of Corpus Christi, a robust baby ready to grow.

The Corpus Christi Caller Times: Government and Grass

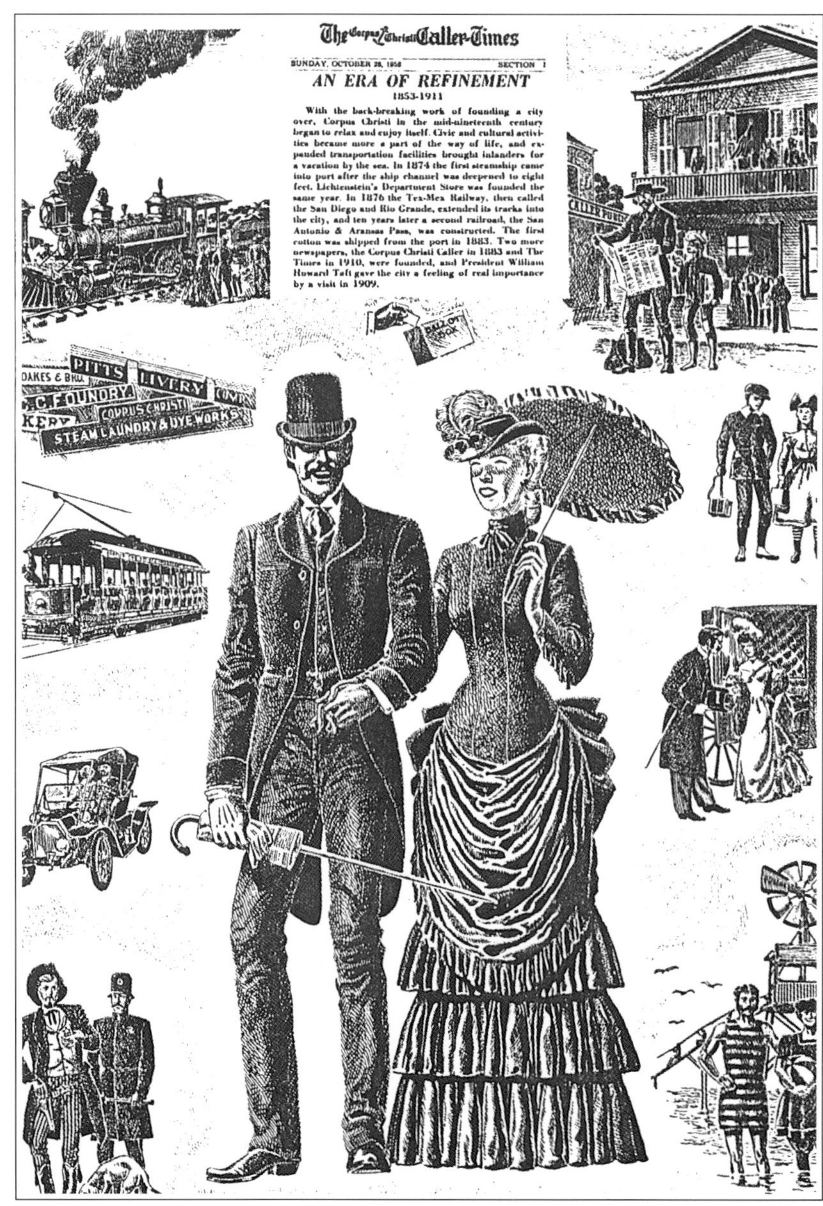

The Corpus Christi Caller-Times

SUNDAY, OCTOBER 26, 1958 — SECTION 1

AN ERA OF REFINEMENT

1853-1911

With the back-breaking work of founding a city over, Corpus Christi in the mid-nineteenth century began to relax and enjoy itself. Civic and cultural activities became more a part of the way of life, and expanded transportation facilities brought inlanders for a vacation by the sea. In 1874 the first steamship came into port after the ship channel was deepened to eight feet. Lichtenstein's Department Store was founded the same year. In 1876 the Tex-Mex Railway, then called the San Diego and Rio Grande, extended its tracks into the city, and ten years later a second railroad, the San Antonio & Aransas Pass, was constructed. The first cotton was shipped from the port in 1883. Two more newspapers, the Corpus Christi Caller in 1883 and The Times in 1910, were founded, and President William Howard Taft gave the city a feeling of real importance by a visit in 1909.

The Corpus Christi Caller Times: An Era of Refinement

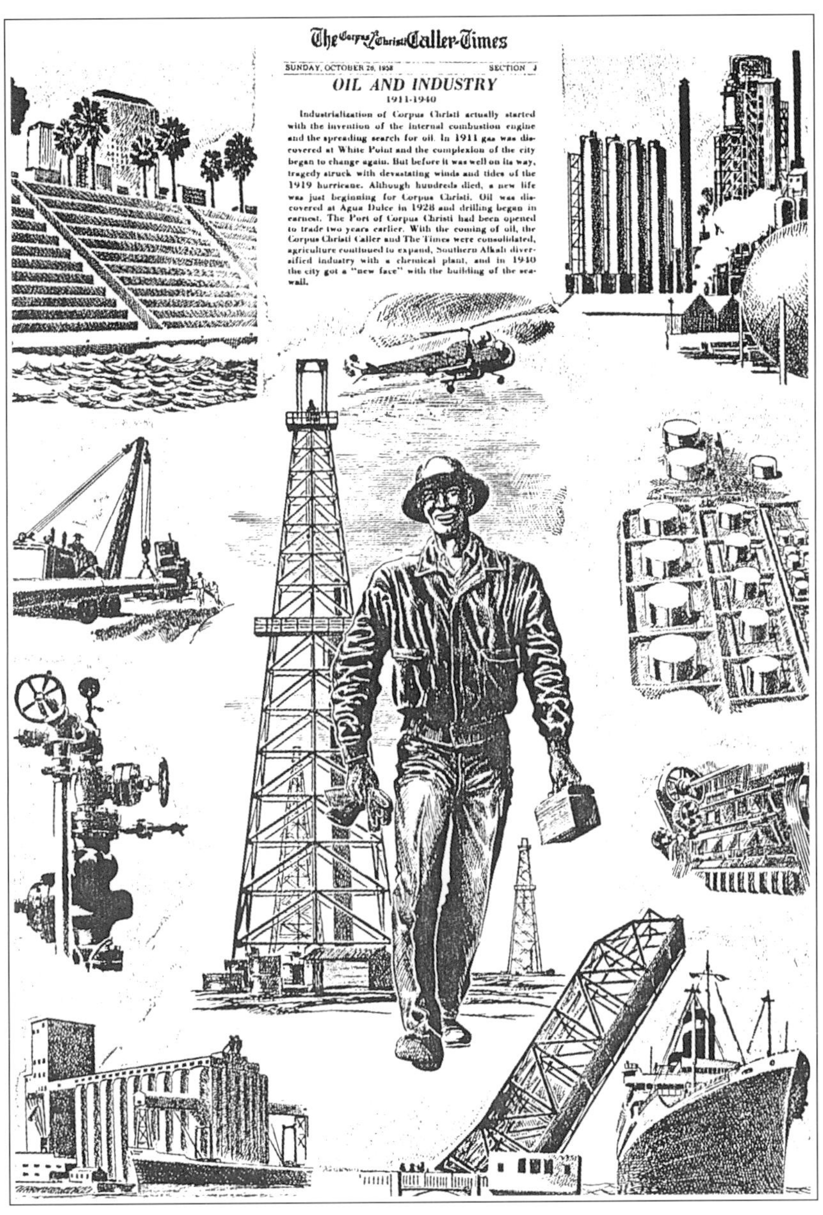

The Corpus Christi Caller-Times

SUNDAY, OCTOBER 26, 1958 SECTION J

OIL AND INDUSTRY

1911-1940

Industrialization of Corpus Christi actually started with the invention of the internal combustion engine and the spreading search for oil. In 1911 gas was discovered at White Point and the complexion of the city began to change again. But before it was well on its way, tragedy struck with devastating winds and tides of the 1919 hurricane. Although hundreds died, a new life was just beginning for Corpus Christi. Oil was discovered at Agua Dulce in 1928 and drilling began in earnest. The Port of Corpus Christi had been opened to trade two years earlier. With the coming of oil, the Corpus Christi Caller and The Times were consolidated, agriculture continued to expand, Southern Alkali diversified industry with a chemical plant, and in 1940 the city got a "new face" with the building of the seawall.

The Corpus Christi Caller Times: Oil and Industry

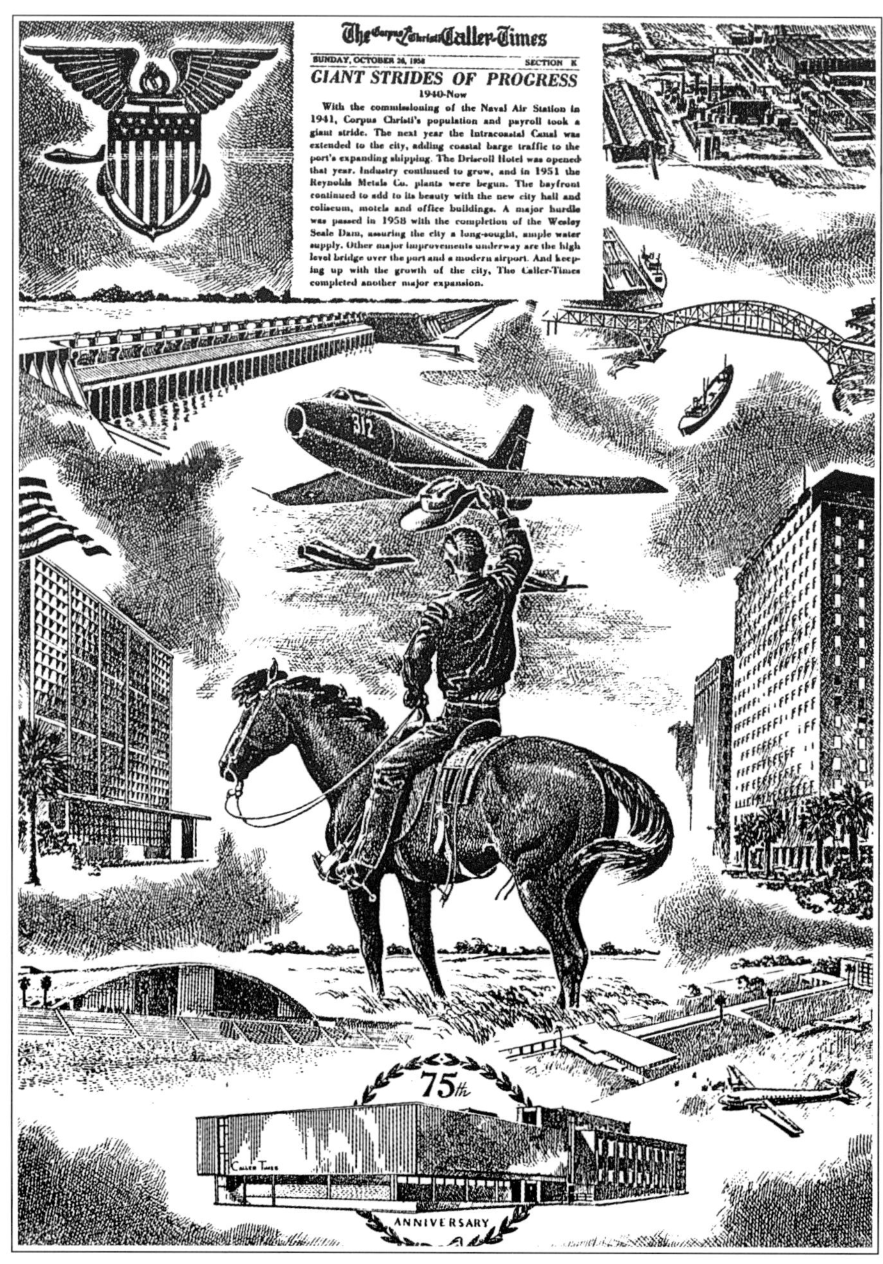

The Corpus Christi Caller-Times

SUNDAY, OCTOBER 26, 1958 — SECTION K

GIANT STRIDES OF PROGRESS

1940-Now

With the commissioning of the Naval Air Station in 1941, Corpus Christi's population and payroll took a giant stride. The next year the Intracoastal Canal was extended to the city, adding coastal barge traffic to the port's expanding shipping. The Driscoll Hotel was opened that year. Industry continued to grow, and in 1951 the Reynolds Metals Co. plants were begun. The bayfront continued to add to its beauty with the new city hall and coliseum, motels and office buildings. A major hurdle was passed in 1958 with the completion of the Wesley Seale Dam, assuring the city a long-sought, ample water supply. Other major improvements underway are the high level bridge over the port and a modern airport. And keeping up with the growth of the city, The Caller-Times completed another major expansion.

The Corpus Christi Caller Times: Giant Strides of Progress

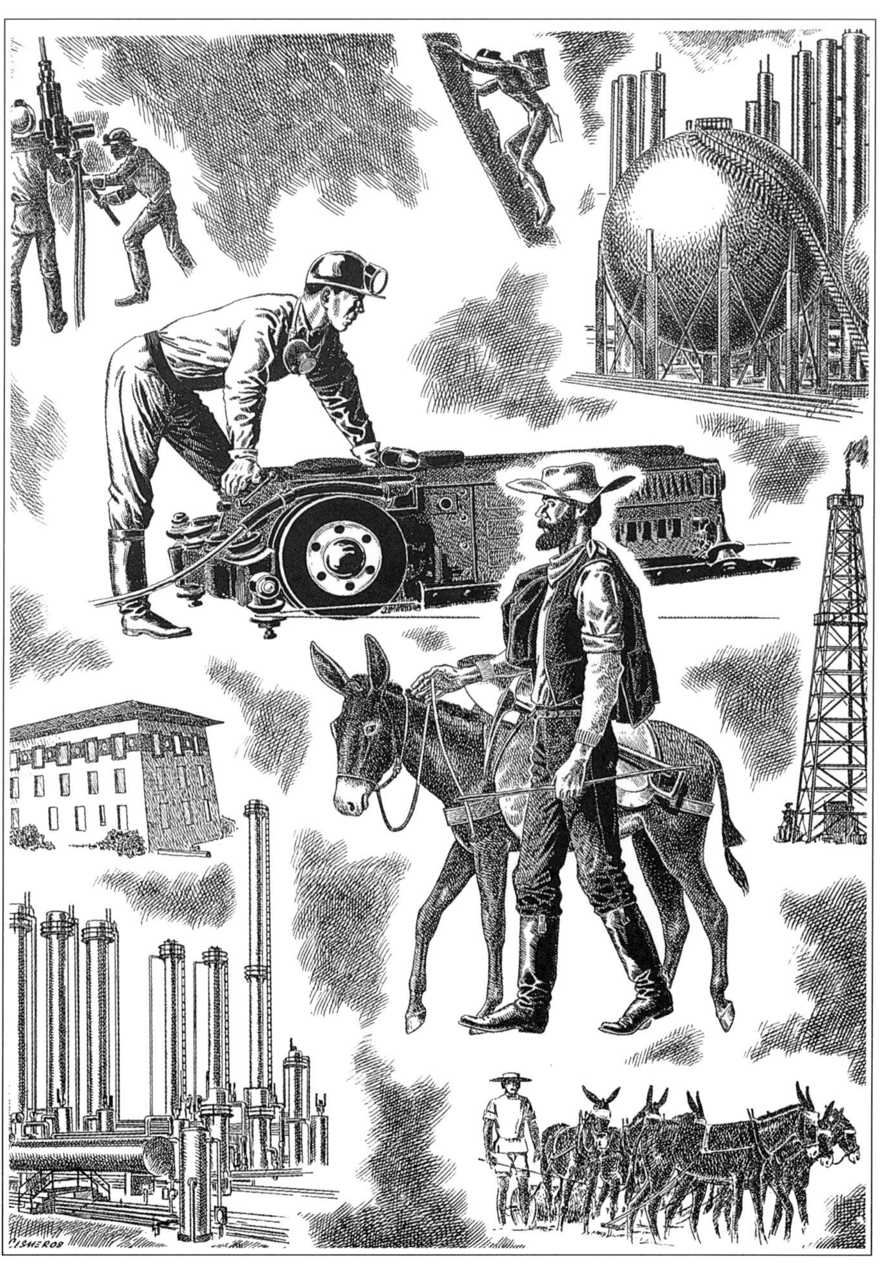

The El Paso Times

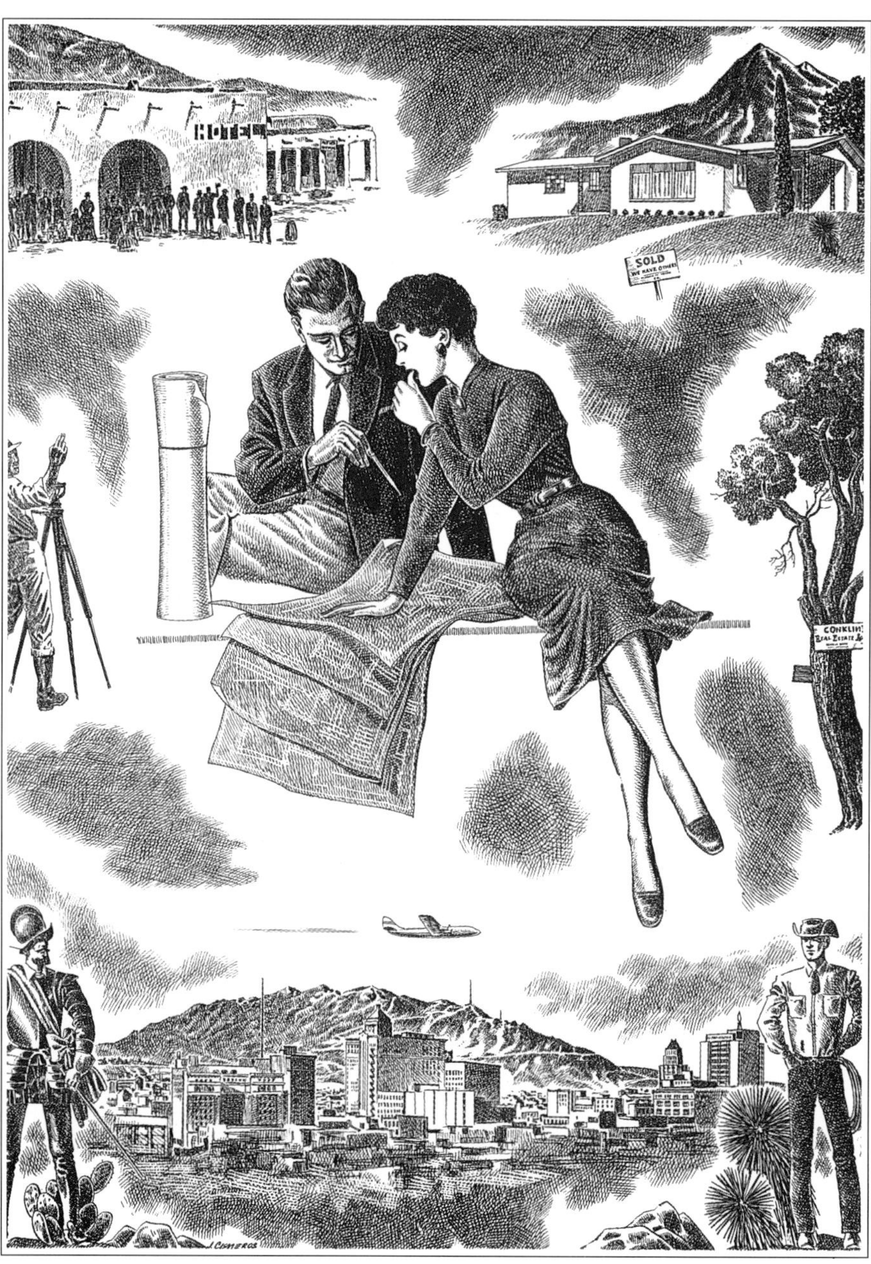

The El Paso Times

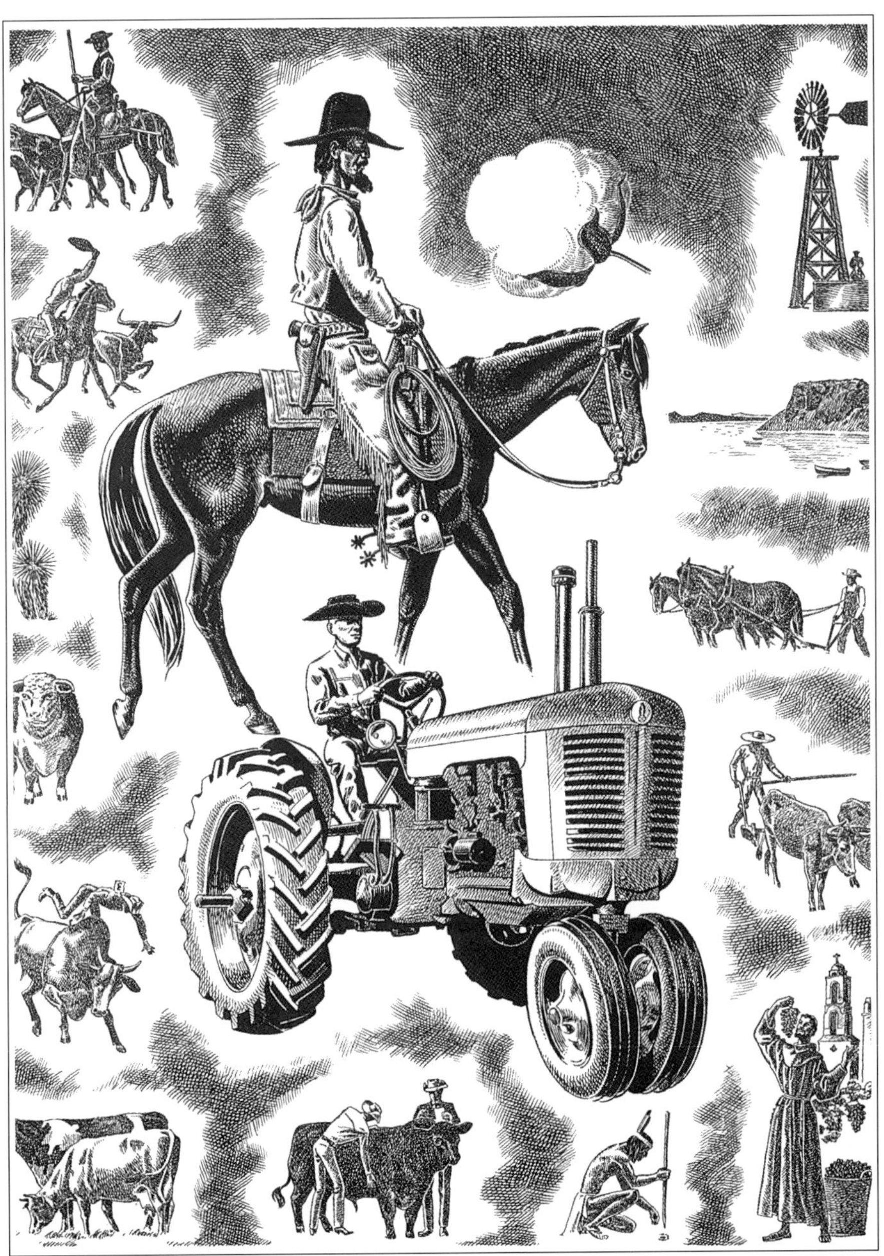

The El Paso Times

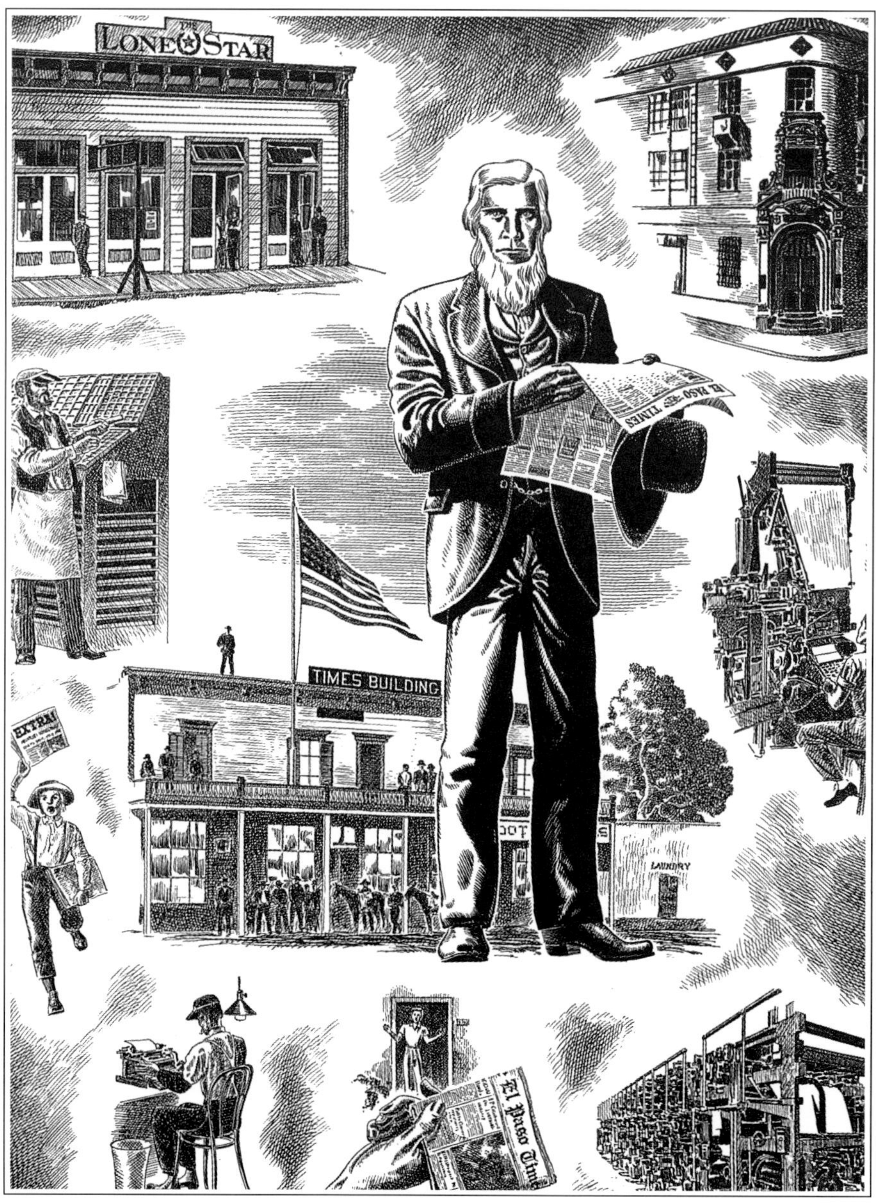

The El Paso Times

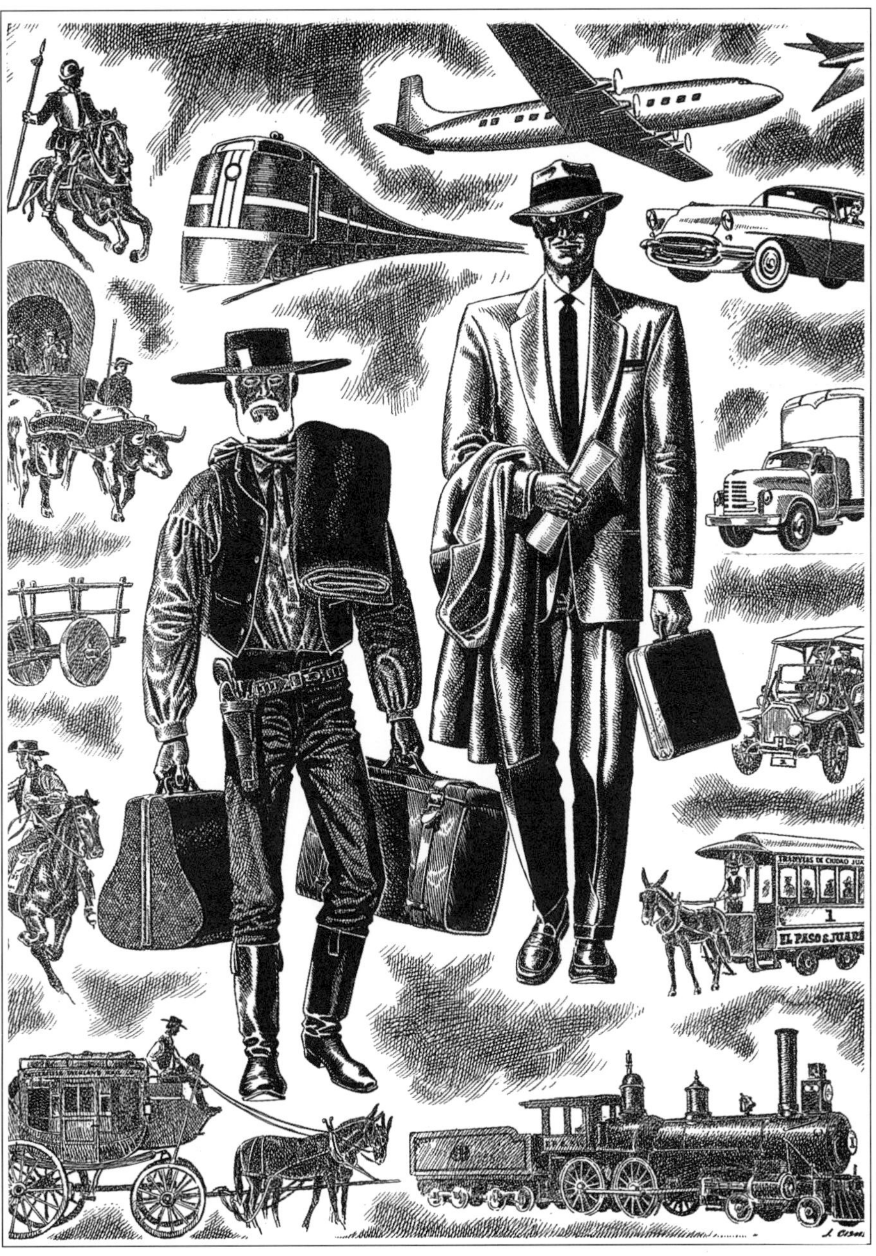

The El PasoTimes

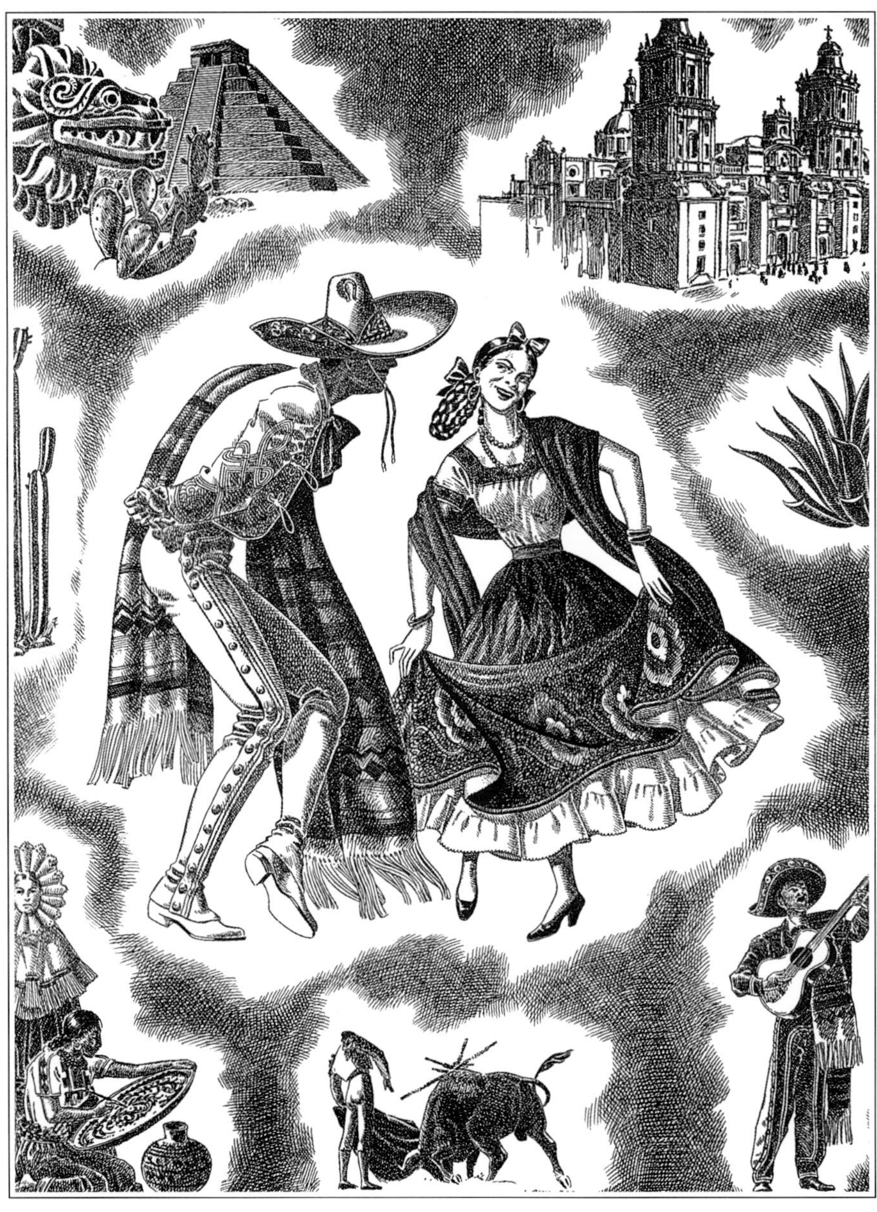

The El Paso Times

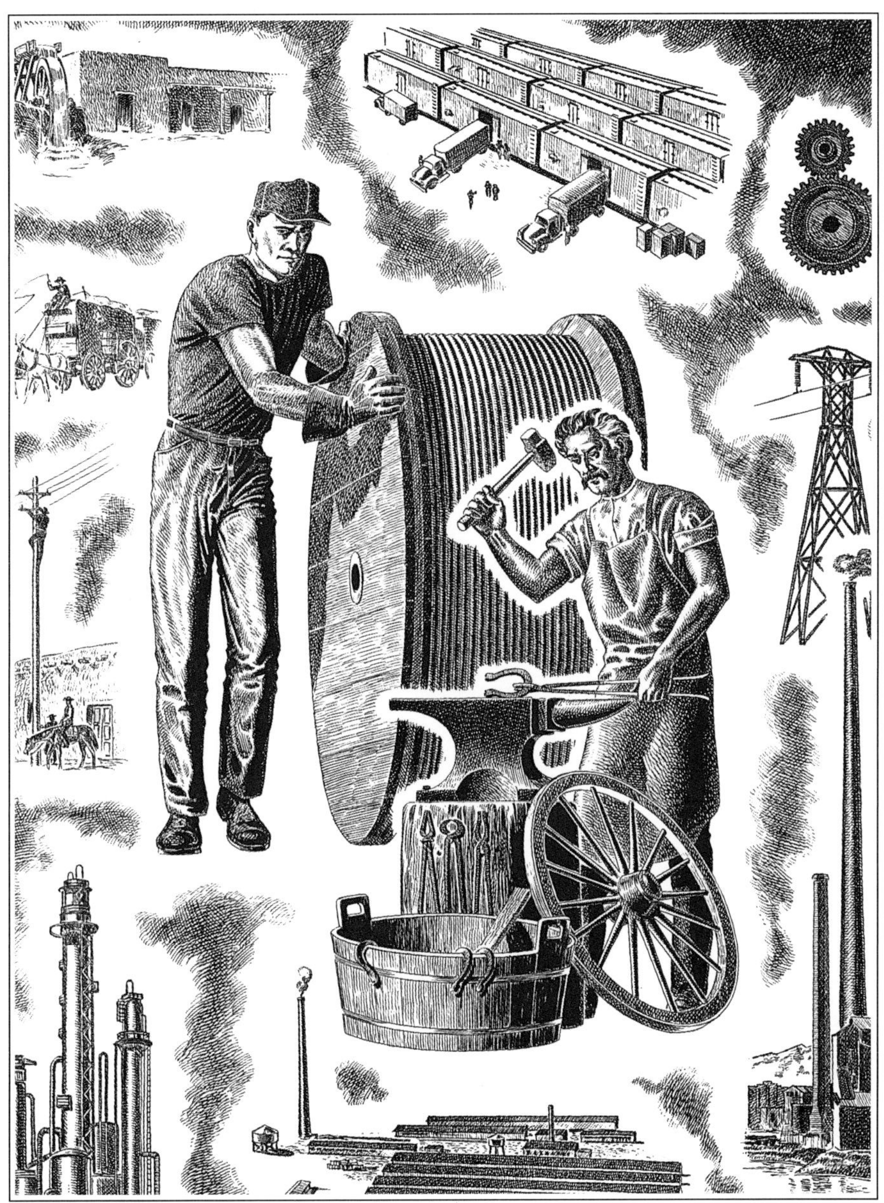

The El Paso Times

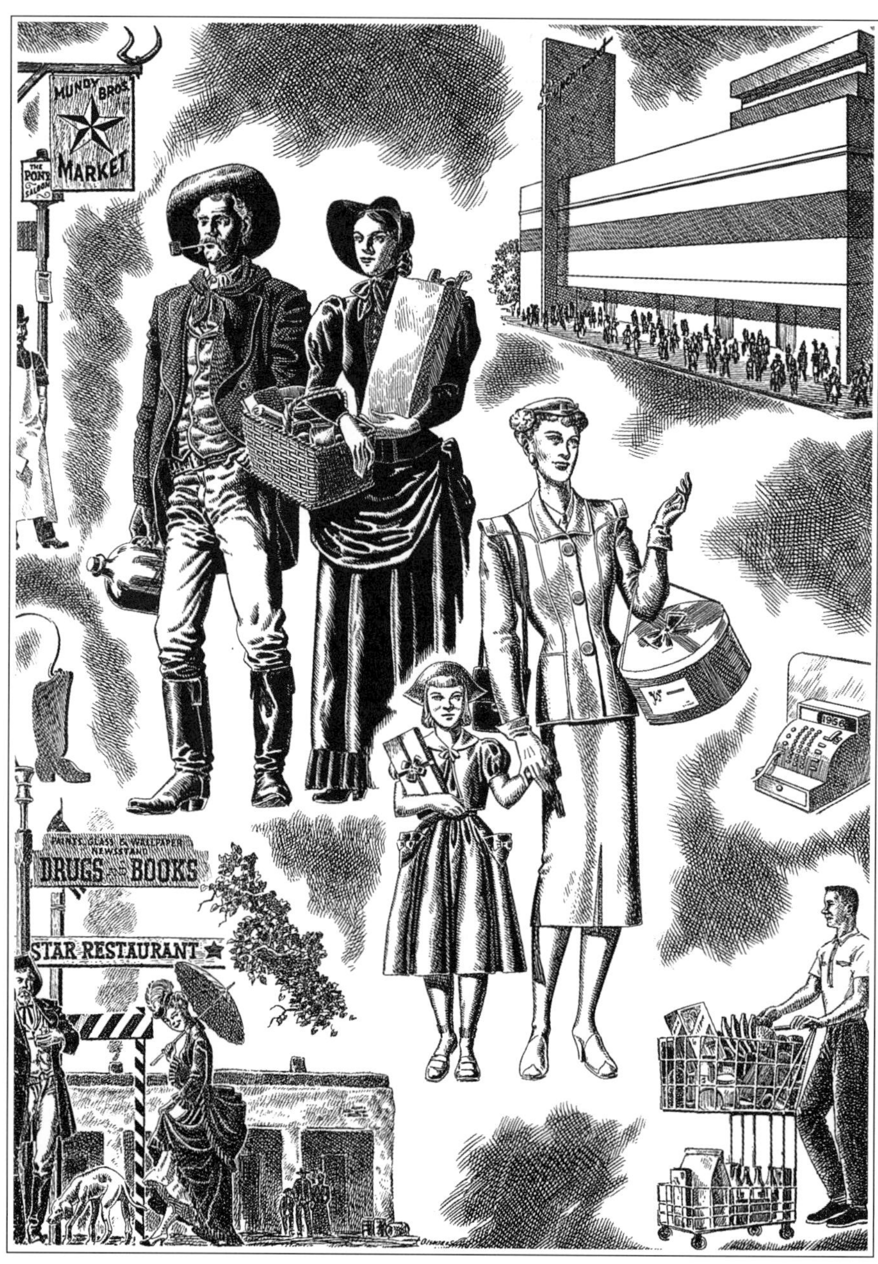

The El Paso Times

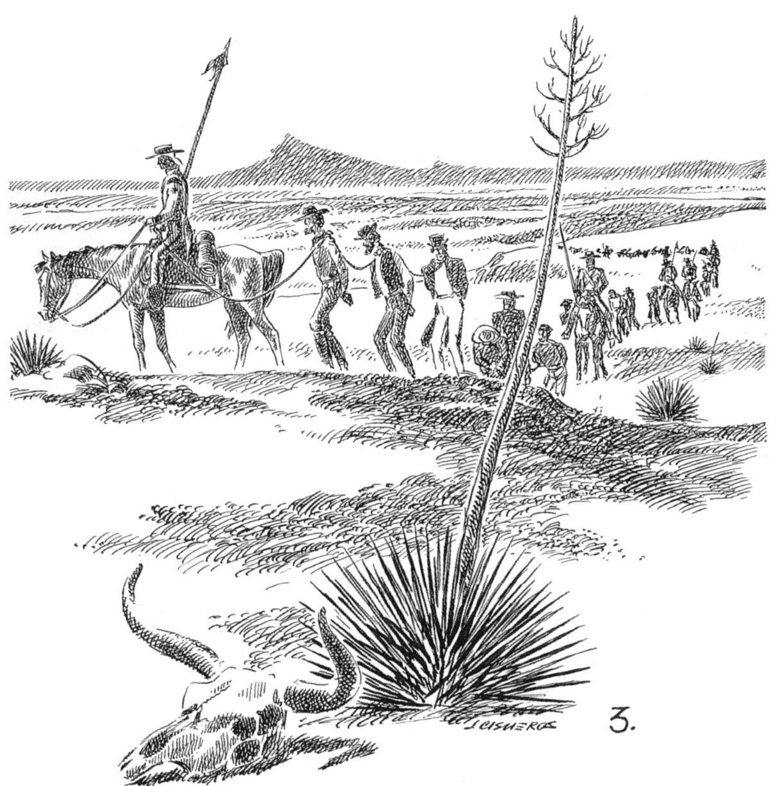

In 1959, Texas Attorney General Will Wilson wrote a series on Texas' boundary troubles, entitled "The Shape of Texas," for state newspapers. (Courtesy of Will Wilson)
above, The ill-fated Santa Fe Expedition sent Texans north to Santa Fe in an attempt to seize the upper Rio Grande area for the Lone Star State; captured and taken to Mexico, the survivors suffered great hardship.

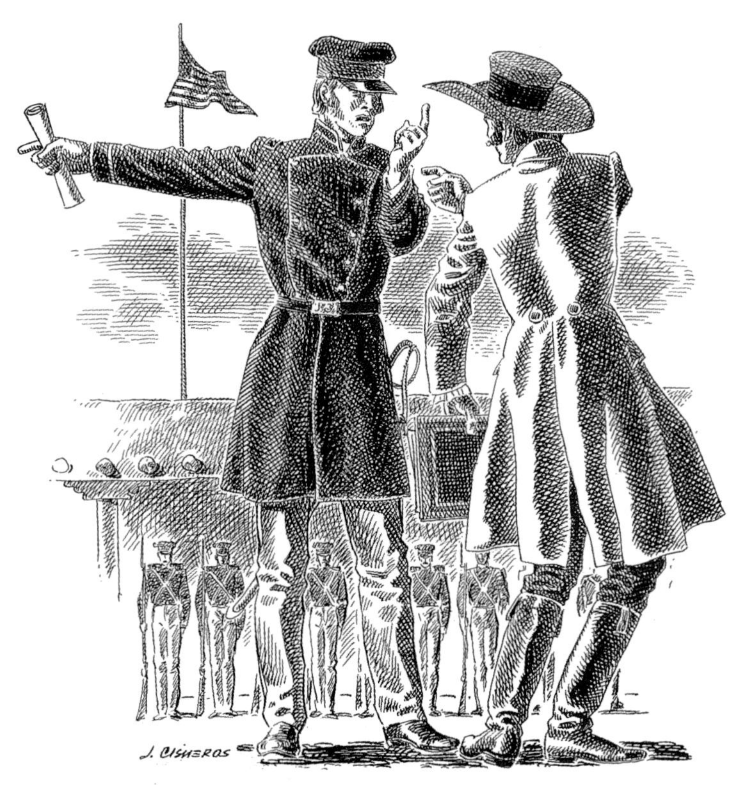

"The Shape of Texas,"
U.S. Army Col. John M. Washington and his troops deposed a Texas county judge in another attempt at making the Santa Fe area a part of Texas.

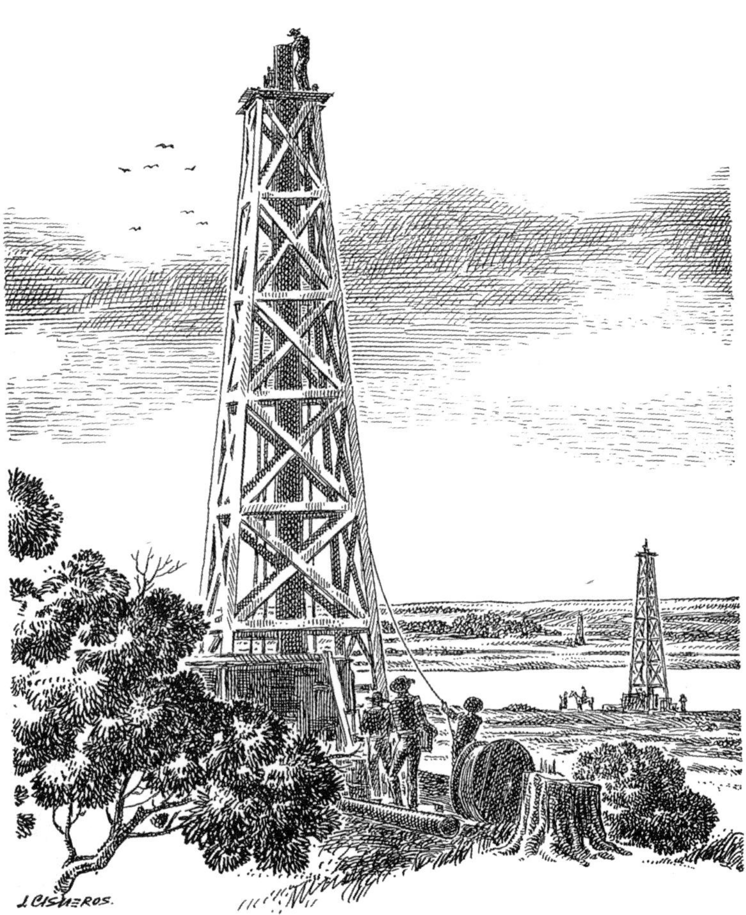

"The Shape of Texas"

The disputed area around the Red River became even more important when oil was discovered on the south bank around 1919.

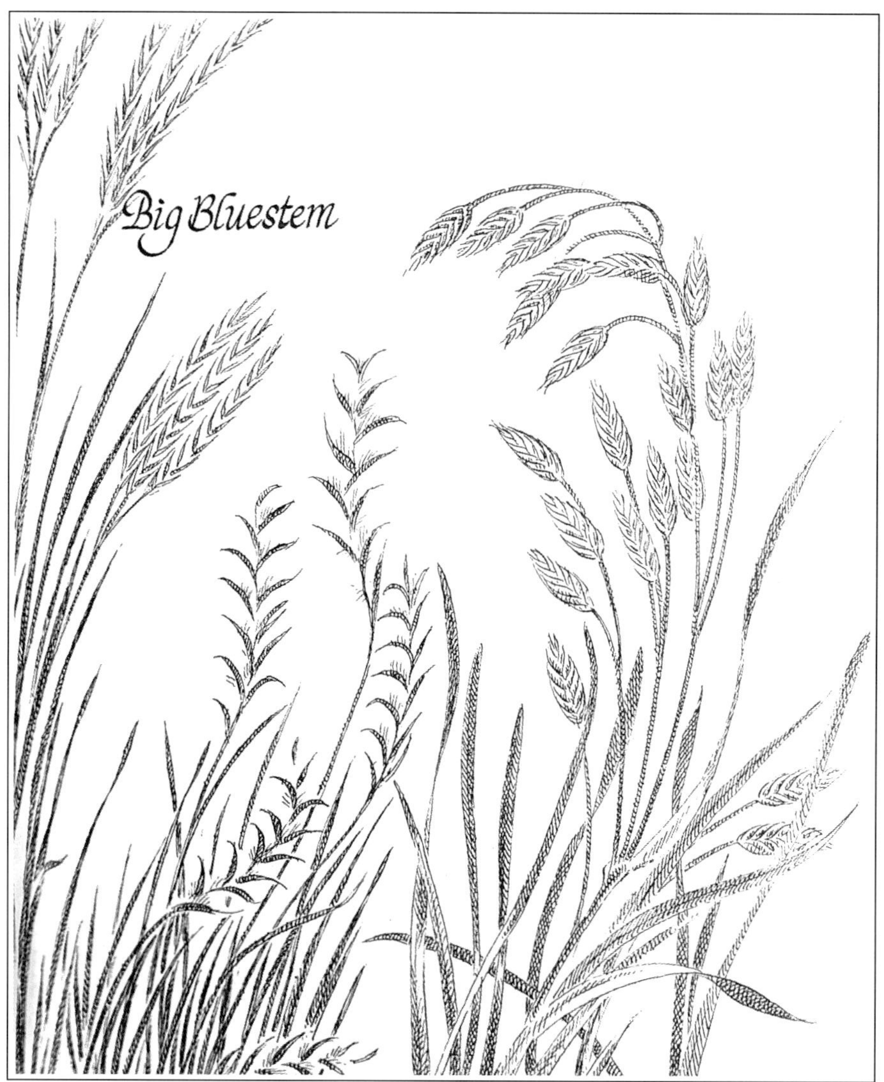

An illustration from a leaflet on Texas grasses, published by Carl Hertzog in the early 1950s.

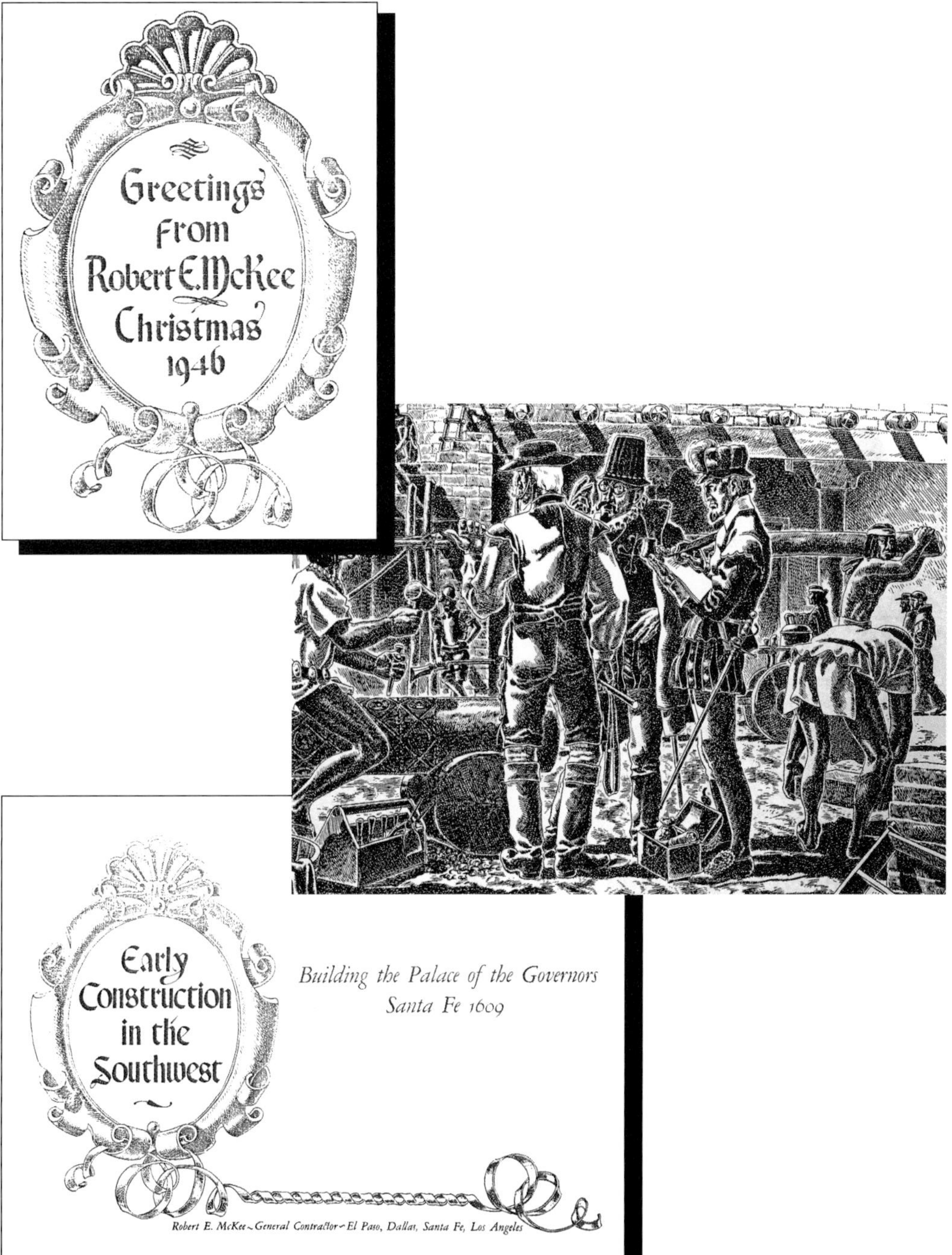

R.E. McKee, prominent Texas builder, called on Cisneros talent to create his 1946 Christmas card, with an illustration of early construction in Santa Fe.

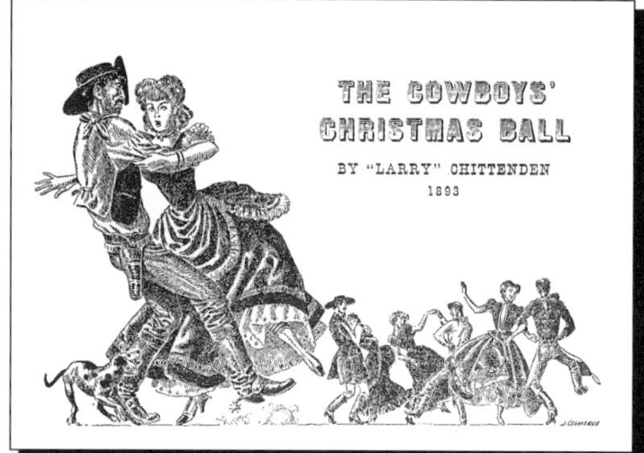

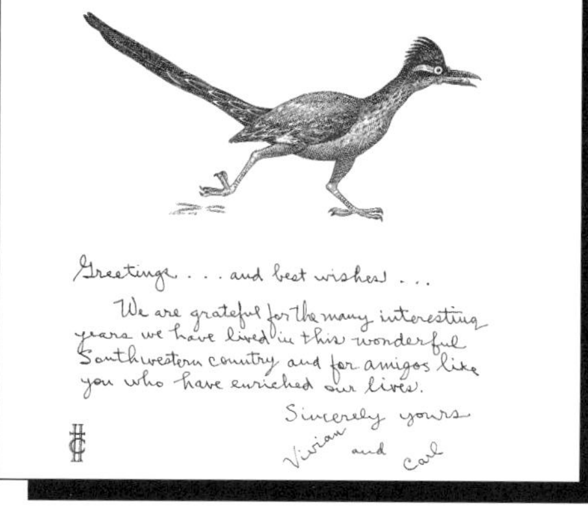

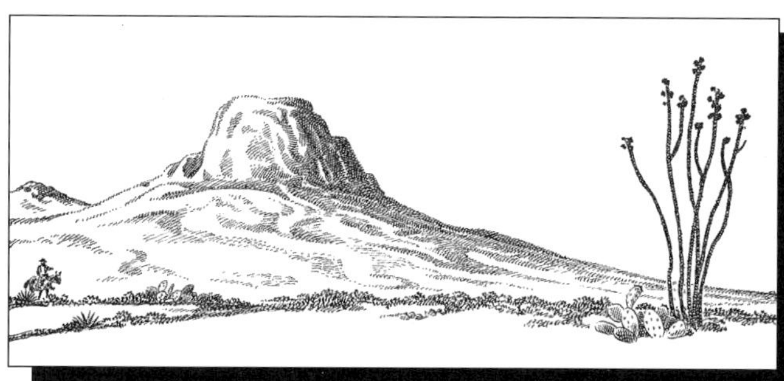

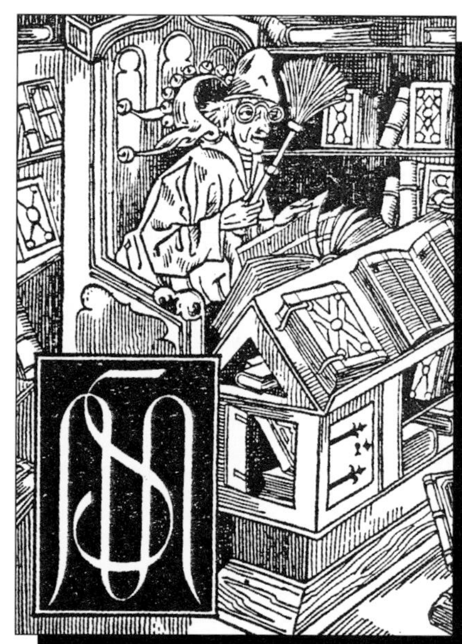

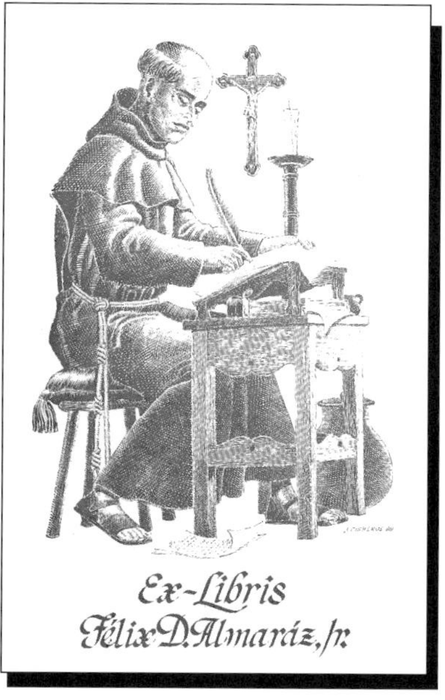

Cisneros Christmas cards and bookplates (Courtesy of Al Lowman)
Top left: Larry Chittenden's poem "The Cowboy's Christmas Ball," card for Southwestern publisher Jack Rittenhouse.
Top right and center: Cisneros designed cards for Carl and Vivian Hertzog.
Bottom left: Stanley Marcus bookplate designed by Cisneros.
Bottom right: Felix Almaráz bookplate.

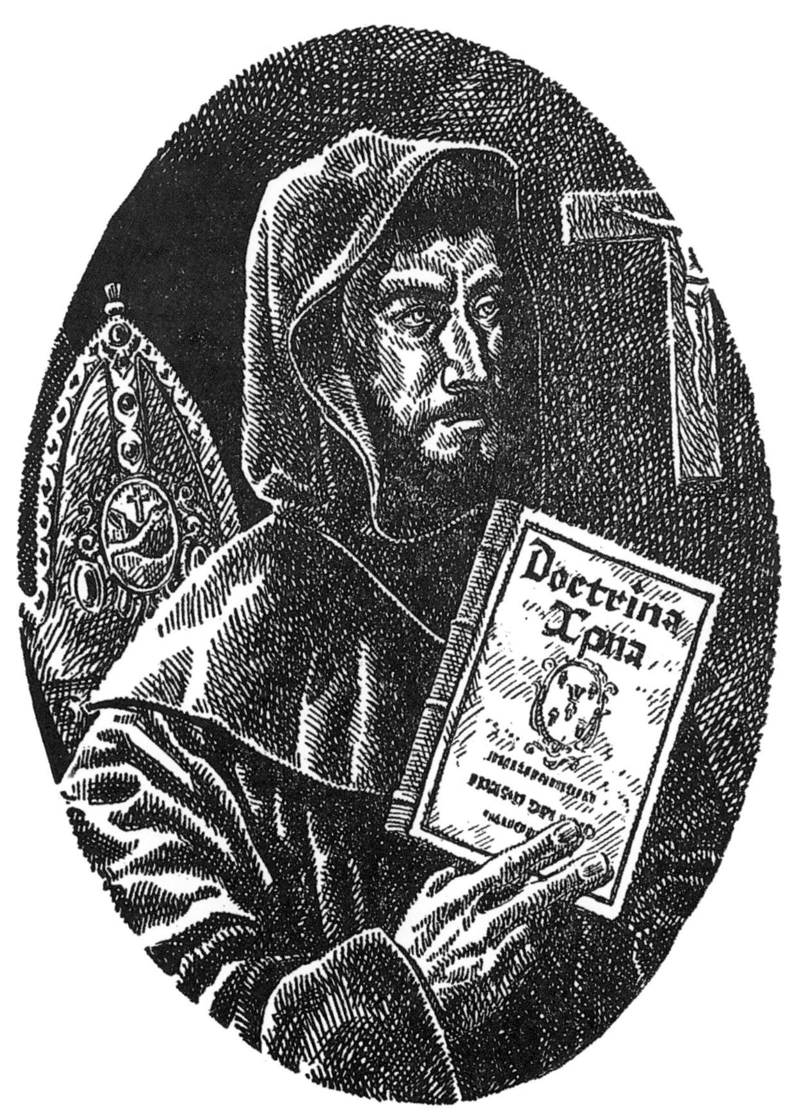

Juan Suárez, O.F.M., named the first bishop of "Rio Panuco y Victoria Garayana," as the lower Rio Grande area was once called, never took charge of his post. (From a 1950s newspaper article by historian Cleofas Calleros)

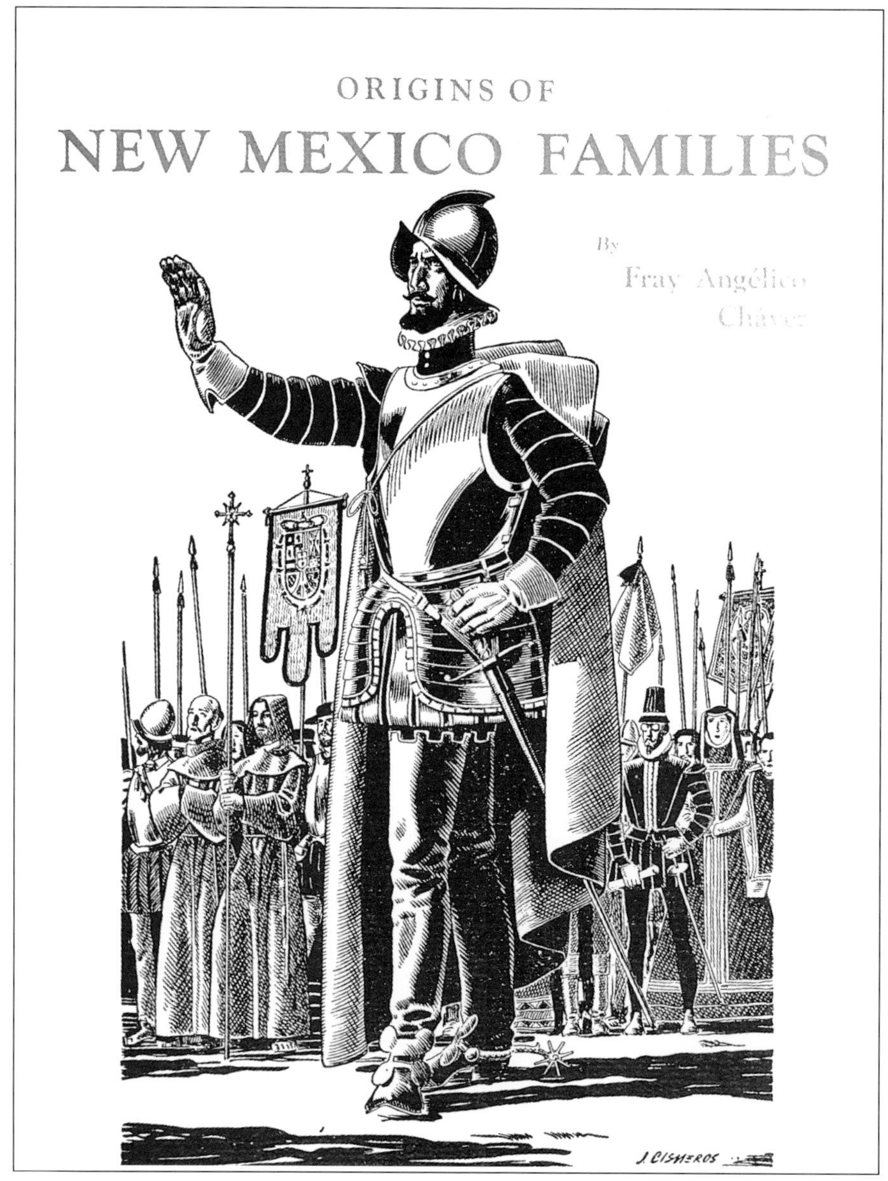

Origins of New Mexico Families (*1954*) *by Fray Angélico Chávez had these illustrations by Cisneros*
The title page

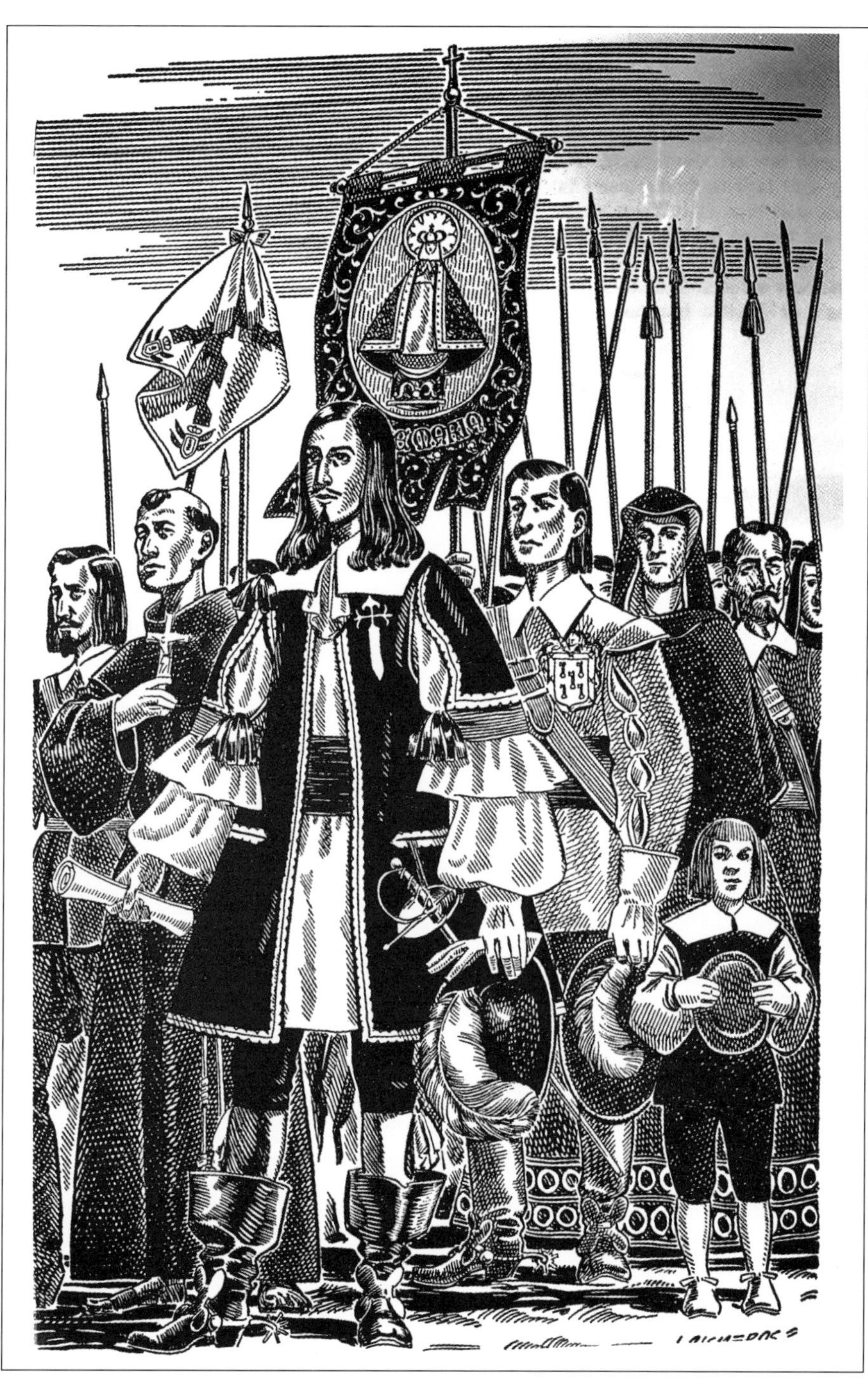

Origins of New Mexico Families: *The frontispiece, depicting a procession of early settlers*

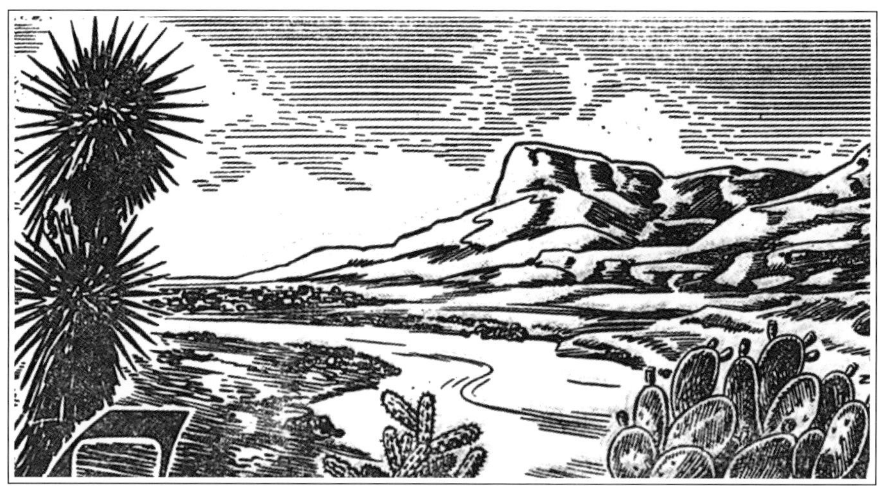

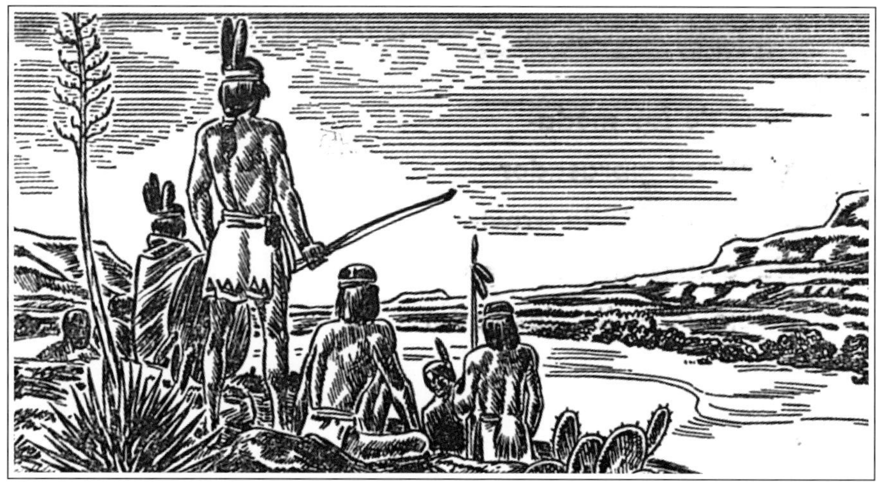

A 1959 epic poem by Cisneros friend and patron Armando B. Chávez inspired these illustrations for Síntesis Gráfica de la Historia de Ciudad Juárez.

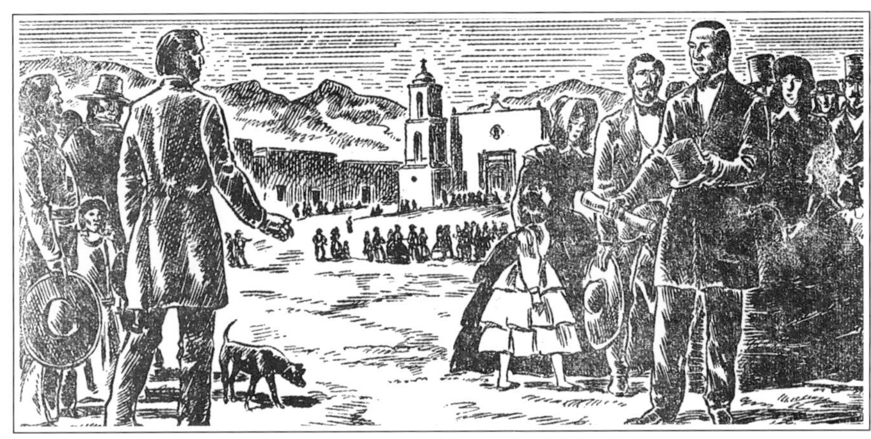

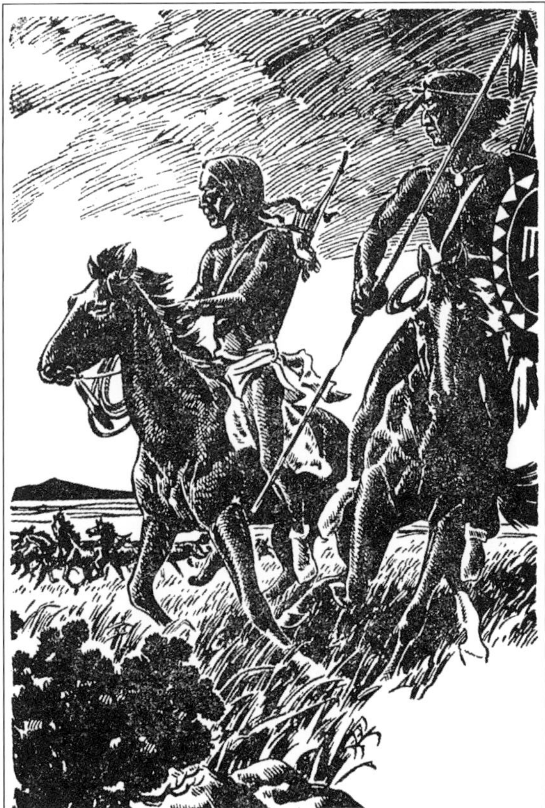

Síntesis Gráfica de la Historia de Ciudad Juárez

by C. L. SONNICHSEN

The

EL PASO SALT WAR

of 1877

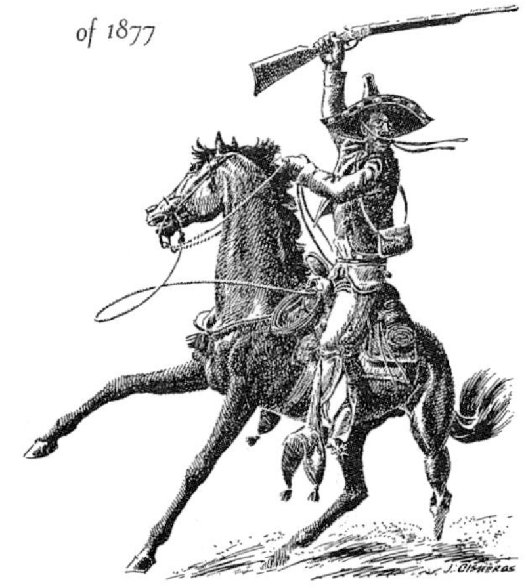

Illustrations by
José Cisneros

Typography by
Carl Hertzog

Carl Hertzog is a nationally known book designer and typographer who is responsible for the format of such books as Tom Lea's *The King Ranch* and John Graves' *Goodbye to a River*. An artist in type, his work commands the highest respect—and the highest prices—among collectors.

Jose Cisneros is an exceptionally talented illustrator who specializes in the Spanish background. His conquistadores, priests and rancheros are right to the last detail. He has made a lifetime study of costumes from the days of Cortés through the nineteenth century.

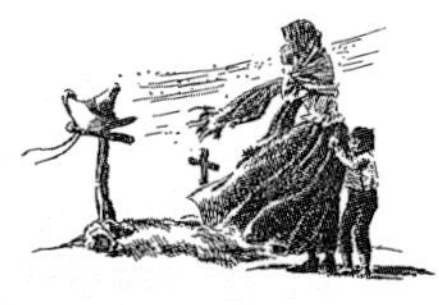

TEXAS WESTERN PRESS
AT THE COLLEGE
EL PASO, TEXAS

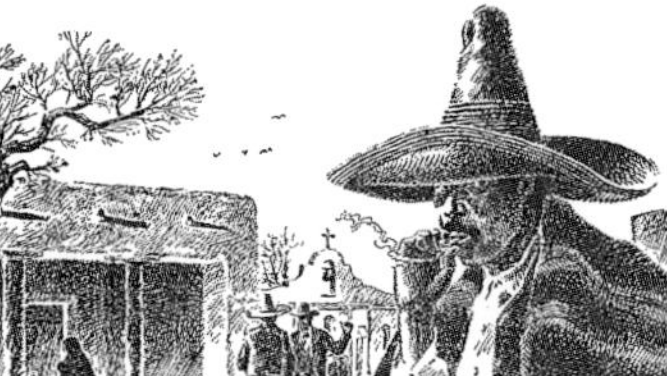

Down the river, at San Elizario, every nerve was taut as an Apache bowstring. By twos and threes men from Mexico plowed across the waterless bed of the Rio Grande, squatted under the cottonwoods with their American *Compadres*, and talked in low bitter tones. Some of them quoted Father Borrajo, who was holding forth these days with redoubled vigor on the wickedness of the Gringos.

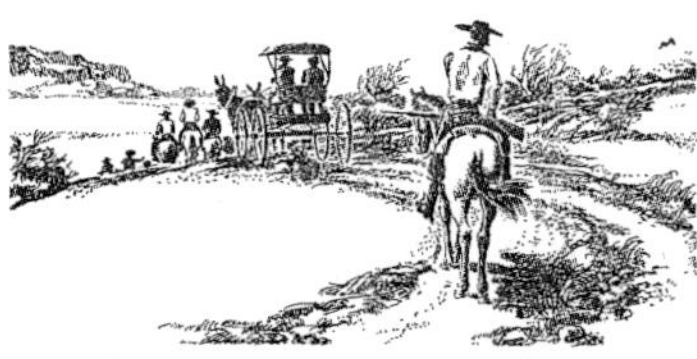

Magoffin stirred his stumps. He squeezed his portly figure and Old Testament beard into a buggy, picked up half a dozen mounted soldiers, and went to have a look. As he passed through Ysleta and Socorro, he questioned and listened, and what he heard made him very uneasy. This was no two-by-four revolt. The entire Mexican population on both sides of the river was mixed up in it.

The EL PASO SALT WAR [1877] – SONNICHSEN

The El Paso Salt War *by C.L. Sonnichsen (1961) dust jacket by Cisneros.*

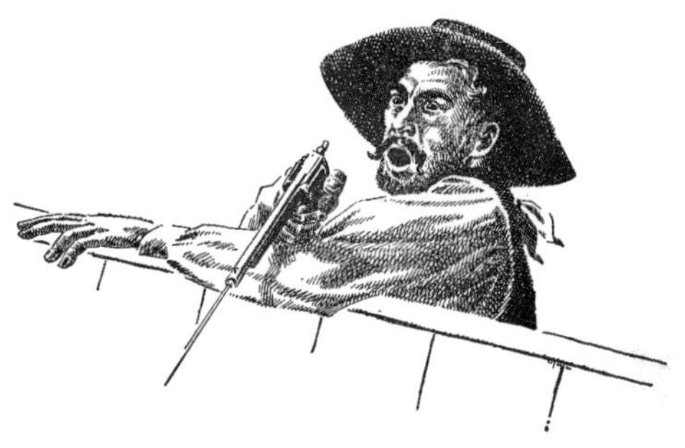

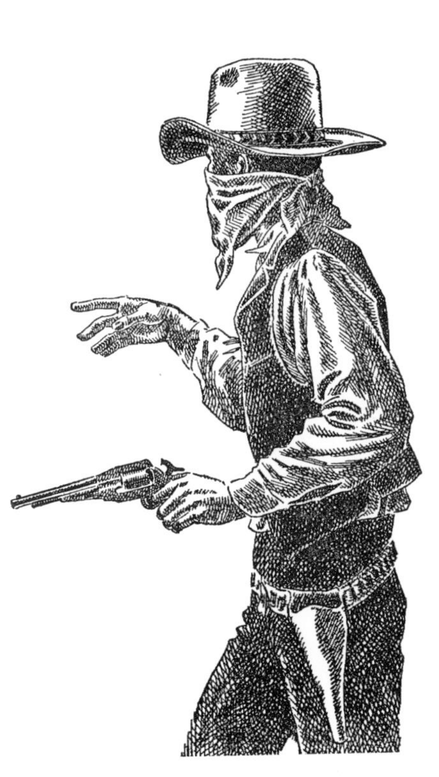

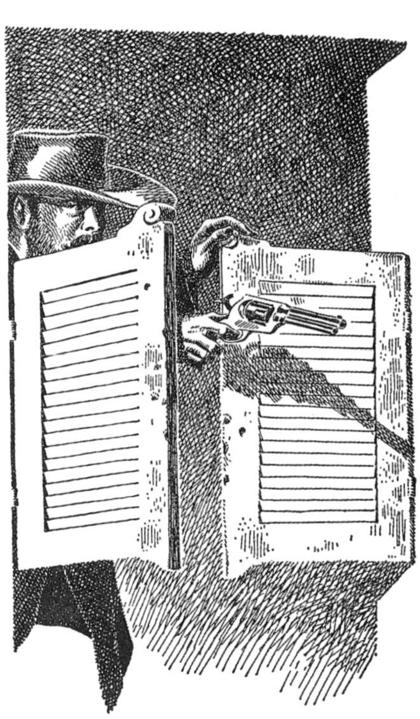

The history of feuding in Texas, captured by C.L. Sonnichsen in I'll Die Before I'll Run *(1962), has a large assortment of Cisneros illustrations.*

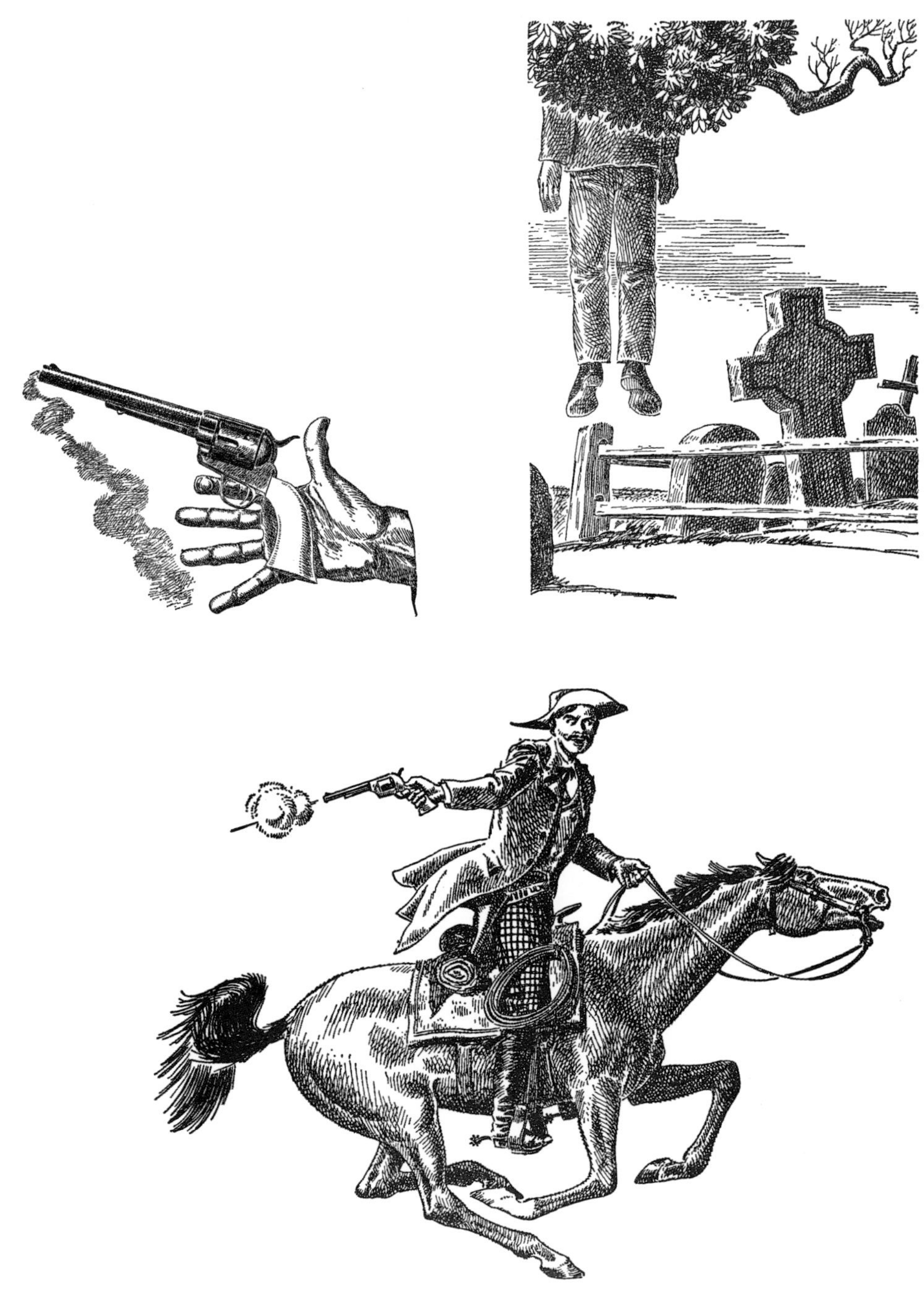

I'll Die Before I'll Run

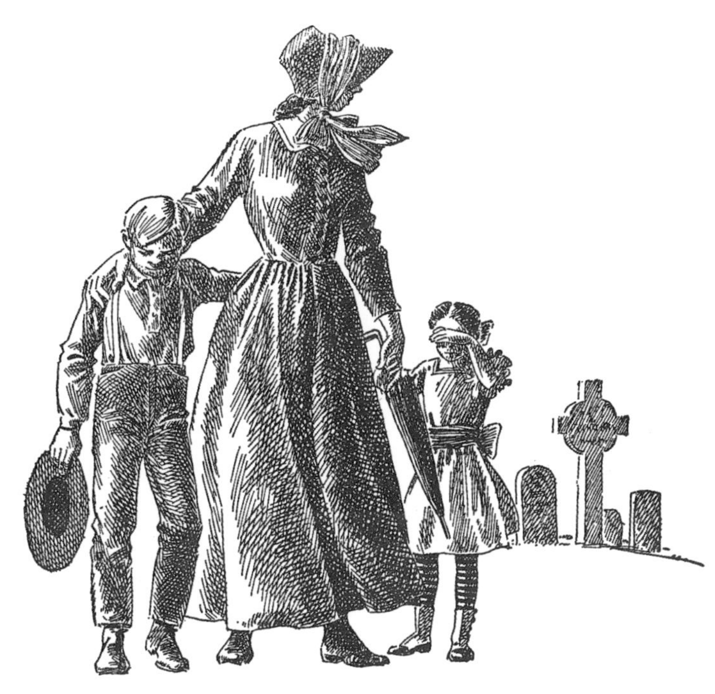

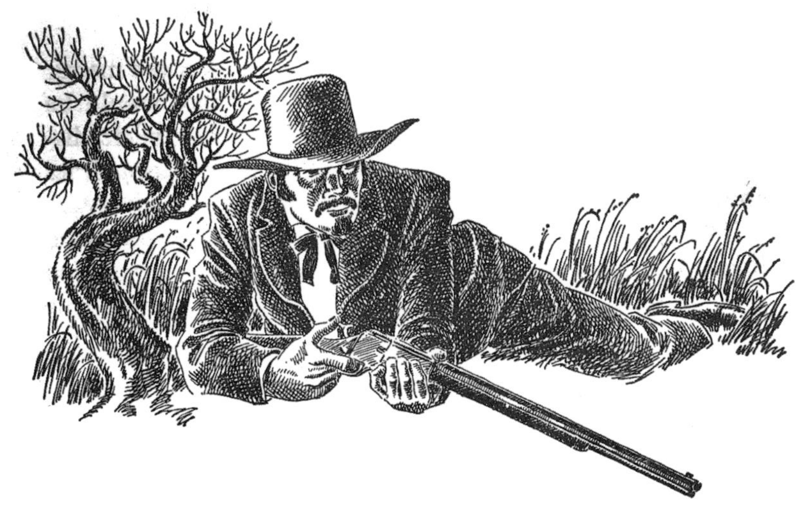

I'll Die Before I'll Run

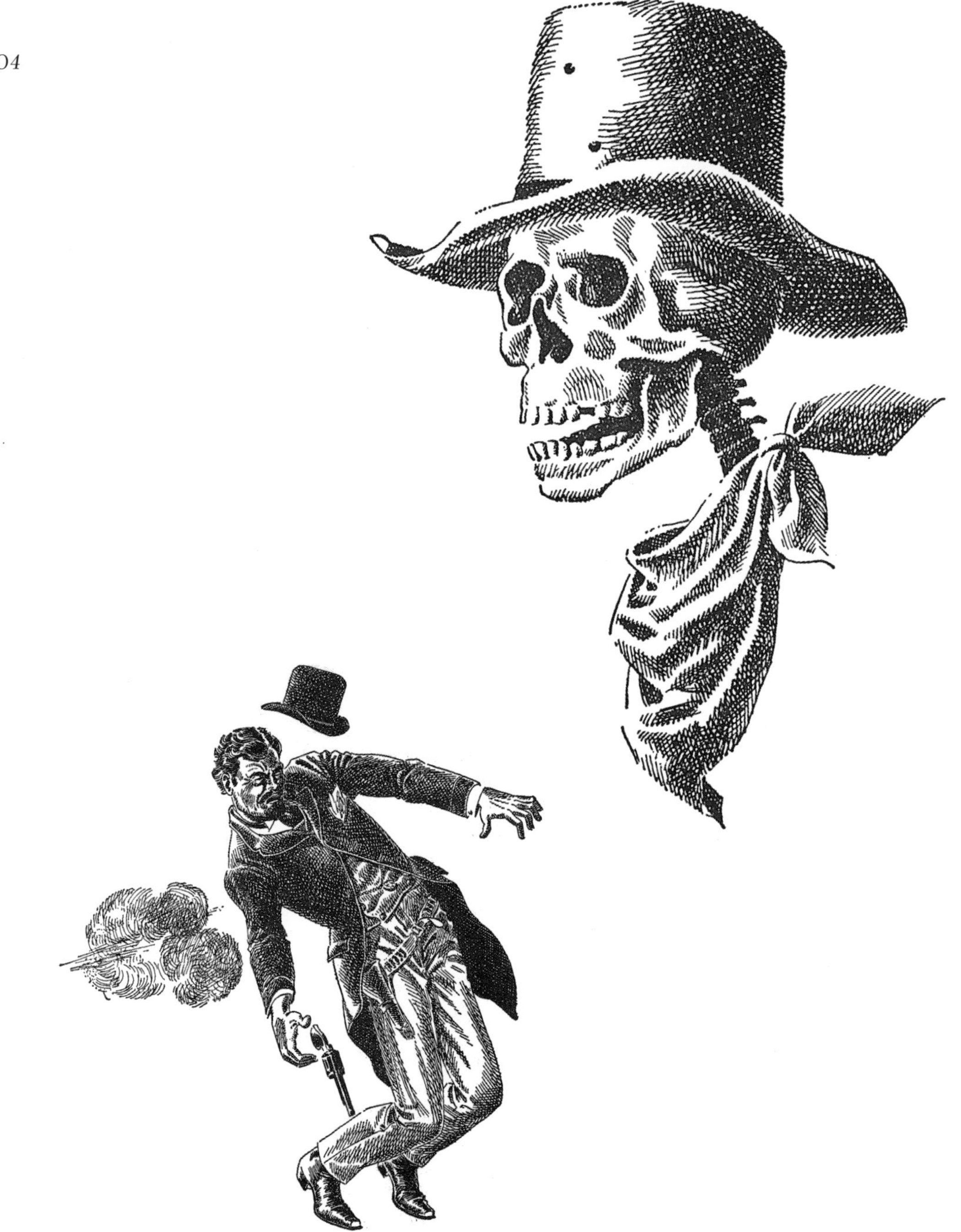

I'll Die Before I'll Run

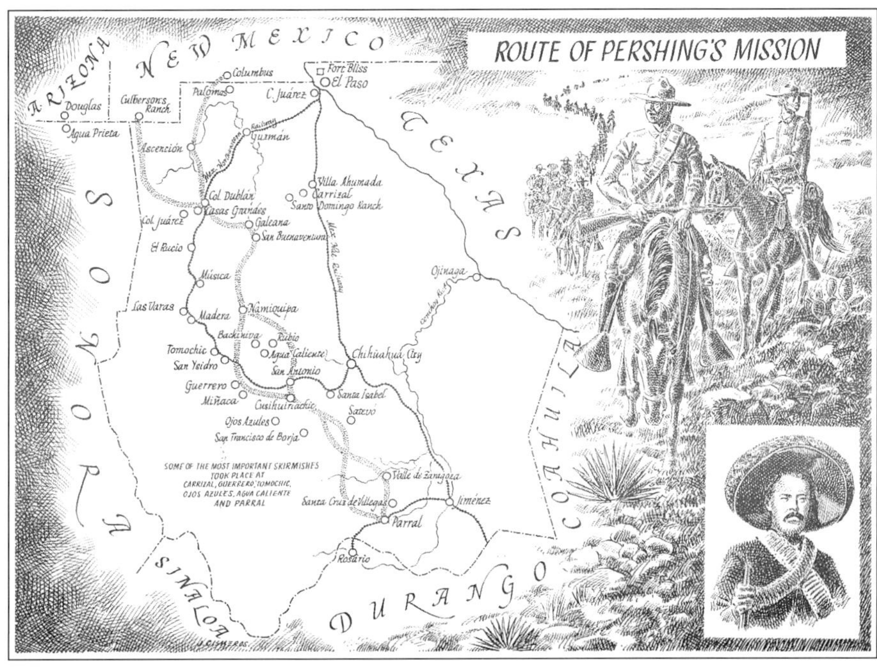

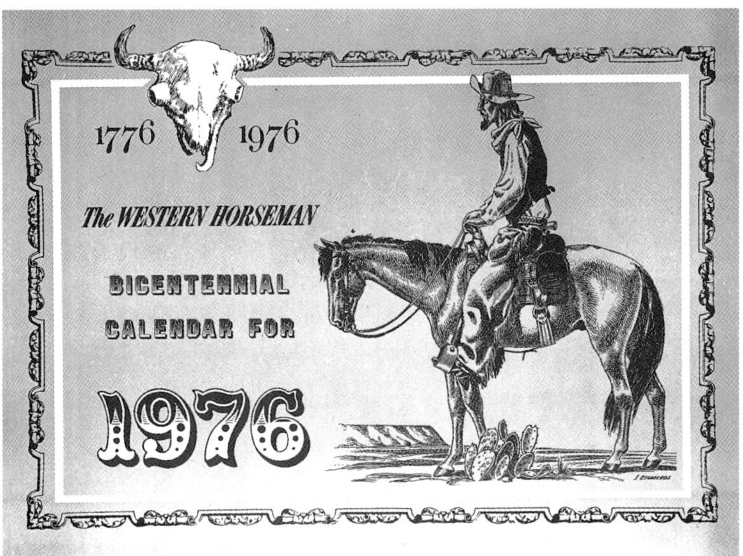

Top: Pershing's Mission to Mexico *(1965) by the late Haldeen Braddy, University of Texas at El Paso author and Pancho Villa authority, has this map showing the route General John J. Pershing followed in pursuing Villa after the 1916 raid on Columbus, New Mexico. Bottom:* Western Horseman Calendar*.*

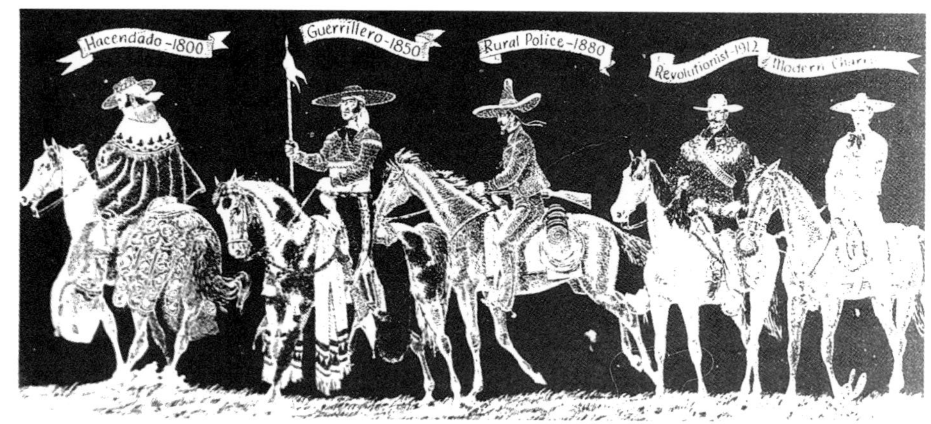

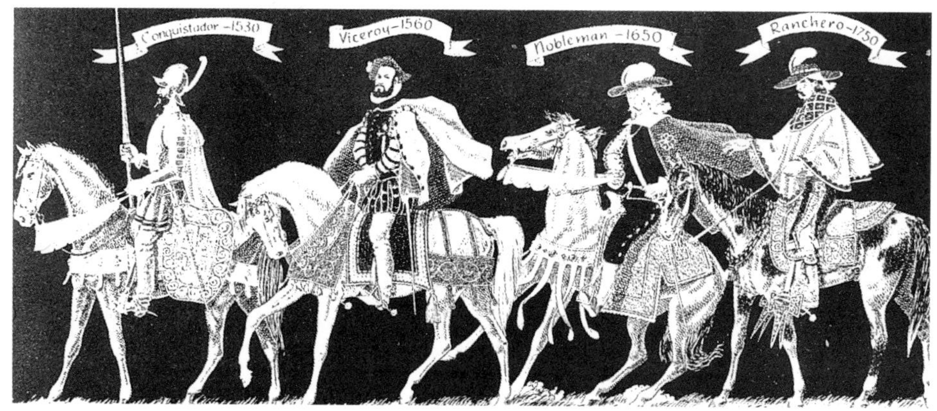

A parade of Cisneros horsemen (reproduced from Western Horseman, *September 1951).*

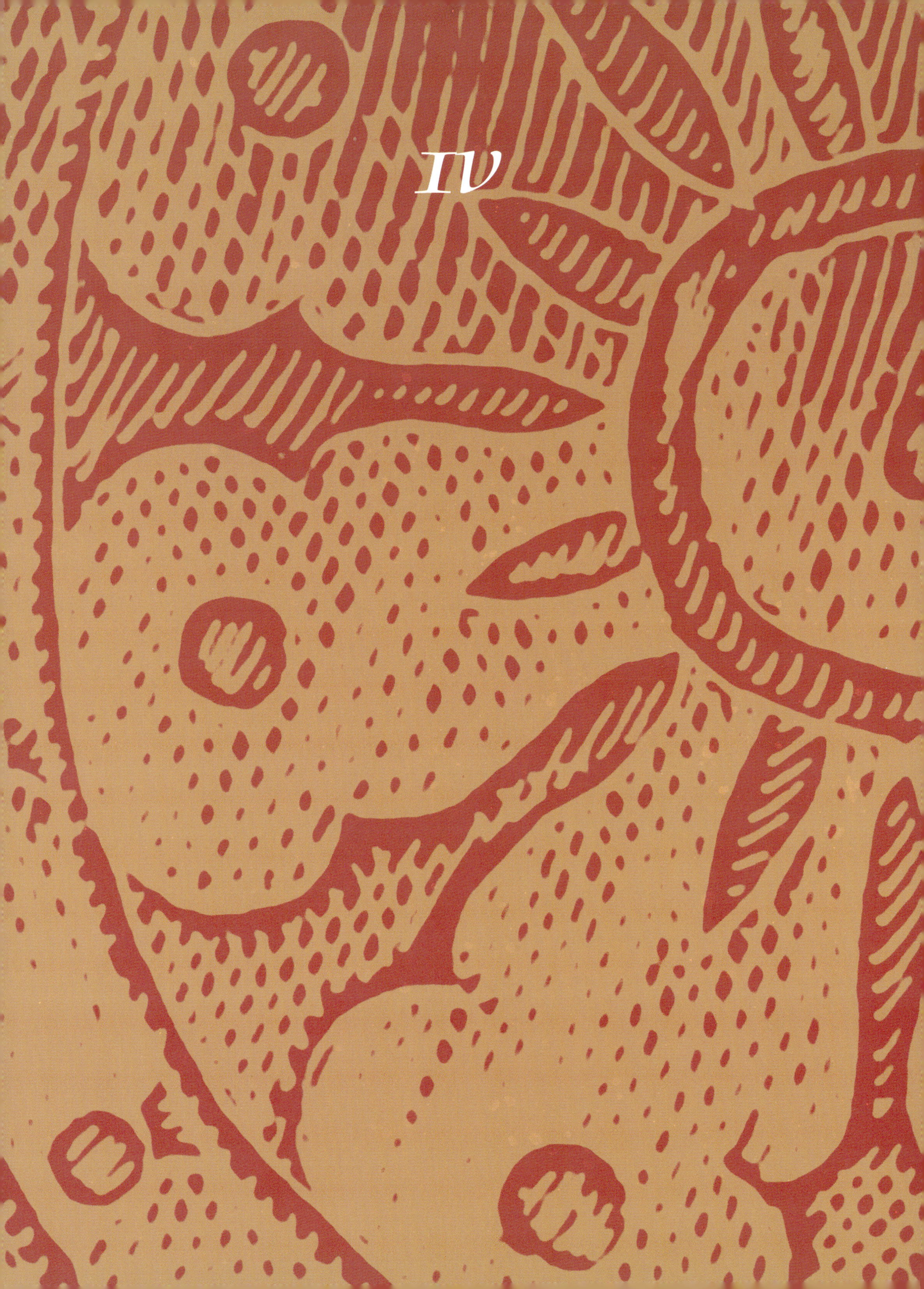

IV

IV

Paisano Turning Point

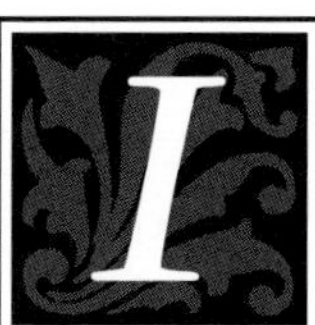

In the late 1960s José Cisneros decided to reach for a star. He knew the value of friends, of making contacts for a budding artist with ambition. The trip he had made with Carl Hertzog to Paris and Austin, Texas, had taught him that. So he offered to take an exhibit of his works, even paying for display space, to the coming meeting of the Western History Association in Tucson, Arizona. Harwood Hinton and the directors decided the offer was too good to pass up, but they insisted on paying for the exhibit and the space it would occupy. Tuffly Ellis and Frank Wardlaw, prominent Texans in the field of publishing history, were among the contacts made in this venture, and they encouraged Cisneros to apply for the Paisano Fellowship being offered to writers and artists who needed time to develop their skills without the strain of earning a daily wage. The suggestion bore fruit soon, and the El Paso artist had earned his chance.

In February, 1969, José Cisneros, his wife Vicenta, his eight-year-old daughter Rita, and his four-year-old grand-daughter Margaret, took up residence for six months at J. Frank Dobie's old ranch, Paisano, on Barton Creek in the Hill Country southwest of Austin. He was working at El Paso City Lines in the painting department when it was announced he won the fellowship, and his immediate supervisor was unwilling to release him for so long, "possibly for reasons of jealousy," Cisneros speculates. Someone farther up the chain of command felt that it was an honor to have an employee so recognized, and he approved a leave of absence for the artist. Cisneros was the fourth recipient (and the first artist) to win a $3000 Paisano Fellowship, enabling him to live and work in a place Dobie described as "a place where I could see all that's going on in the sky around me. Here, at Paisano, I can see the clouds and at night the stars, and I'm near water." The change from the desert/mountain surroundings of northern Chihuahua and El Paso had a great impact upon Cisneros. "We are getting adjusted to the quietude and solemnity of the place," he wrote Carl Hertzog. "We saw a lot of turkeys this morning, and deer jump over our front yard fence every day." Doubtless

Frank Dobie understood the impact Paisano would have on a sensitive artist.

Hertzog had written to Cisneros before the move took place, urging him to take in the Institute of Texan Cultures in San Antonio, only sixty miles away, where he could see "Spanish armor, spurs with those long extensions and wide iron sides and many other items connecting with your Big Project." Cisneros's ambition, his "Big Project," was one he had often discussed with Hertzog. They had described it as "Cortez to Cowboys" as the two traveled from Paris to Austin back in 1948. His aim was to focus upon accurate, historically correct depictions of the horsemen of the Spanish Southwest. For years he had haunted museums when he was near them, and pored over illustrated books of horses and horsemen, learning about the riders' costumes, horse gear, the spurs and equipment of some four hundred years of Southwestern history. Of course, given the historical nature of his major subjects over the years, he had drawn a multitude of horses as they fitted into historic sites and scenes. But the horses he had drawn for *El Léon Juarense*, for example, or *Mexico* magazine, had tended to be stylized. Costumes of the riders were dramatic and full of the flavor of Spain and Mexico, but he was driven—ever since his days at San Miguel de Allende—to be accurate, placing each detail in its proper time frame. And since horses had been so closely related for so long to the history of mankind, they were truly special to the budding artist. "The horse is God's most beautiful animal. I have always admired the 'architecture' of horses, the way they move, how their muscles work," he said recently, "and I was never able to learn enough about them." The stay at Paisano gave him the opportunity to concentrate on what was to become his most notable subject matter, one which added to his already established fame, and one for which many historians have cited him as an excellent illustrator of the Borderlands and its history.

The Institute of Texan Cultures in San Antonio, where Cisneros did much of his research, not only provided an early exhibit of ninety-two of his horsemen; it also published a sampling of that exhibit, under the

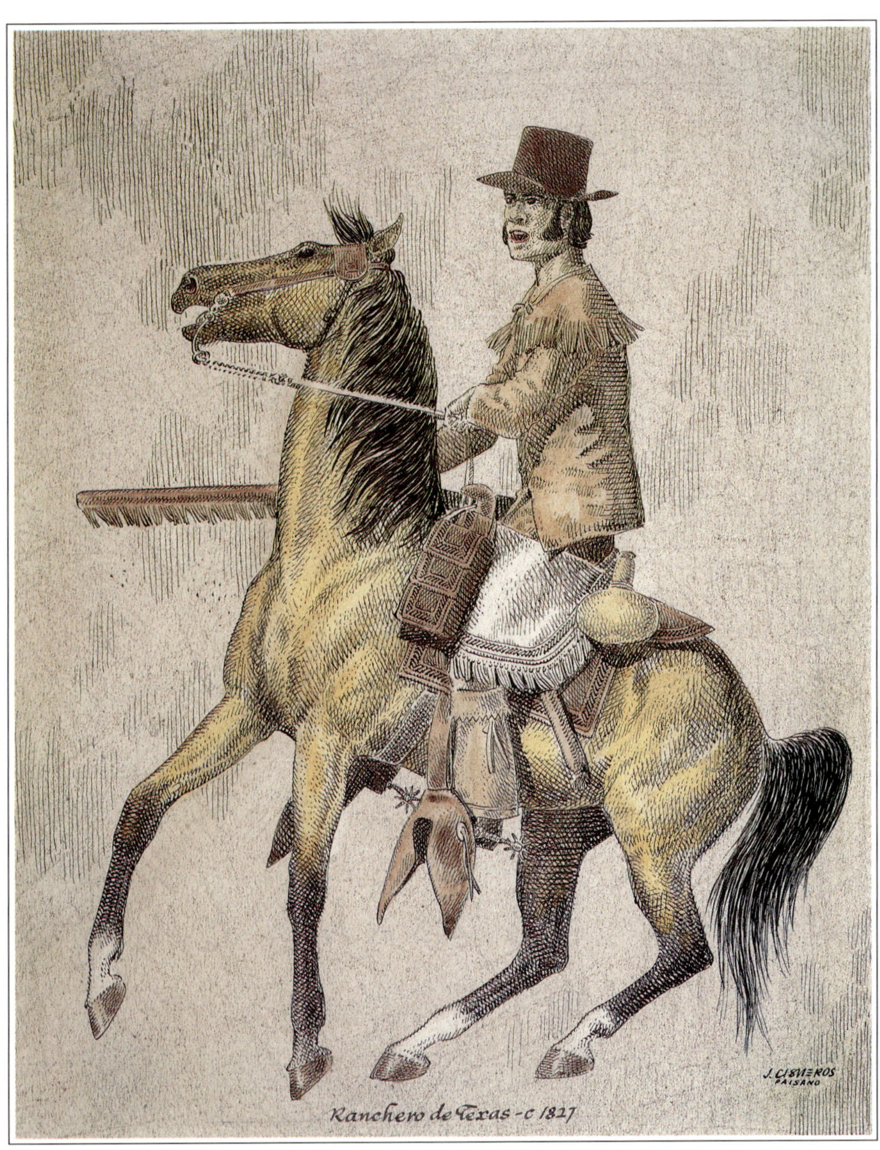

The artist's horse illustrations began to evolve from stylized, static figures to lifelike images during the time he spent at Frank Dobie's Paisano Ranch in 1969.
One of the first of the artist's Paisano Ranch horsemen.

title *José Cisneros at Paisano, an exhibit: Riders of the Spanish Borderlands*, with a biographical introduction by Al Lowman and a description of the Dobie-Paisano Project by Bertha McKee Dobie. The title, "Riders of the Borderlands," in one form or another, and the subject matter of that exhibit and that booklet have been Cisneros's main concern ever since. A feature article in a 1974 issue of *Southwestern Art*, "The Horsemen of Cisneros," spelled out his strong interest (a direct but unacknowledged quote from the artist): "His aim and intense desire has been to reconstruct and depict to the best of his ability the pageantry of horsemanship of Mexico and the southwestern border states of the U.S." Such was his "Big Project" that began, for all practical purposes, with the stimulation his imagination had received from the eloquence of Don Manuel Villaraus in Escuela Primaria No. 190, back in historic Valle de Allende.

In 1981 an exhibition of 112 of Cisneros's horsemen at the Centennial Museum at the University of Texas at El Paso bore fruit in a Hertzog-designed catalog with twenty-one of his drawings entitled *Riders of the Borderlands*, ranging from a soldier with Cortez to a West Texas cowboy of the current century, as he and Hertzog had discussed so many years ago: "Cortez to Cowboys." By 1984 the collection had found its focus and was reduced to one hundred horsemen that now hang on permanent display on the walls of the University of Texas at El Paso Library, a collection culminating in the Texas Western Press classic *Riders Across the Centuries* of that year, thanks to the spiritual and financial support of UTEP president and historian Haskell Monroe (who, upon arriving at U T El Paso, sought out and introduced himself to the artist of whom he had heard so much, even before Carl Hertzog could manage to introduce the two).

Of that first book of horsemen published by the Institute of Texan Cultures (but still applicable to his later work), writer Mike Cox of the San Angelo *Standard Times* marveled over the various types of horsemen Cisneros drew, including a drawing of a typical Cuera Dragoon, the Spanish cavalry charged with the protection of the missions in Texas. Unknown to most amateur historians, incidentally, is the fact that these

Spanish soldiers did not wear the lobster-shell-like armor usually depicted in the cinema. Instead, the frontier Spanish horseman wore thick leather armor—a protection much more practical and comfortable for Texas.

That description was accurate as far as it went, since from decade to decade and area to area entirely different styles of armor and protection devices were worn on the frontier. Cisneros keeps them all straight in his encyclopedic mind, earning from art historian Paul Rossi the praise that he is "beyond any doubt, the leading authority in the country concerning the many varied horsemen of Spanish American history and horsemen of our Southwest."

A visit to Cisneros's basement studio is a trip back in time for the lover of horses or history. His grandson, Robert Villareal, in an eloquent essay written for a class at U T El Paso, revealed that the crawl space beneath the house was carved out by his grandparents, José and Vicenta, the dirt carried out in buckets and dumped in the unpaved alley behind the house, to create that studio. That effort, and the support that Vicenta has provided to her husband over the years, makes that studio even more precious to one who knows its history. However, the contents of the studio are impressive enough by themselves: there one finds literally hundreds of books on horses and horsemen, on different aspects of history (especially Hispanic and Southwestern). Here are the tools used for reference materials by this artist who insists on being accurate. Cisneros loves to recall that his granddaughter, Christie, was once sent downstairs to see if he was asleep. She was soon back reporting to the family "He's not asleep. He's working, as he always is."

The basement studio is also a treasure store, with a wealth of books with dust jackets, frontispieces, or full illustration treatment by the artist. If a visitor should ask a question, for example why a Mexican soldier still carried a lance years after such a weapon would seem to be out of date, or why a tough frontier soldier has lace drawers visible above his boots, then the questioner is in for a lengthy history lesson. *Vaqueros*, one learns, pull their *sombreros* down close over their eyes; Texas cowboys tip their hats back, as a part perhaps, of their devil-may-care image. Cisneros knows his subject, and welcomes the opportunity to display with precision the manner in which people, history, costume, and horse "furniture" have grown and developed over the centuries.

Recently he noted how a variety of costume details have lasted beyond their origins:

> Many details of horsemen's costume have prevailed through the centuries. For example, in the 17th century when men's coats began to grow downward, it was necessary to split the back in order for the wearer to ride horses; that vent is still with us in modern men's jackets. Also during the 17th century the French started to wear ruffles at the bottom of their drawers. That fad was prevalent in Argentina, Mexico, and other Latin American countries in the 18th and 19th centuries. Many Indian tribes in Mexico still use them as a part of their typical attire. In the early 16th century Don Vasco de Quiroga, bishop of Michoacán in Mexico, taught the natives of the towns around Lake Patzcúaro different trades and crafts. One of the villages was chosen to make hats, which the Indians never wore before. Since they had no models to follow, they chose Don Vasco's hat, which had tassels around its crown as insignia of his office. After almost five centuries the hats that come fom Patzcúaro still carry a little tassel in the back.

Ever since the Cisneros's family's stay at Paisano, public interest has grown in his art as *art*, with collectors far beyond the Southwest taking pride in their Cisneros horsemen. An assortment of Cisneros drawings has been collected by former President and Mrs. George Bush, some of them were displayed on the walls of the White House in Washington (one picture, "The Sheriff Got His Man," was a gift from the artist on the occasion of Mr. Bush's second inauguration as vice-president in 1985). People from many walks of life order his drawings. A prominent dentist in Santa Barbara, California, has twenty-six Cisneros horsemen prancing on his office wall, and other art lovers are enraptured with his work, in the original black and white or augmented with watercolor or colored pencils. However, the artist's main interest continues to be the accurate historical illustration of books, magazines, and other works on the Spanish Southwest. Regional history, intertwined as it has been with horses and horsemen for four centuries, has such a strong hold on his imagination that a horse and rider are likely to appear in almost any scene he is commissioned to depict.

Some years ago a book dealer decided to produce a catalog of books focusing on Texas, and asked Cisneros to draw a cover depicting the famous oil well Santa Rita Number One. It was the first producing well on University of Texas property, the beginning of the University's permanent endowment fund. As ordered, the Cisneros cover accurately presented the well in full flow, gushing crude oil all over the derrick, while a *vaquero* sat on his horse nearby, quietly watching all the excitement. Perhaps, in addition to his interest in horses, the drawing reveals the active sense of humor that pervades Cisneros art. Very frequently, a drawing of almost any historical scene that leaves José Cisneros's pen will include a scrawny dog, ribs protruding in mute testimony to his malnourished condition. The horses are almost always well cared for, sleek and fat, while the dogs like those in his experience—especially in his childhood during the Mexican Revolution—had to fend for themselves.

Cisneros supporter Félix Almaráz delights in sharing a story involving Cisneros's design of a certificate for the Texas State Historical Association—a project that illustrates the artist's strong sense of humor. The organization was meeting in El Paso that year, and an outgoing president was complaining that former presidents received little respect. He called an impromptu reception at Martino's Restaurant in Juárez to remedy the situation, but he expected all concerned to pay for their own refreshments. Much to his surprise, he got stuck with the bill for $66—which in 1981 paid for a lot of *margaritas*. As Almaráz reports the results, that night in his presidential address, the victim complained that he had

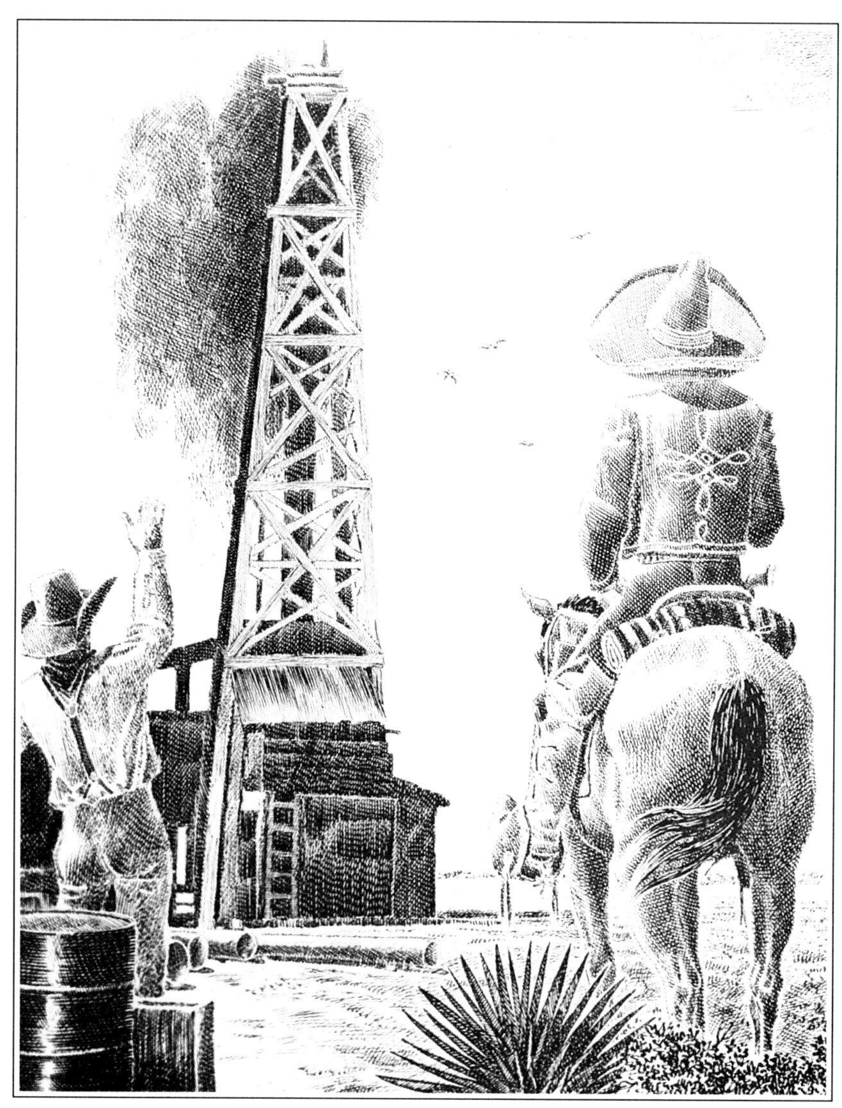

Santa Rita #1, first well brought in on University of Texas oil lands.

been taken advantage of; the following morning, a presentation of sixty-six one dollar bills greeted the complainer, and an announcement that he was the first Pigeon of the Year.

Almaráz says:

> The next year in Austin, Dr. Ben Proctor organized the Pigeon of the Year dinner and the group spontaneously selected the Pigeon of the Year (1982) honoree. The frolicking and festivities continued year after year without standard ceremony until 1986 when I persuaded José to design a special certificate to present with appropriate suspense and pomp.

The resulting certificate is a delightful piece of whimsy, and a sought-after sample of Cisneros art, presented in 1992 to Cisneros booster Al Lowman.

Marc Simmons, Southwestern historian and author of a score of books, has only the highest praise for the work of the El Paso artist:

> José Cisneros is without question the leading historical illustrator of the Southwest. His skill as an artist, combined with his meticulous research, have led to the production of a body of work that must be considered unsurpasssed in its field. Cisneros's contribution to the imagery of the Spanish Borderlands is large, impressive, and should prove lasting.

In the face of such recognition, of which Rossi and Simmons' evaluations are typical, one might expect a man of eighty-three to rest on his laurels. Yet the struggle goes on in the Cisneros studio, the fight for improvement. With such a record of excellence behind him, Cisneros continues to work toward greater skill, greater accuracy, and better renditions of his beloved horsemen. "I continue to strive to sharpen my lines, to make each line count; I am still trying to recreate the people of the past," he says, and then launches into another history lesson for his fascinated listener. A more accurate positioning of a horse's muscle, or a detail in a nineteenth century cavalry uniform insignia, or even the expression on a scrawny dog's face—all these are matters of concern for this accomplished artist. He might well be haunted by the quote he so often heard from his friend Carl Hertzog about trifles making perfection.

Many years ago, in a series of historical drawings he produced for one of the special publications of a local newspaper, Cisneros was anxious about the possibility of cutlines showing up under the wrong illustrations, and inevitably, one did. The newspaperman in charge tried to relieve his mind: "Not one reader in a hundred will notice," he said.

"That is the reader I'm concerned about," the artist answered.

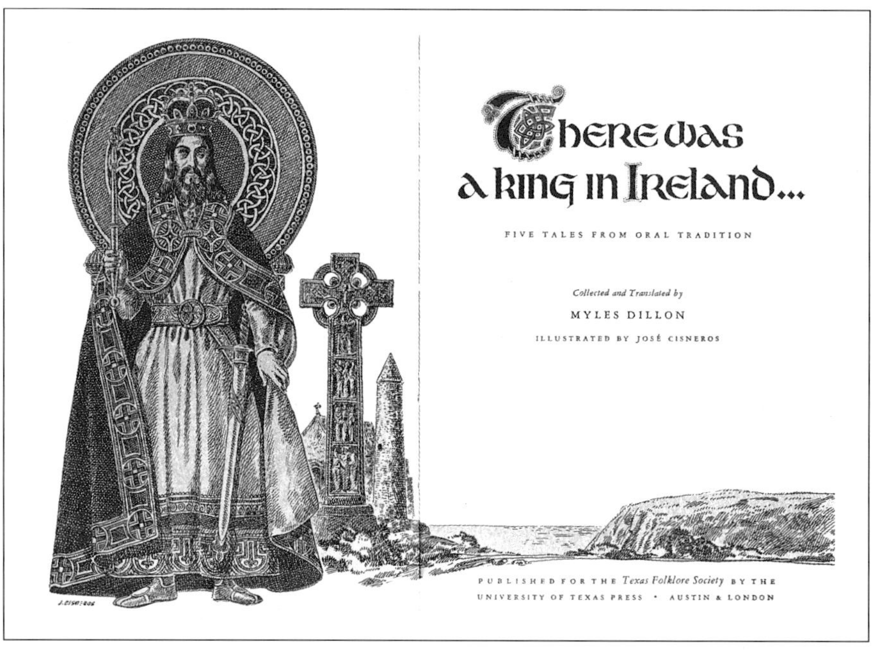

There was a King in Ireland...

FIVE TALES FROM ORAL TRADITION

Collected and Translated by

MYLES DILLON

ILLUSTRATED BY JOSÉ CISNEROS

PUBLISHED FOR THE *Texas Folklore Society* BY THE UNIVERSITY OF TEXAS PRESS · AUSTIN & LONDON

There Was a King in Ireland *(1971), a publication of the Texas Folklore Society, demonstrates the artist's attention to detail in works far from the Spanish Southwest.*

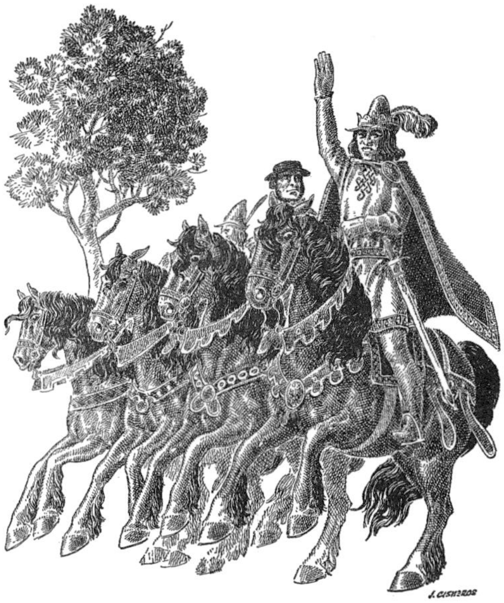

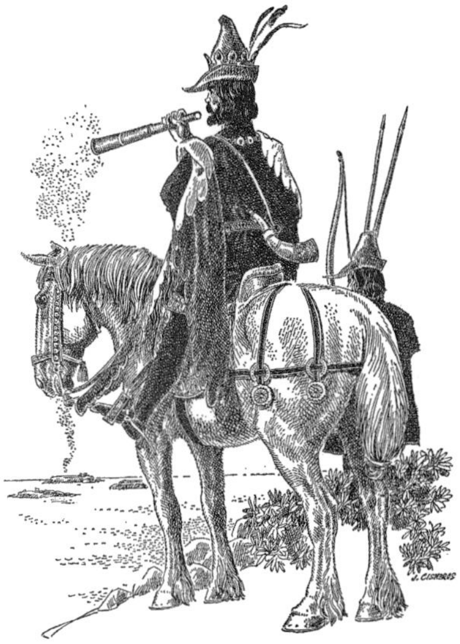

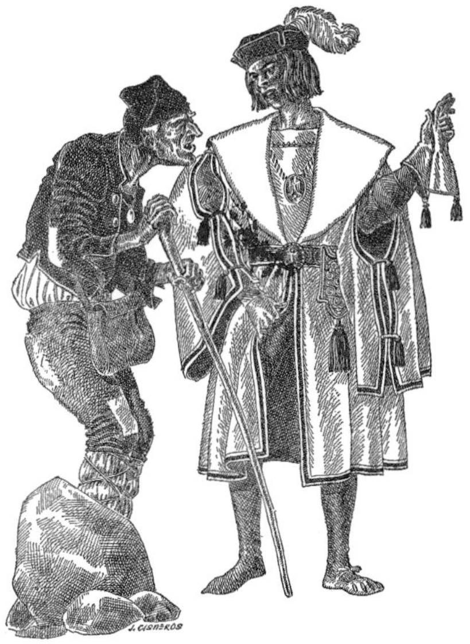

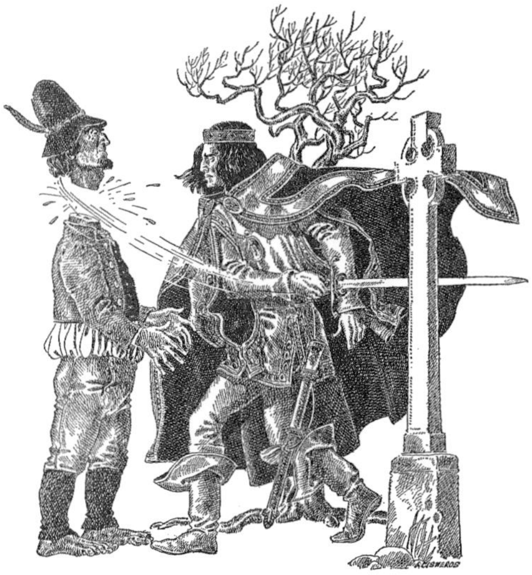

There Was a King in Ireland

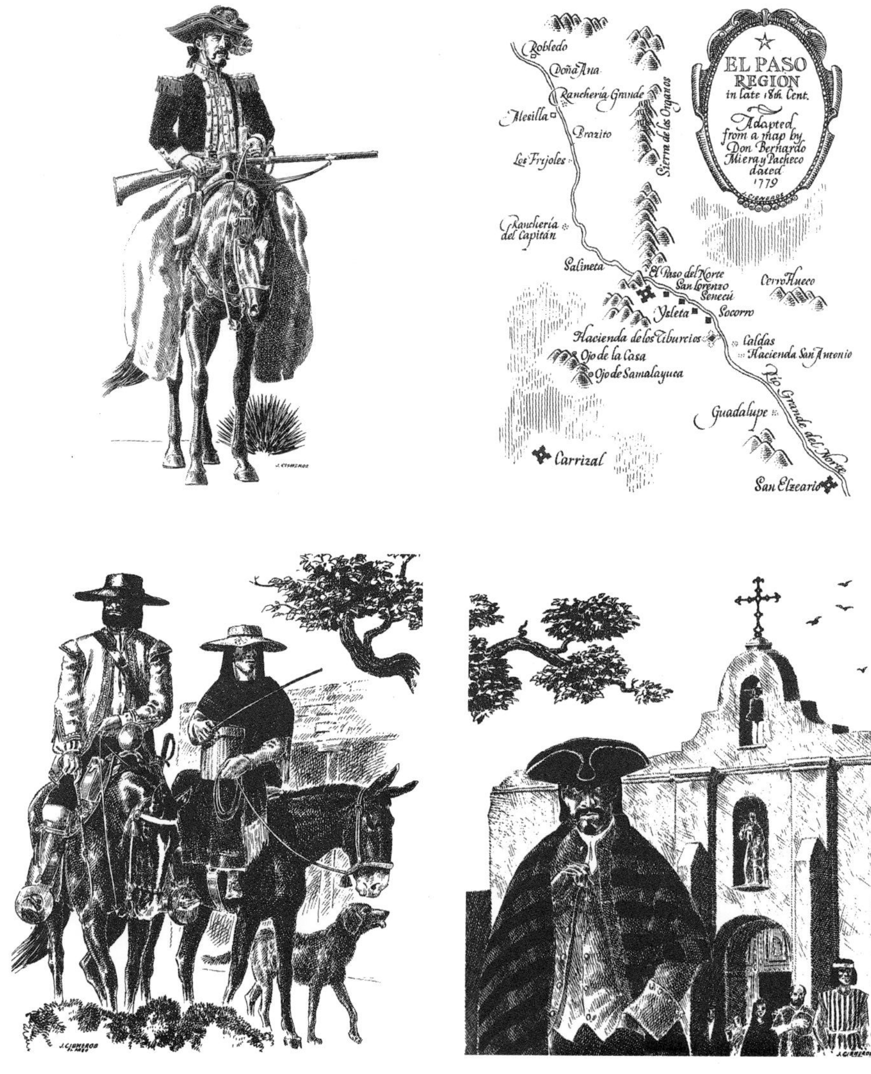

Eugene Porter's San Elizario *(1973) relates the story of the Spanish presidial town and the soldiers sent there to guard against raiding Comanches. Upper left: Dust jacket, a presidial officer, upper right: Map of the El Paso region, 18th century, lower left: Settlers and soldiers of San Elizario, lower right: The presidial chapel was the center of life in the settlement.*

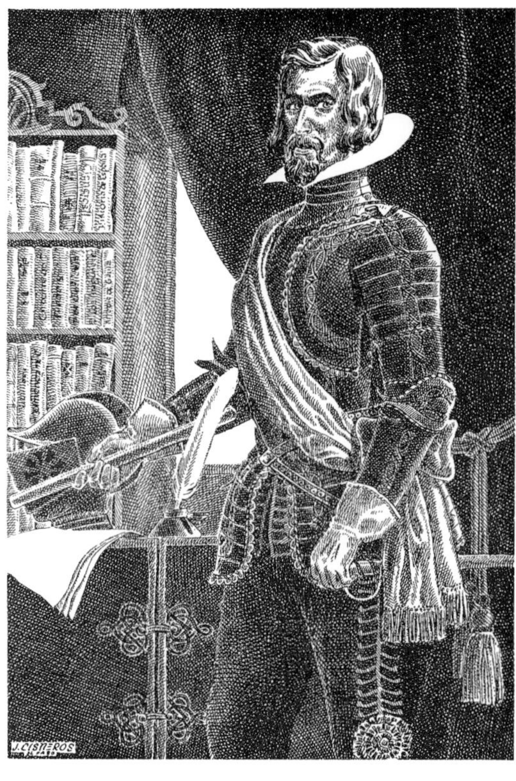

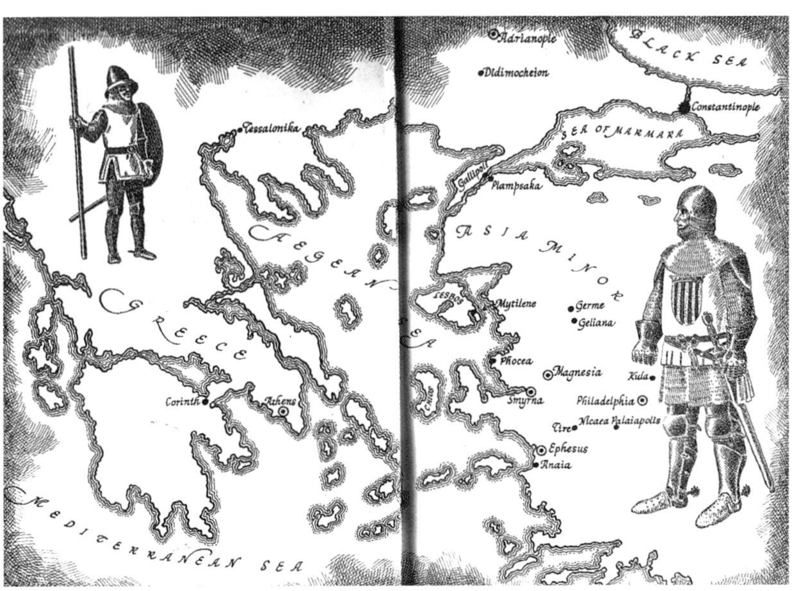

Adventurers from Catalonia departed from Spain in the 14th century to fight Greeks and Turks around the eastern Mediterranean. The Catalan Chronicle *(1975), translated by Frances Hernández and edited by John Sharp, brings their valorous deeds into focus.*
Top: Don Francisco de Moncada, author of the chronicle; bottom: map of Greece and Asia Minor.

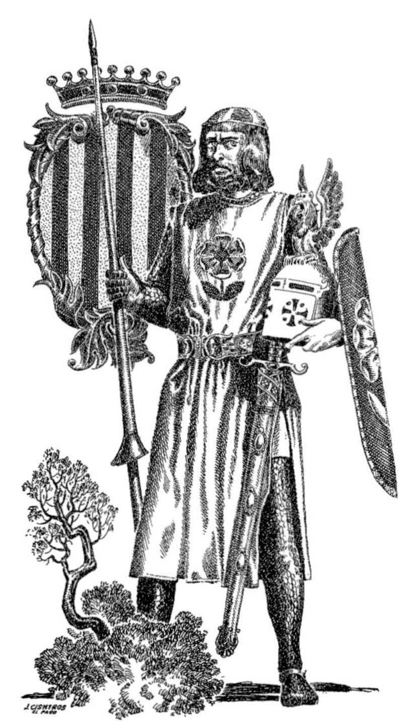

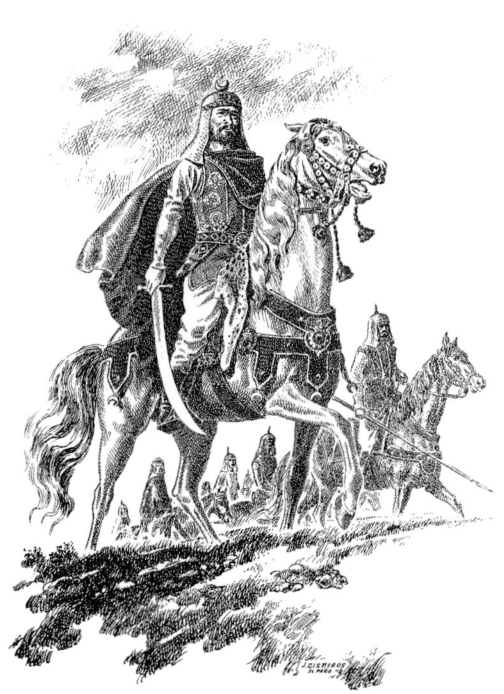

The Catalan Chronicle
Top: Catalonian Knight Roger de Flor; bottom: the opposition—Karaman the Turk.

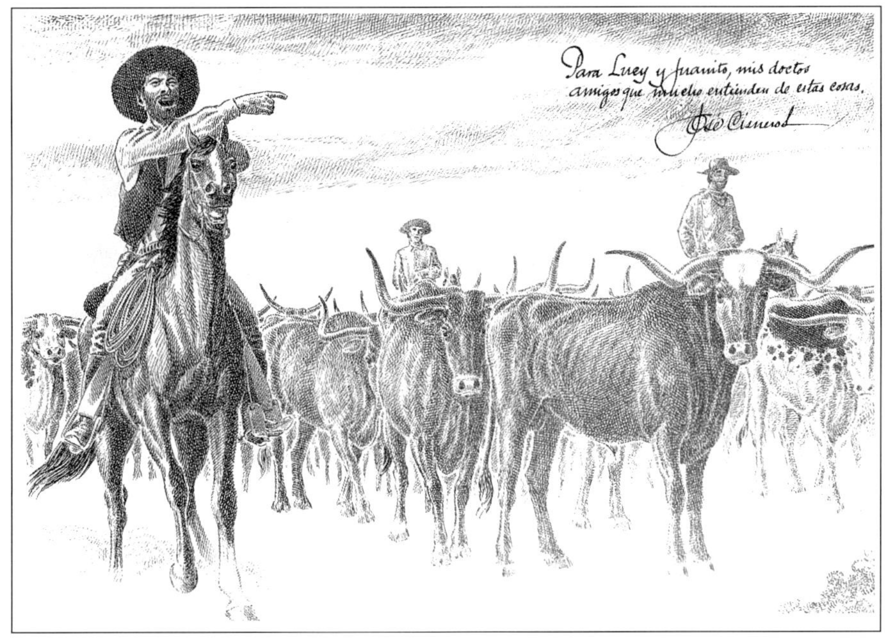

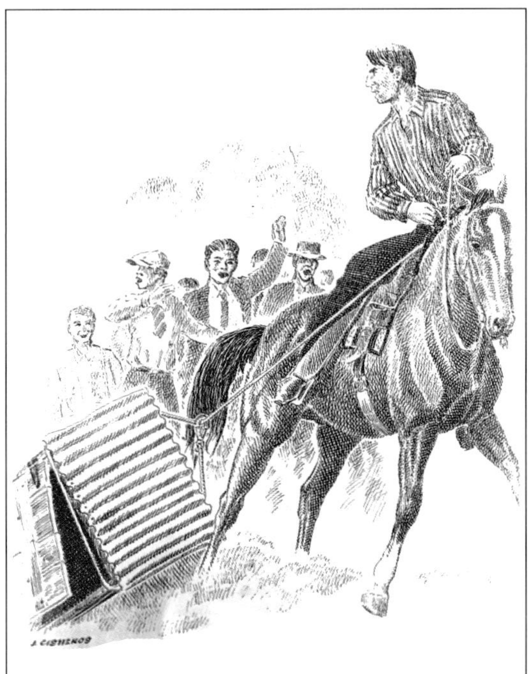

A Ranching Saga *(1976) by W.C. Holden tells the story of the Halsell cattle empire, everyday life on the range.*

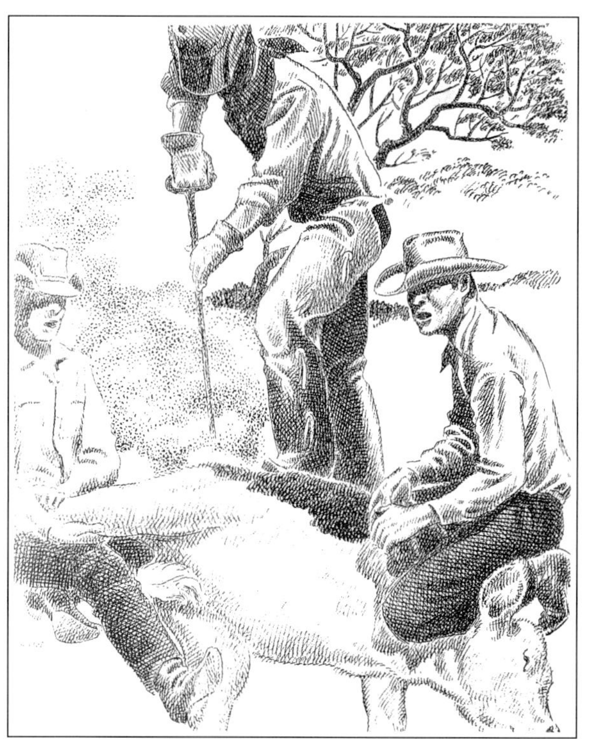

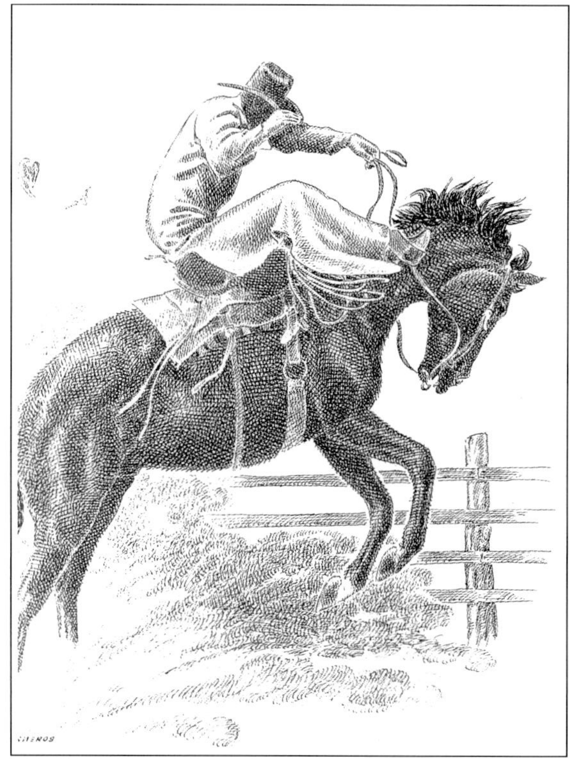

A Ranching Saga

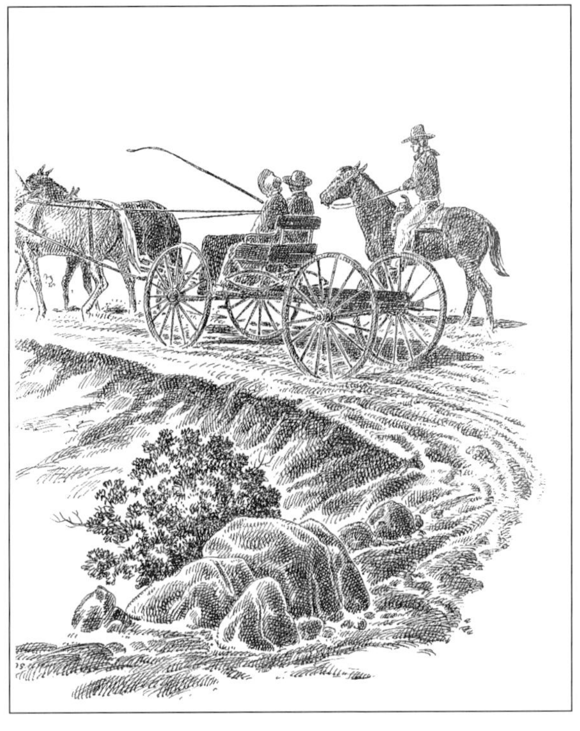

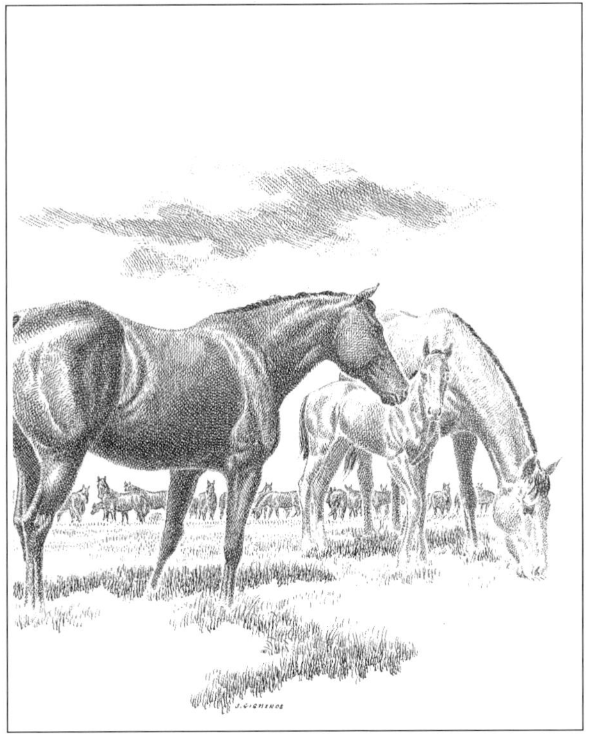

A Ranching Saga

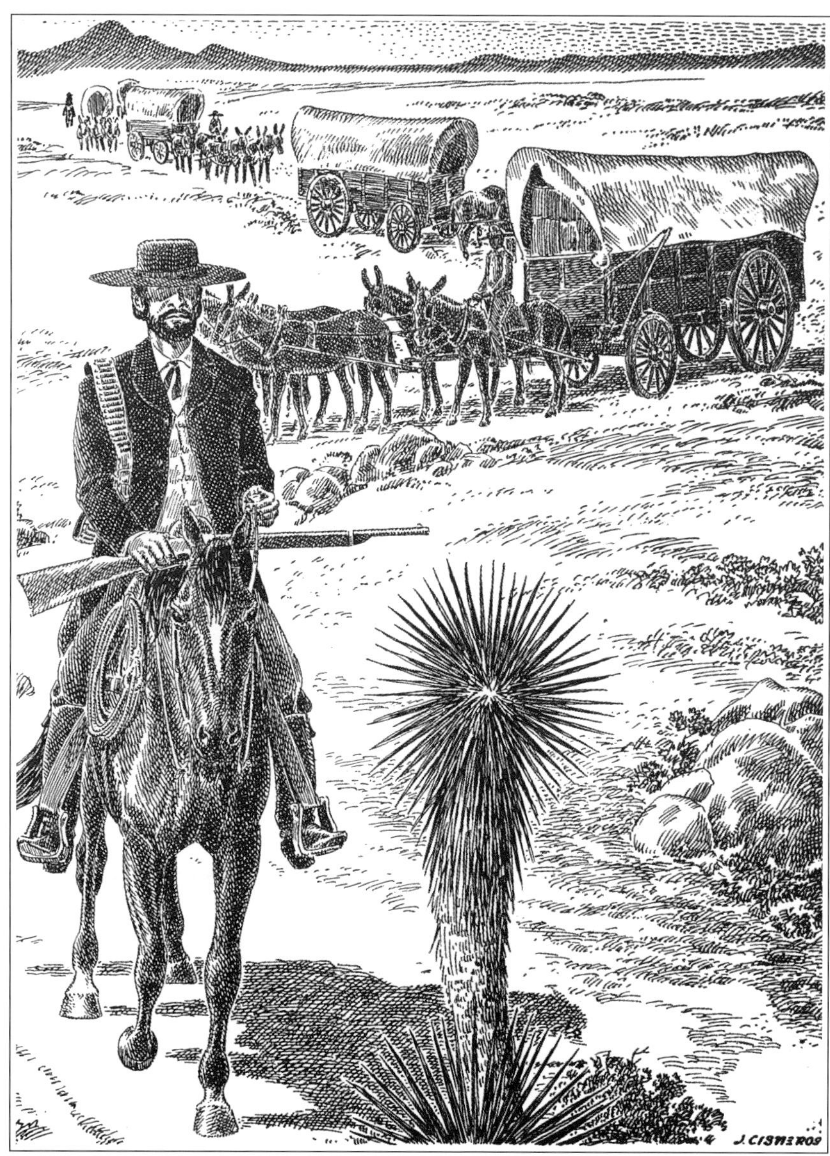
J. CISNEROS

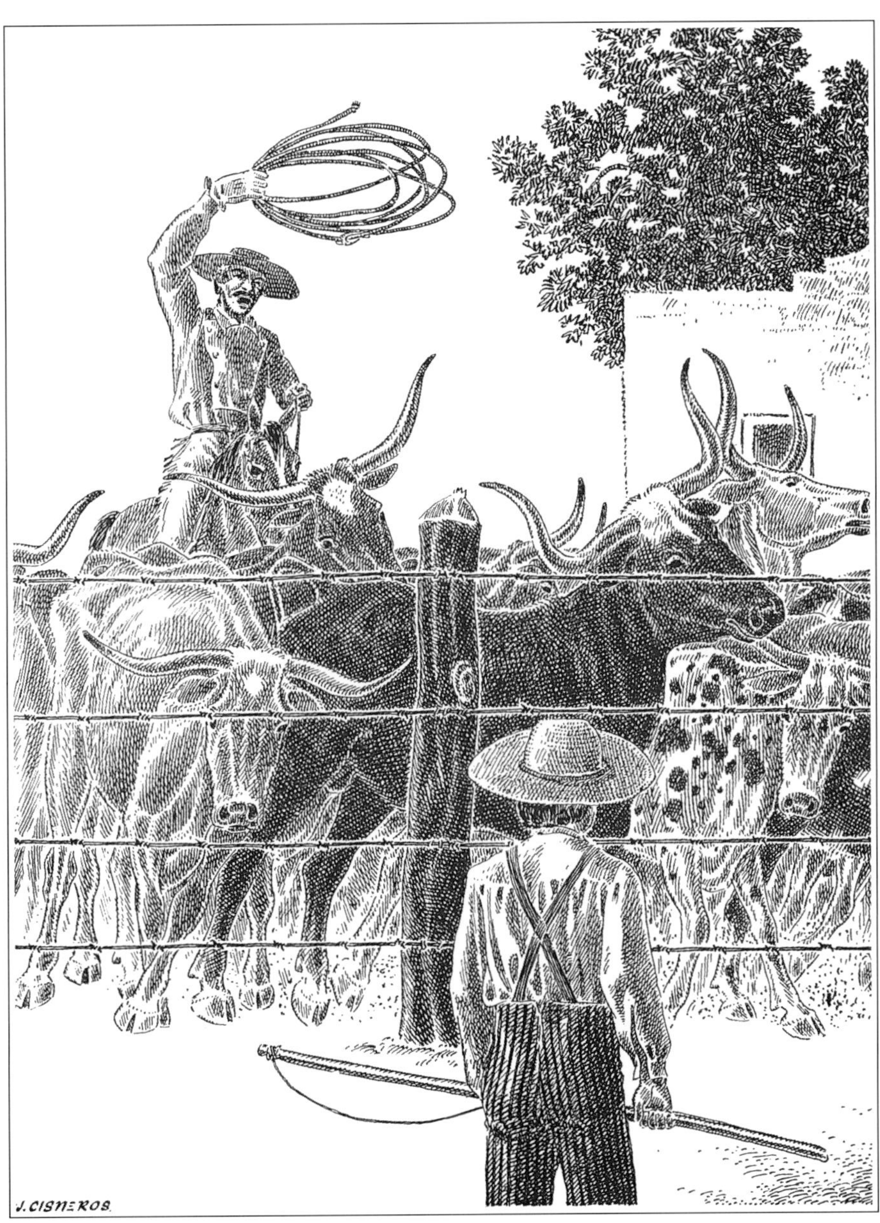

San Antonio Legacy

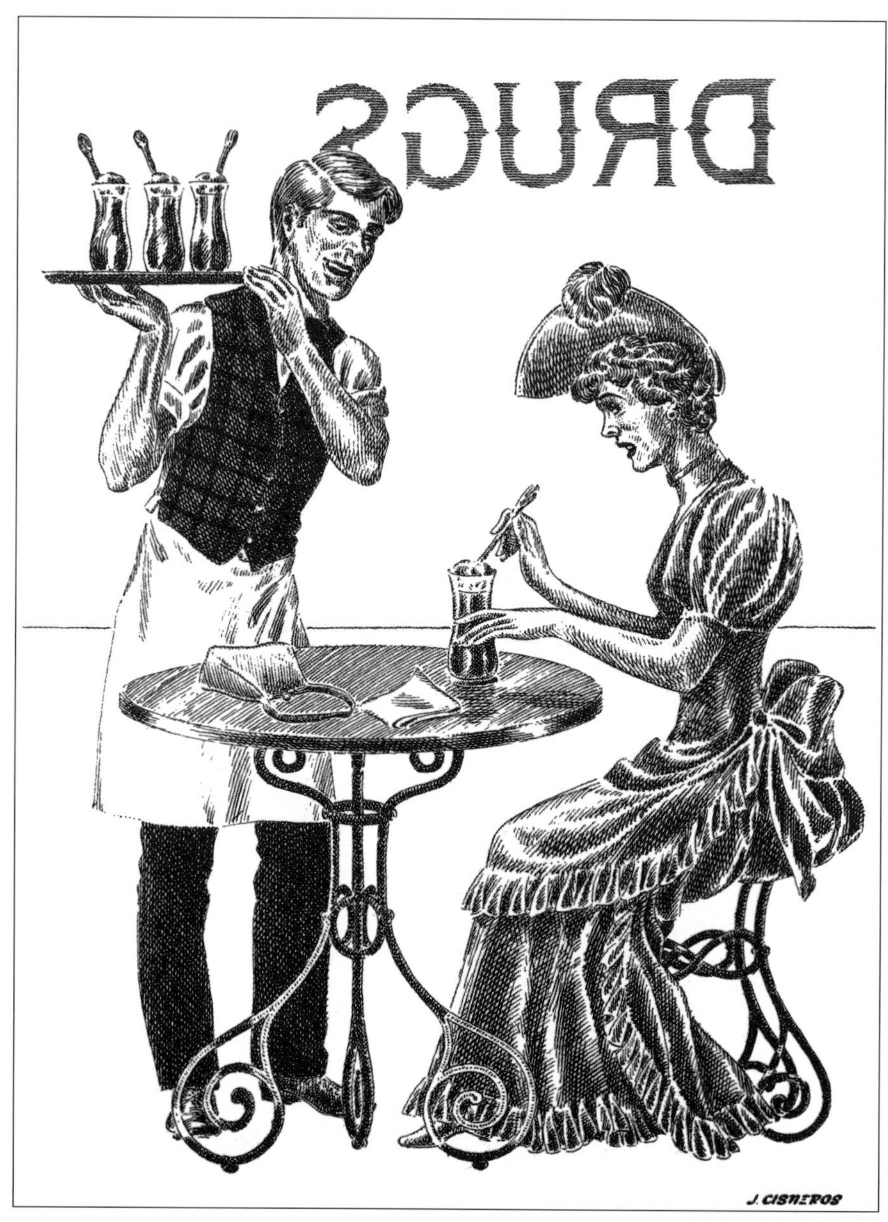
DRUGS
J. CISNEROS

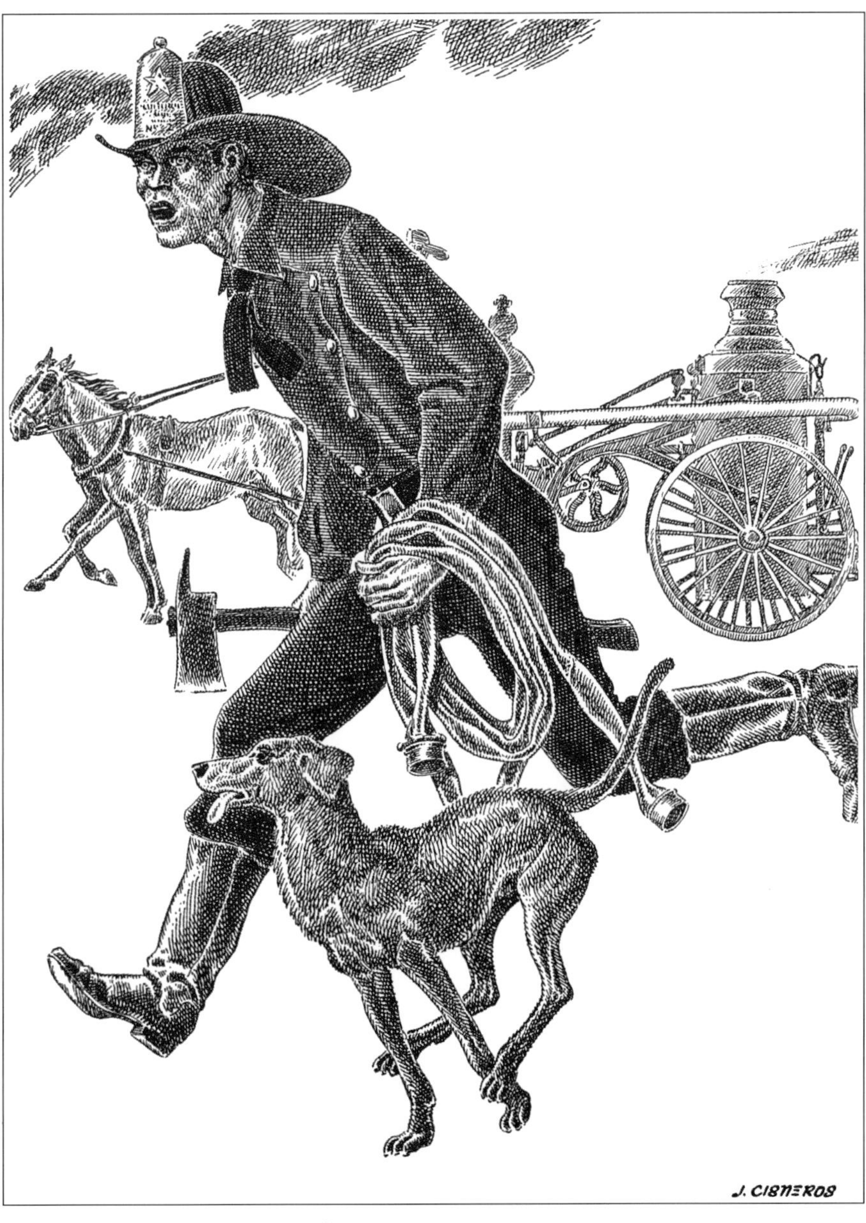

San Antonio Legacy

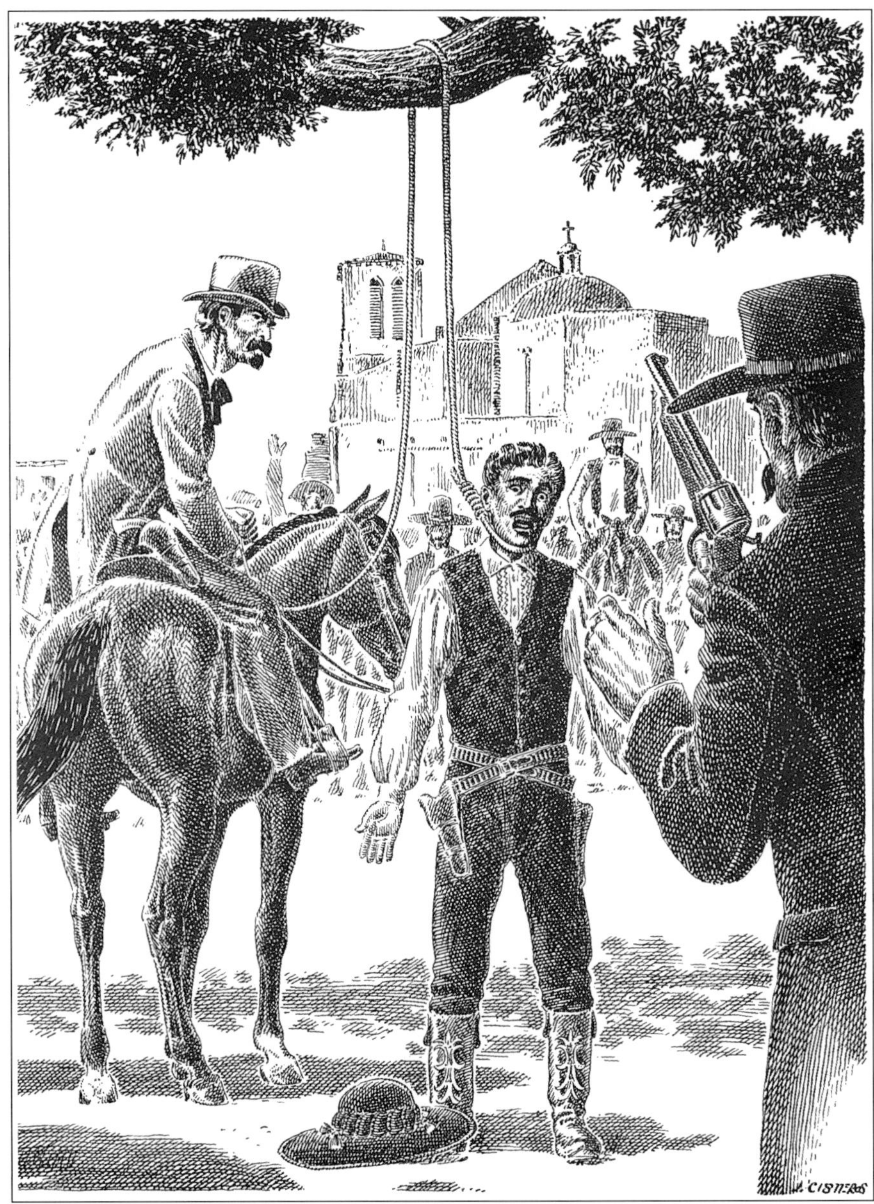

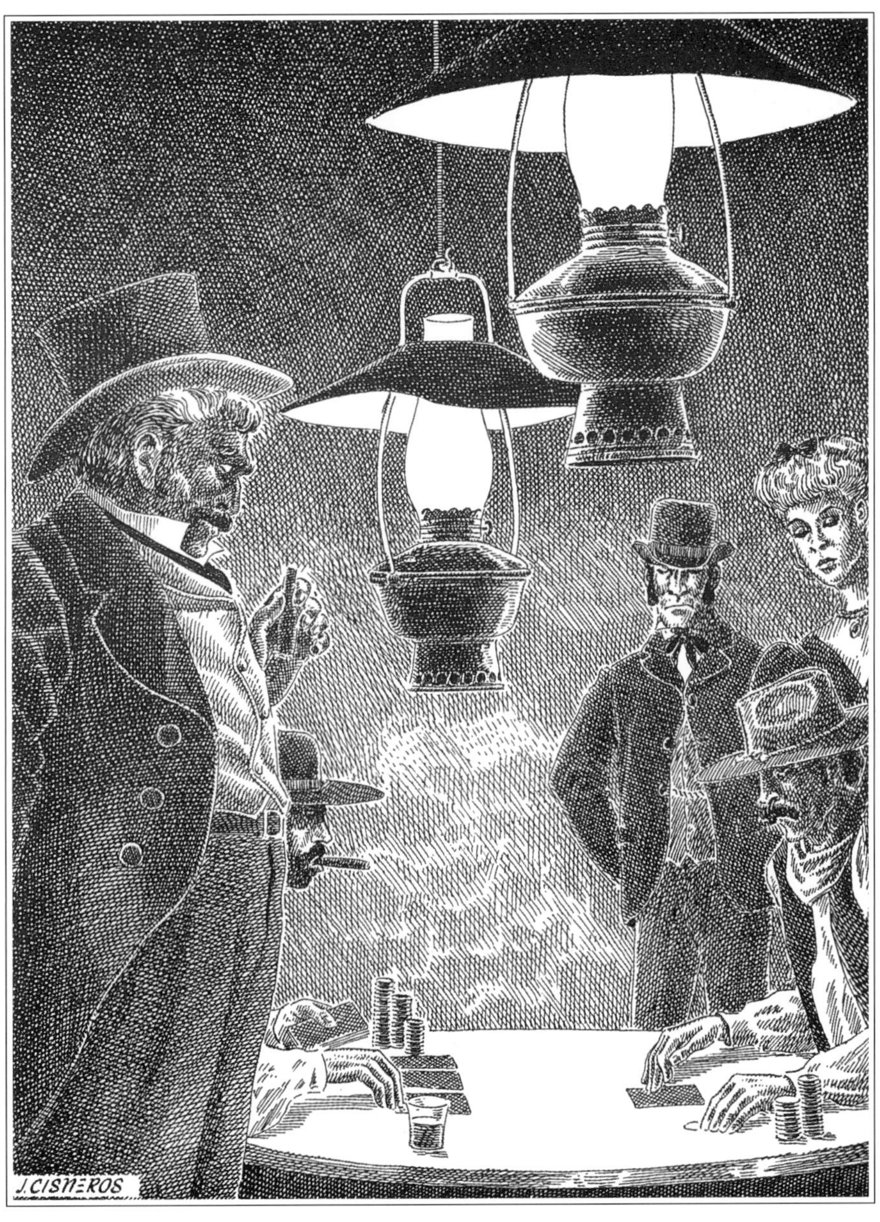

San Antonio Legacy

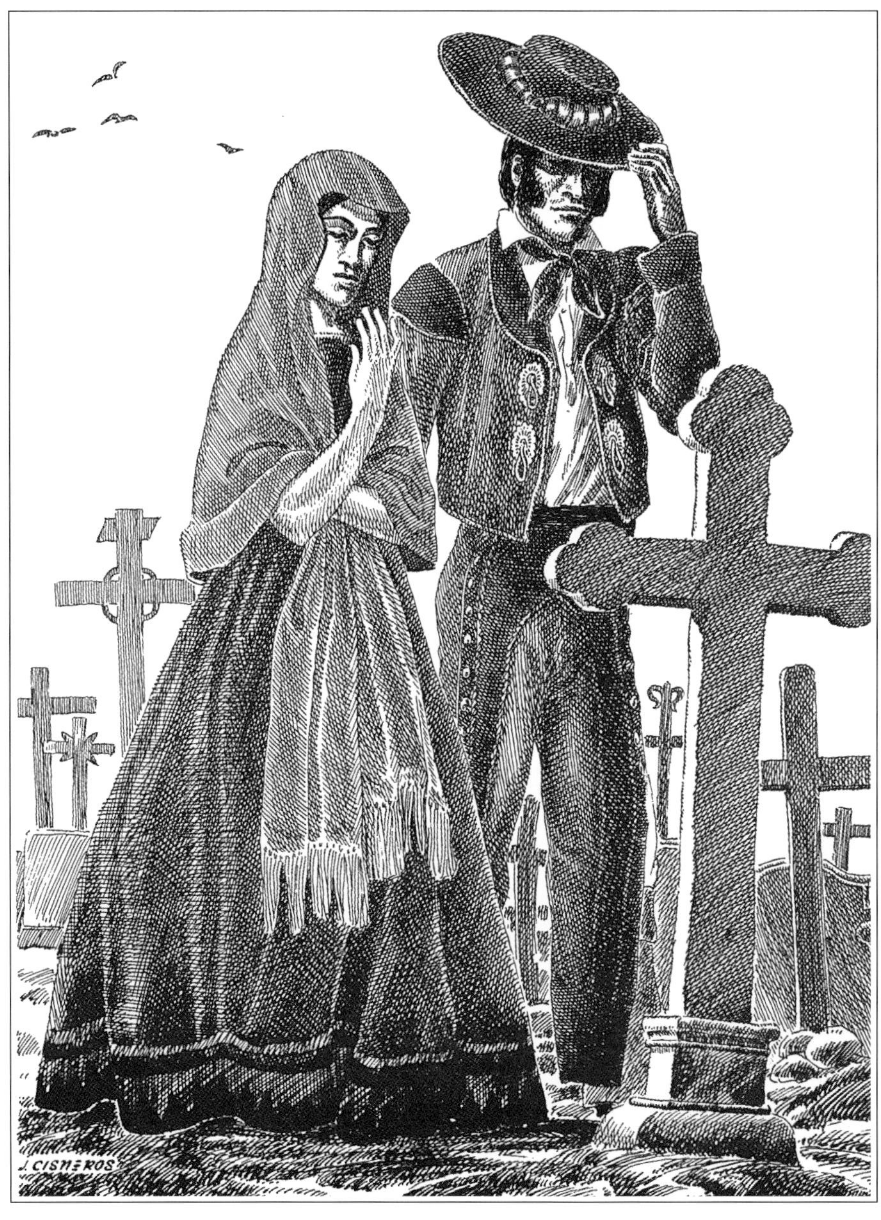
J. CISNEROS

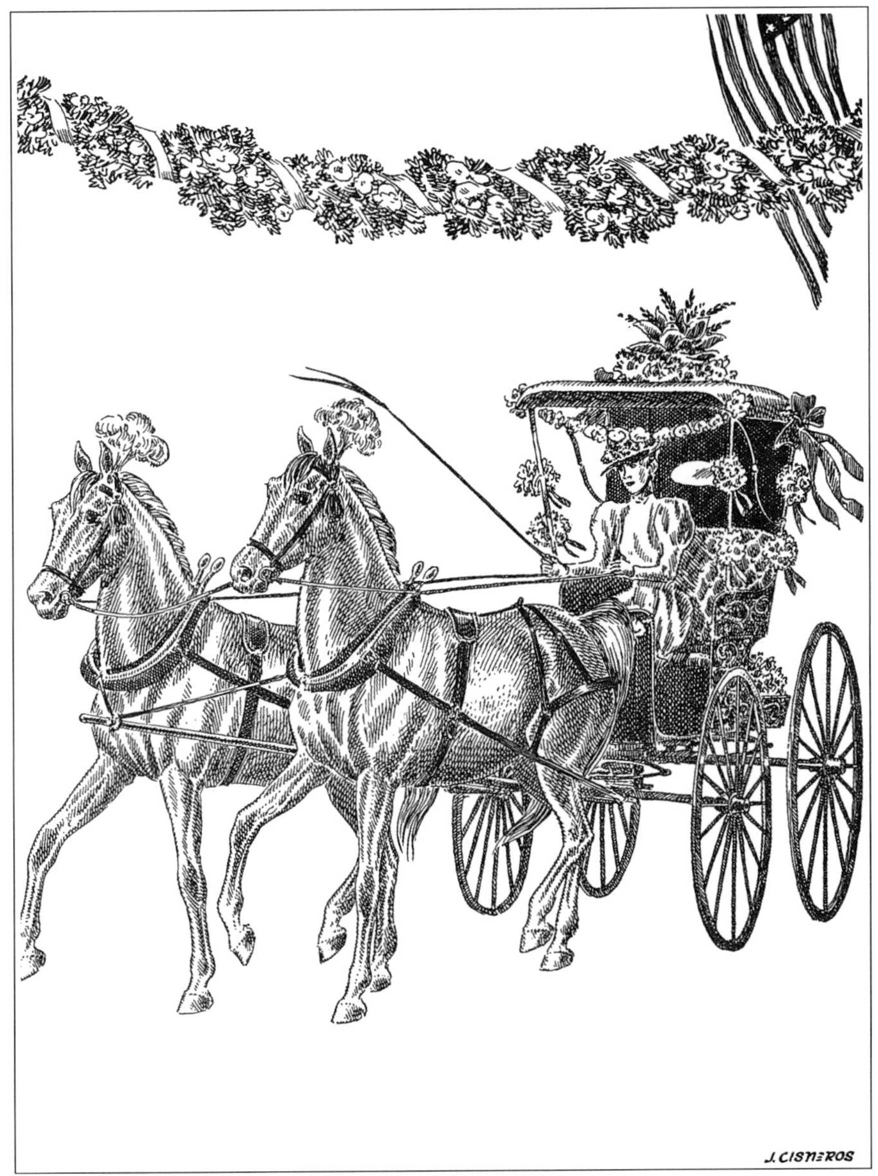

San Antonio Legacy

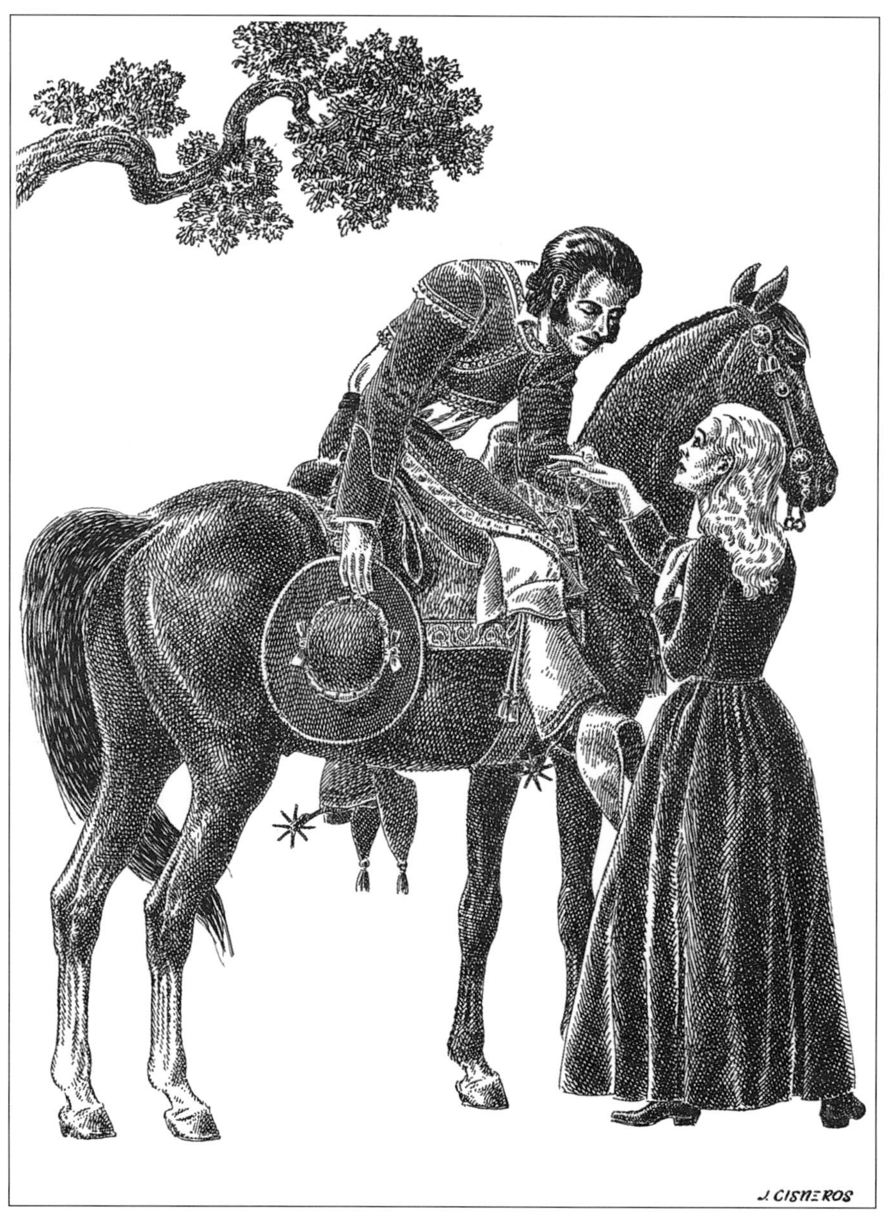
J. CISNEROS

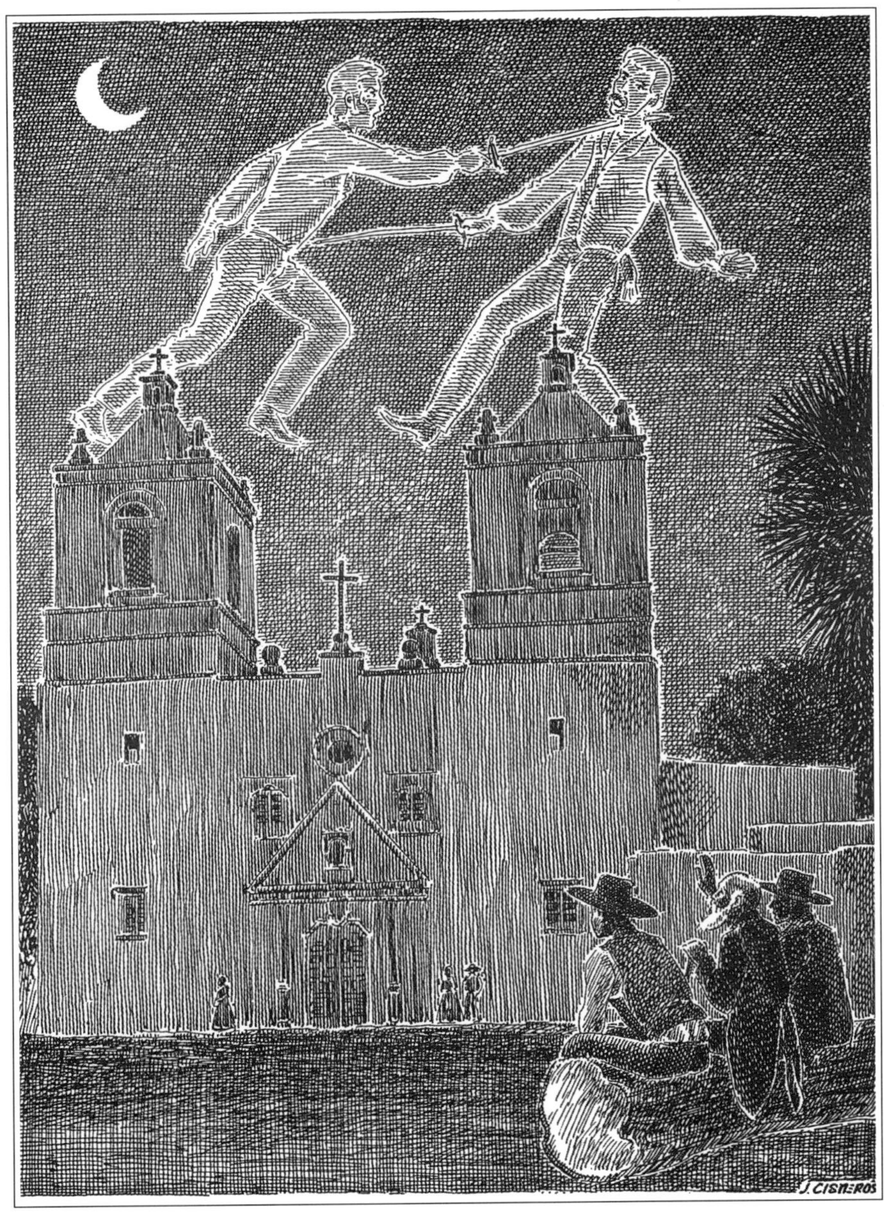

San Antonio Legacy

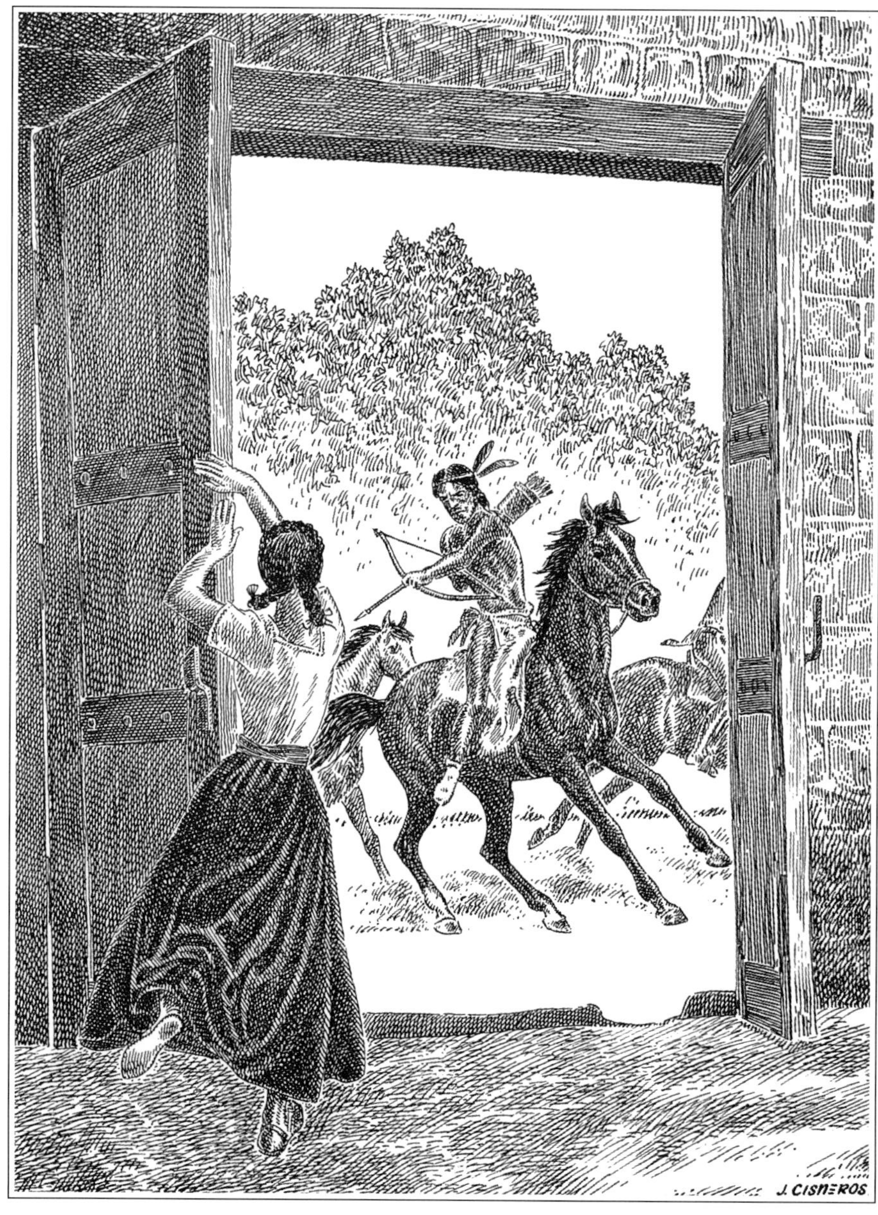
J. CISNEROS

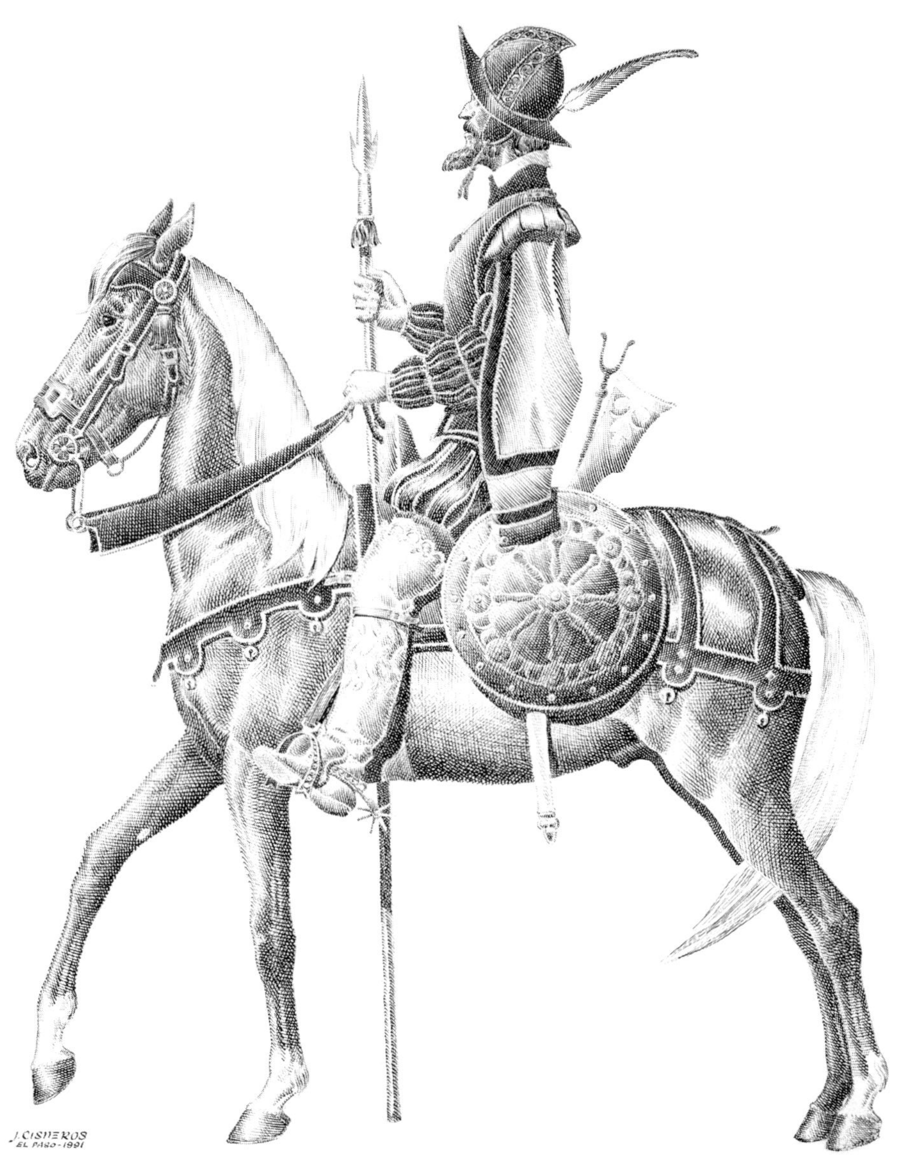

Cisneros's book, Riders Across the Centuries *(1984) spans a four-hundred year period of history.*
above, A conquistador out of the 17th century

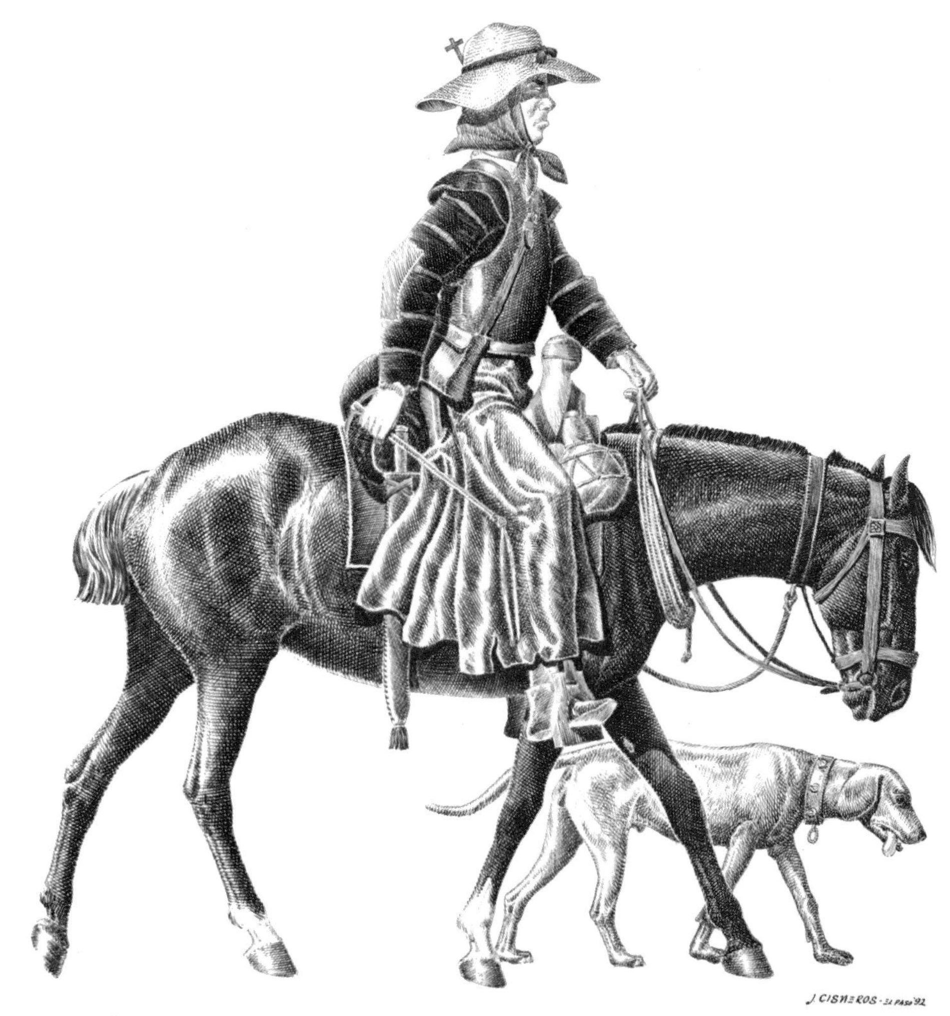

Riders Across the Centuries: *A ranch woman*

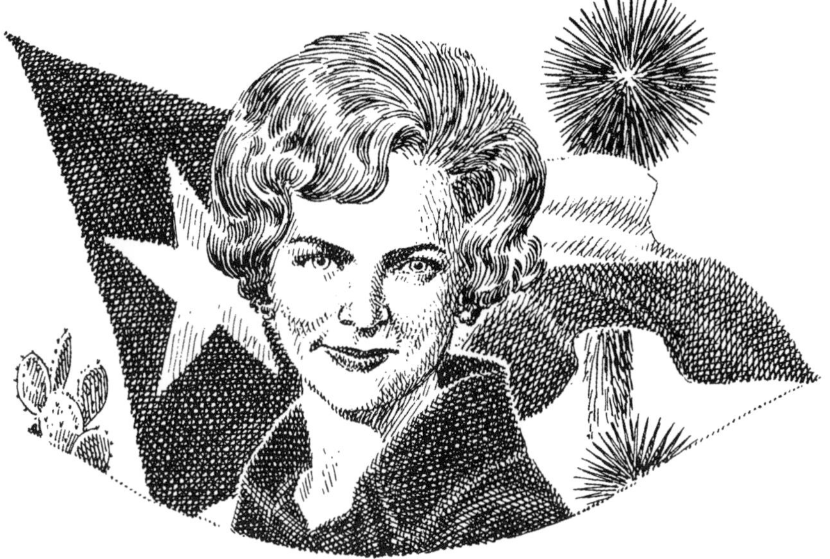

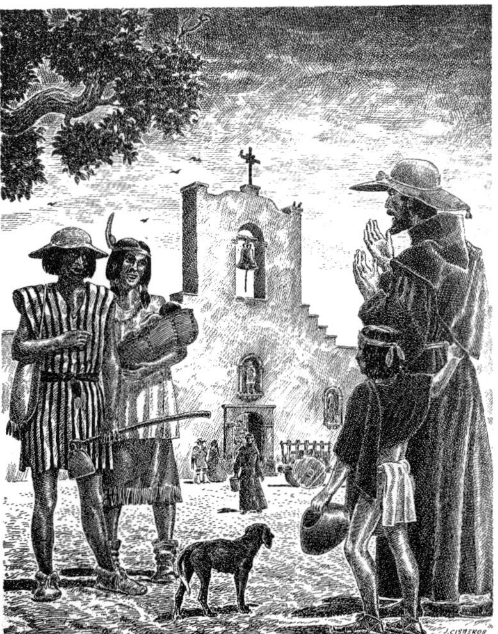

The Pueblo de Socorro Grant (*1987*) *by Katherine White provides historians with details of the past, with the help of Cisneros drawings. (Courtesy of Richard C. White)*
Top: the author, Katherine Hope Huffman White, 1929-1972;
bottom: a padre and Piro townspeople gather in front of the Socorro mission, second oldest in the state of Texas.

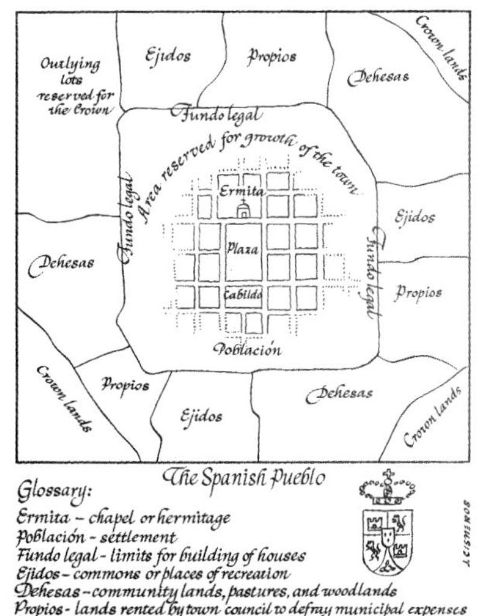

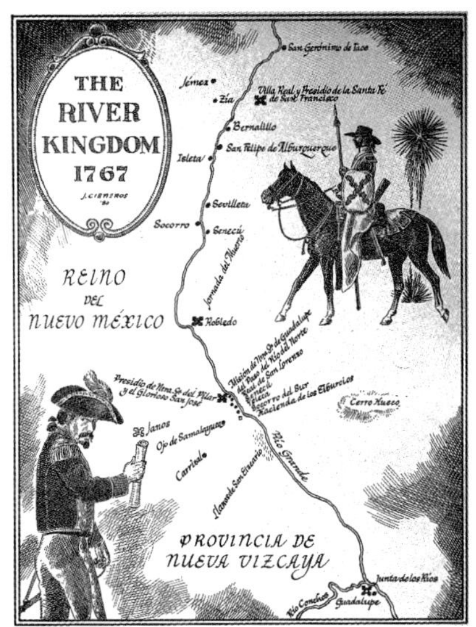

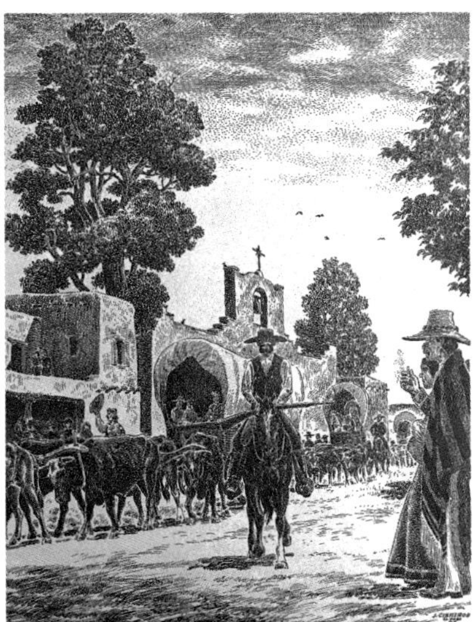

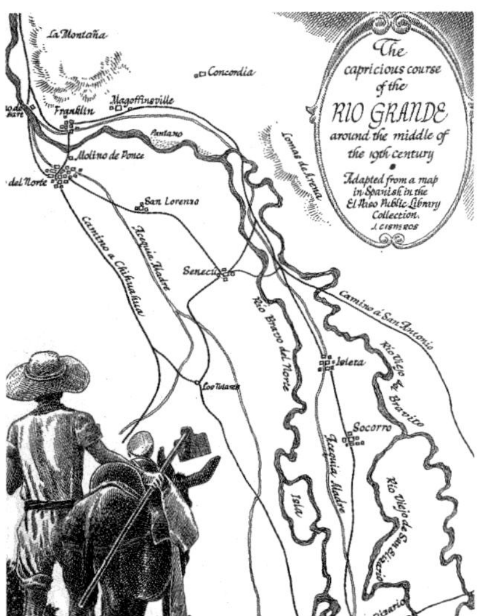

The Pueblo de Socorro Grant

Top left: the Spanish pueblo in the New World. Top right: the River Kingdom in 1767, with settlements from Taos southwards. The Spanish gentleman (lower left) has the face of the artist, José Cisneros.

Bottom left: wagons westward passed through Socorro in the nineteenth century.

Bottom right: the Rio Grande created difficulties with land titles because it would regularly wander out of its banks.

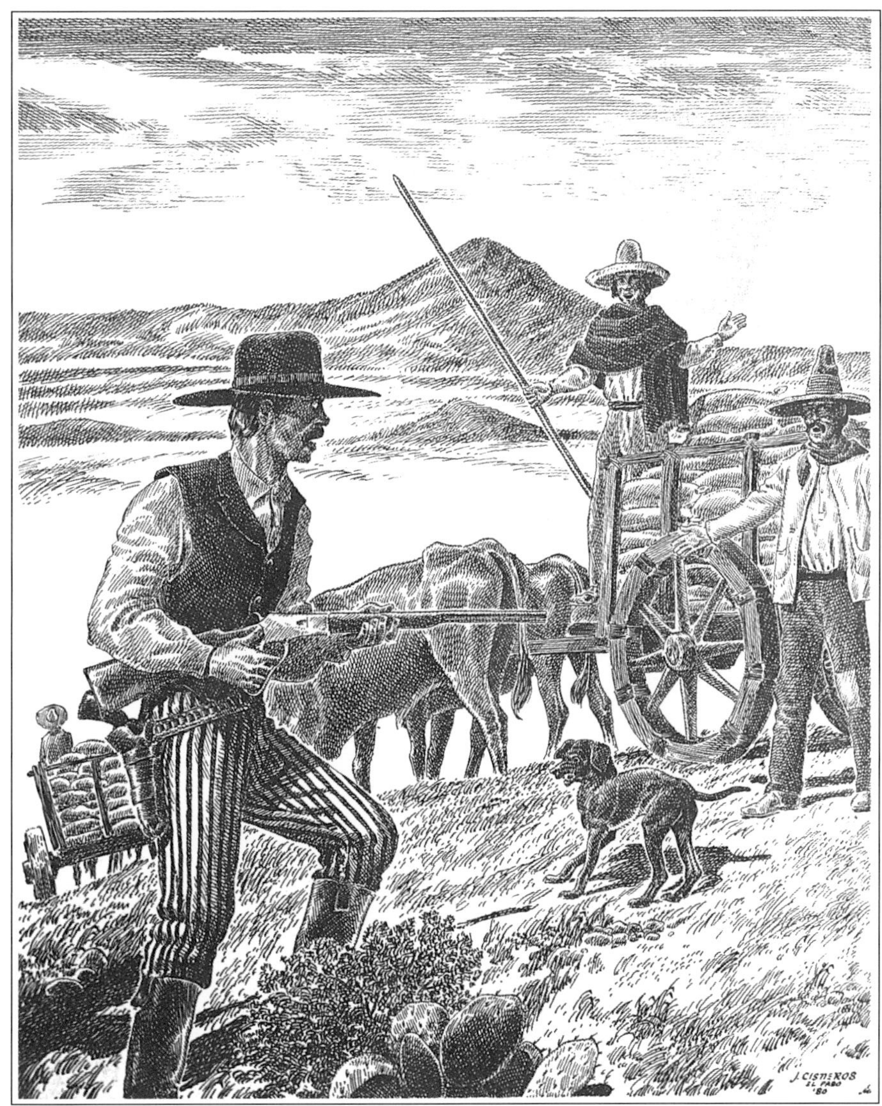

The Pueblo de Socorro Grant

A confrontation between a Texan and salt gatherers at the salt flats near Socorro. (Author's collection)

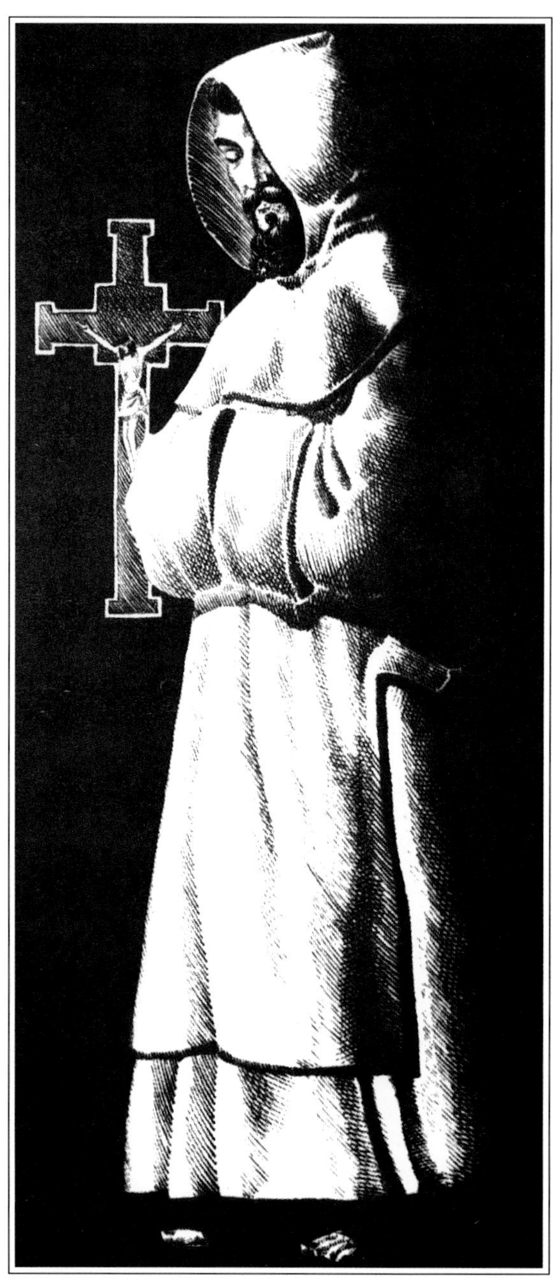

The Questing Beast *(1990) by Brother Paul reveals the pains of a questioning religious brother.*

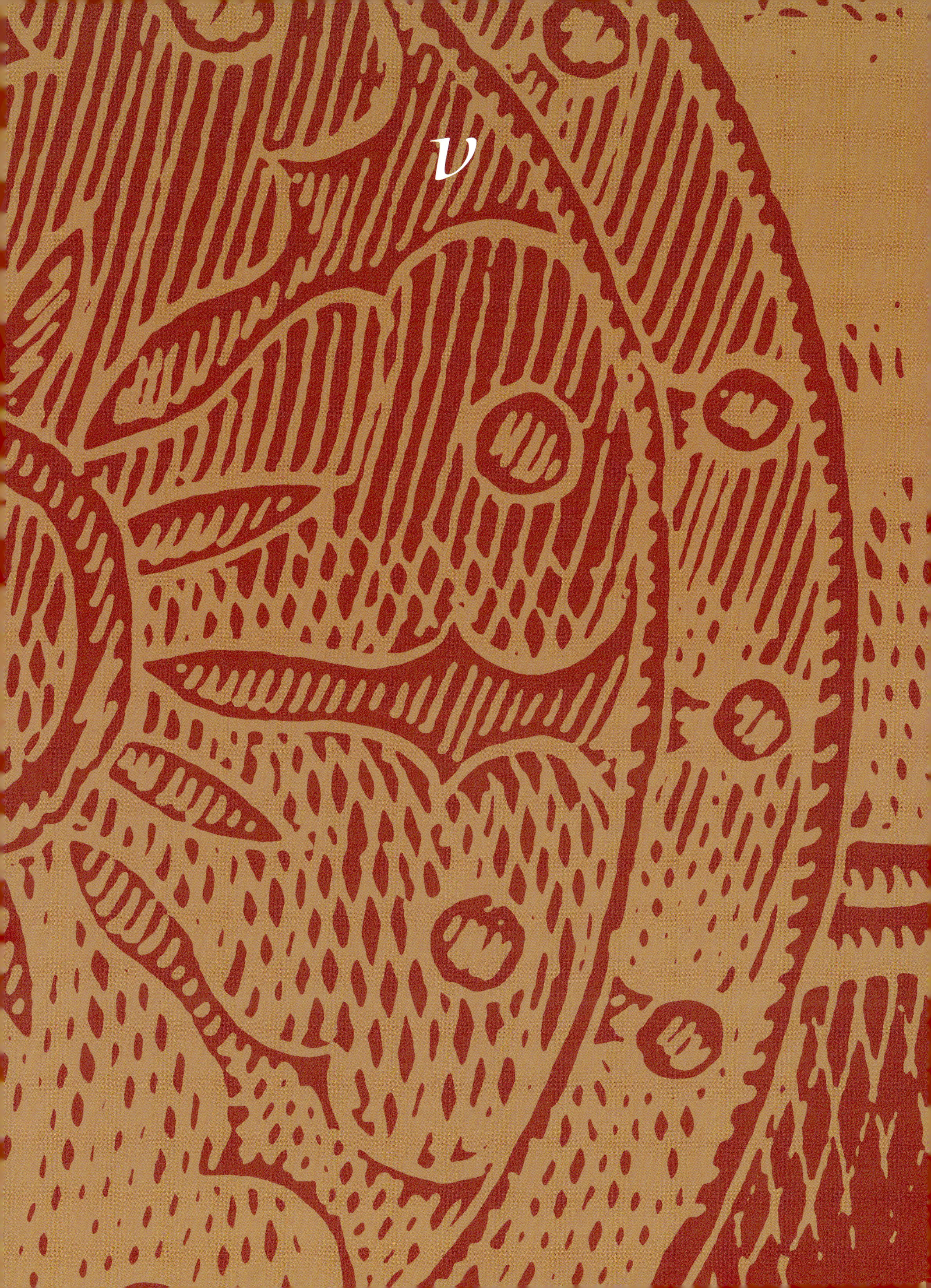

v

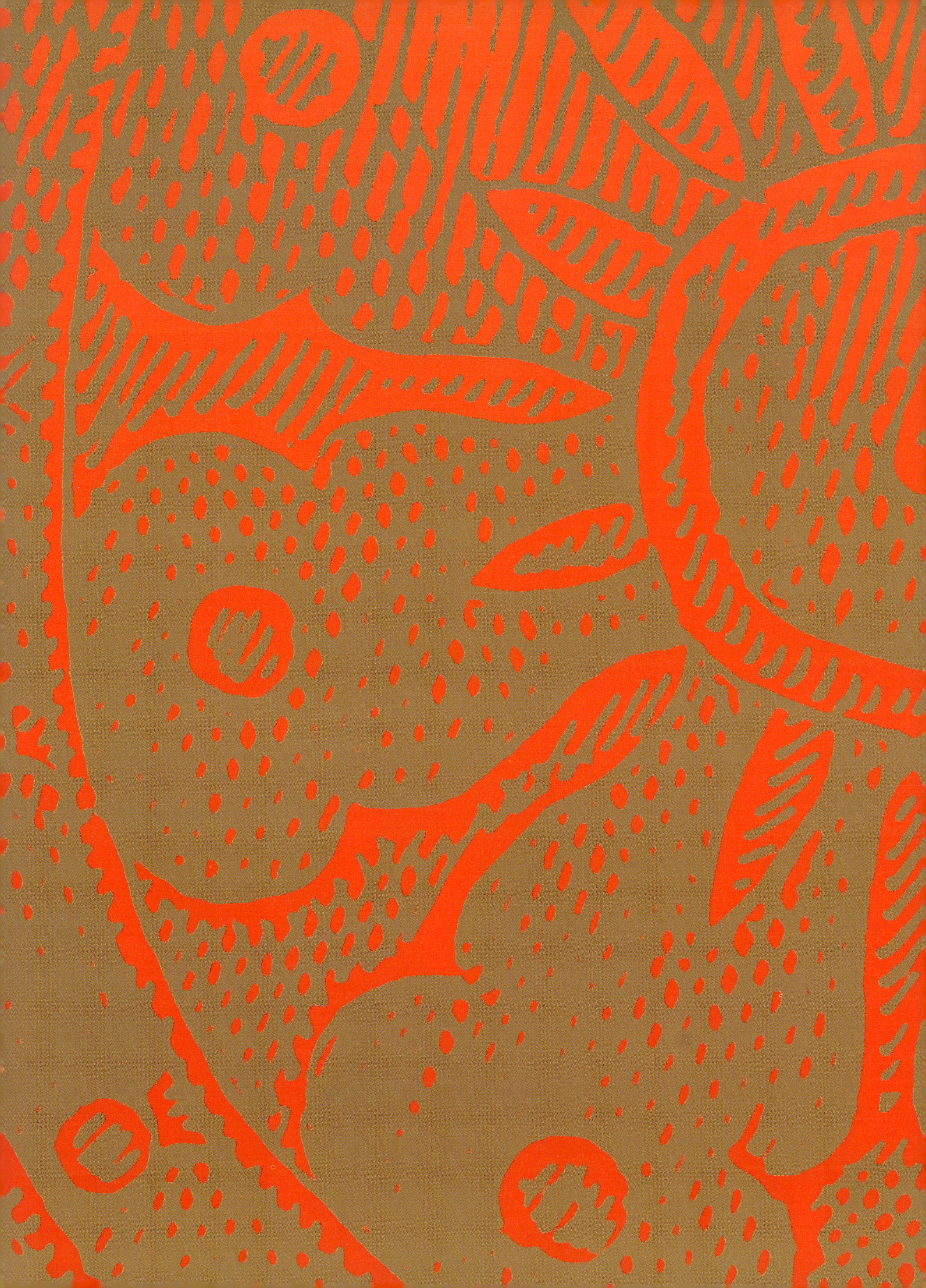

V

A Knight and a Tejano Hero

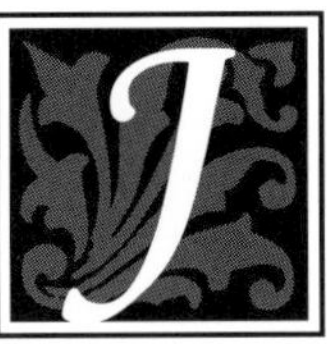

osé Cisneros has been noticed, and his talents have been utilized, for more than half a century in his adopted "home town" of El Paso, Texas. His close association with the University of Texas at El Paso is readily seen in his design of the seal for the University, with its Texas star and Pass of the North with the Rio Grande flowing through it all; the seal is an adaptation of the emblem he had created in 1950 when it was Texas Western College. His hundred horsemen hanging on the walls of the U T El Paso Library attract attention daily.

When the Southern Pacific Railroad donated the El Paso and Southwestern Locomotive No. 1 to the college in 1960, a Cisneros rendition of the engine graced the top of the souvenir program distributed at the El Paso Centennial Museum; retired from active service in 1903, the ancient locomotive was certainly an important part of the history of El Paso that Cisneros was so involved in recording.

The official logo for the El Paso County Historical Society, as has been noted, is the work of the El Paso artist; so is the El Paso Public Library bookplate, in part a gift in gratitude for the library's having hosted the young unknown artist's first public exhibition. Almost everywhere in El Paso, the work of José Cisneros can be seen. Ask a native or a newcomer if he or she knows the artist's work and a blank stare may surface; describe that work and a look of glad recognition appears.

Cisneros has had many formal exhibitions of his work in his adopted city, from the first one arranged by Librarian Maud Durlin Sullivan (at the suggestion of artist Tom Lea), to the most recent at the El Paso Museum of History sponsored by the El Paso County Historical Society in the Spring of 1992—with numerous exhibitions in between. One noteworthy event occurred at the 1939 art show of the Woman's Club of El Paso. Cisneros was not the only artist whose work was displayed, quite naturally, since many members of the organization were artists too, but *The El Paso Times* reported that among the surprises of the day were "the clever little costume pictures and street scene sketches shown on the screen in the main auditorium, the work of José Cisneros." In addition to the attention created by the young artist's work, Mrs. Lloyd Burlingham (herself an artist with works in the show, and co-editor of *Mexico* magazine, which would soon begin purchasing Cisneros's drawings for publication) wrote Cisneros, informing him that Dr. and Mrs. J. W. Cathcart were interested in buying some of his works for a daughter living in Caracas, Venezuela. Thus, José Cisneros made his first sale to an individual, and his professional career was launched. (Two of those drawings were reproduced in *Riders Across the Centuries* in 1984 as exemplary of some of Cisneros's "other" work besides horsemen.)

Among many other exhibitions of Cisneros art in El Paso over the years are included: several each at the El Paso Museum of Art, the University of Texas at El Paso, and the Cavalry Museum (now the El Paso Museum of History). Cisneros recalls with pride one special event: "After our stay in Paisano the El Paso Public Library organized a very beautiful and significant party of recognition which Carl Hertzog commented on in a very exuberant manner." Other displays include one in the Gallery of the Consulate General of Mexico in 1983; the state Senate Gallery in Austin, Texas, in 1986 and 1987; the El Paso Mayor's Invitational Art Exhibit; and an array of thirty-one of his riders at the El Paso City Hall in 1991, sponsored by the City of El Paso Arts Resources Department. Other exhibits have been shown far from the City at the Pass—by the State Department in Mexico City in the 1970s, arranged by U. S. Rep. Richard White; the University of the Pacific in Stockton, California; and twice at the Hidalgo County Historical Museum in Edinburg, Texas, featuring a permanent display of more than a score of his works commissioned to present the history of the Lower Rio Grande area.

Cisneros's stay at Paisano began bearing fruit even during his time there: two exhibits were hosted by the University of Texas in Austin in the spring of 1969; one at St. Mary's University in San Antonio and another at St. Edward's University in Austin; and the one mentioned earlier at the Institute of Texan Cultures in San Antonio (plus others later). The Witte Museum; the Panhandle Plains Museum in Canyon,

Texas; the *Centro Cultural Mexicano* in San Antonio; Eastern New Mexico University in Portales, New Mexico; the Harlingen, Texas, Springfest; the Westerners Corral in San Marino, California—the list of showings of his horsemen is almost endless. One exhibit that was planned at the Smithsonian in Washington, was unfortunately thwarted by a well-meaning friend who wanted to handle the details himself.

On October 12 and 13, 1990, in a Quincentenary Celebration of Columbus' discovery of America, Sul Ross State University and the Center for Big Bend Studies not only presented an exhibition of José Cisneros's works, but included him as a speaker in a conference advertised as consisting of "outstanding scholars on the history of the borderlands." Perhaps because he was the only speaker without a Ph.D., he recalls,

> I was nervous, but I told them of my work with the history of the horses of the Southwest. Very early I made a commitment to follow their hoof prints along and across the land, . . . to restore, visualize and create the physical appearance of their riders was my aim.

After detailing some of the outstanding people who had led the way in civilizing the area, especially the Franciscan fathers who often found martyrdom in their efforts to save souls, this artist without a Ph.D. received a standing ovation—the only speaker so honored.

Although José Cisneros feels very strongly about the O. F. M. (Order of Minor Friars, as the Franciscans are properly called), and takes a special pleasure in illustrating works connected with them, he also respects highly those who bore arms instead of Bibles in their attempts at pacifying the frontiers of New Spain. At the 1992 meeting of the Texas State Historical Association in Austin, he was asked to provide a cover illustration for the program—and to bring an assortment of his horsemen drawings for a silent auction. His description of the soldier he singled out for display on the cover is reflective of his respect for the past and those who shaped it, especially the unsung hero of the Spanish

The Texas State Historical Association

Auction of Texana

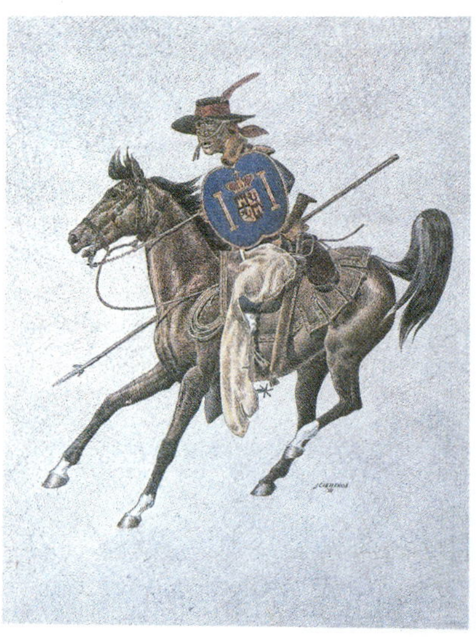

February 28, 1992
Hyatt Regency Hotel, Austin

Cover for the Texas State Historical Association

frontier, the "Cuera" Dragoon. Chief supporter of the Spanish military hold on the northern frontier of New Spain was the "Cuera" or buckskin, leather-and rawhide-clad presidial soldier. Due to the unattractiveness and lack of interest in the interior of the country for the remote posts, the "Cueras" had to be recruited largely from among the inhabitants of the region. Few of these rough and enduring individuals were pure Spaniards; most came from the "mestizo" and mixed blood groups. On account of their small numbers and poor equipment, these true frontiersmen were never able to conquer the Indians, but for the length of the Spanish occupation of the Southwest, they kept the edge of the borderlands from receding.

Romantic he may be in his love of the historical past, but artist Cisneros definitely has a deep knowledge of the reality of those bygone days. Perhaps it is this mix of the romantic and the realist that makes him such an excellent interpreter of that era.

The Hon. Julian Nava, former United States ambassador to Mexico, is among those who truly understand and appreciate the work José Cisneros has pursued throughout his life. In a recent publication he described the artist and his achievement:

> In his work he emphasizes the brotherhood of human beings. Cisneros has been honored by various groups, and his work has been displayed before many groups. Young people, especially children, enjoy his illustrations very much.
>
> The work of Cisneros will keep alive the interest in the theme of the Southwest that he has awakened. In addition, with the passage of time, the work of José Cisneros will become even more important. The heritage of three great people—the Spanish, the Mexican, and those of the Southwestern United States—lives in the work of this artist born in Durango.

Such a tribute is particularly significant in assessing the honors earned over the years by José Cisneros. Those honors have come from all

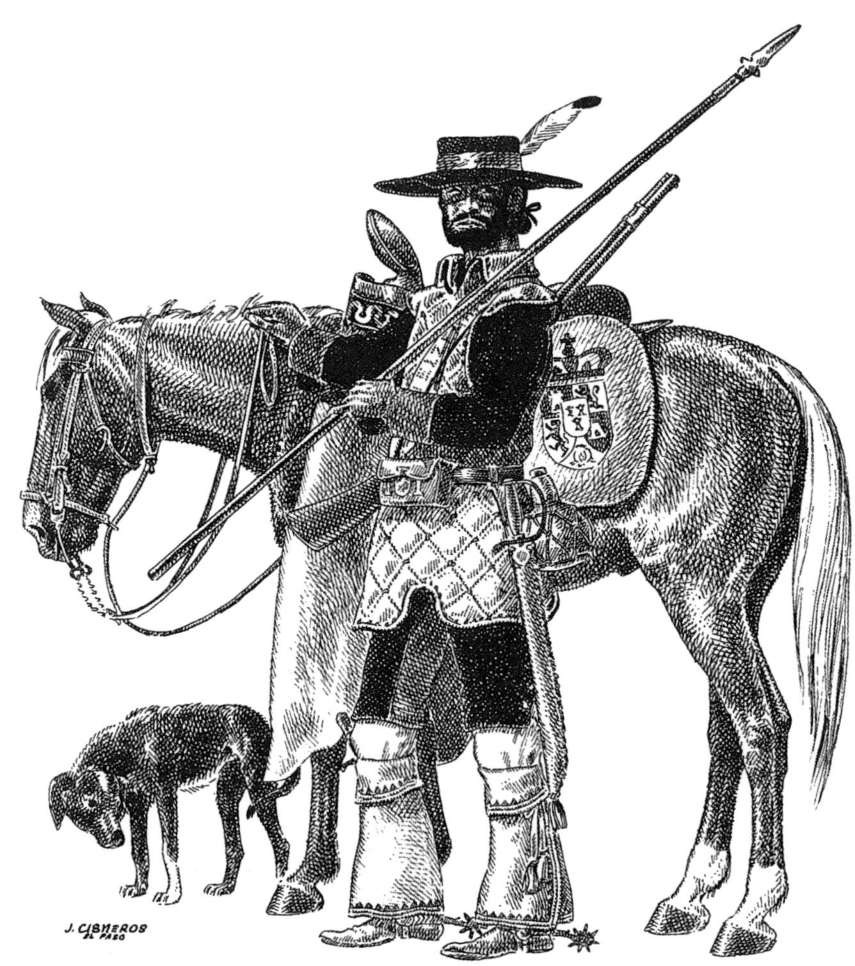

A tough cuera *soldier helped guard the frontier, protected by rawhide armor. From Eugene Porter,* San Elizario *(1973).*

levels, ecclesiastic, lay, scholar, and casual viewer of his art alike. The fact that he has been selected so often to illustrate works of such different types suggests to a large degree the respect he has earned over the years. Still, it is of value to enumerate some of those honors.

José Cisneros has repeatedly been chosen to create certificates to be awarded to people of merit. The first came in 1954 when he was asked to design a recognition certificate for the local branch of the League of Latin American Citizens—LULAC. When the certificate was reproduced and he was inscribing the names of the honorees, he was astounded to be asked to execute one for himself. His excitement was dampened considerably when the master of ceremonies at the LULAC banquet couldn't figure out who this "José Cisneros" was, and Father Harold Rahm, the honoree, had to make the presentation. Cisneros designed the Hall of Honor certificate for the El Paso County Historical Society (and was named to that honor in 1974; in addition he was added in 1979, with his wife Vicenta, to the roll of charter members); the El Paso County Historical Commission recognized him in 1990 for his life's work; he designed the mayor's Conquistador Award for outstanding contribution by citizens (and has received the award from three mayors: Peter DeWetter, Fred Hervey, and Tom E. Rogers); the Gran Paseño Award created by U T El Paso President Haskell Monroe was designed by Cisneros and he was one of the first two recipients, along with Mayor Fred Hervey; the El Paso Corral of the Westerners awarded him a citation and a life membership in 1975, during Sheriff Leon Metz's tenure. He was chosen the Outstanding Ex-Student in 1985 by his alma mater, Lydia Patterson Institute, where he had studied for several years while struggling to educate himself, delivering newspapers and sweeping the halls to pay his tuition. And in 1990 he was one of seven senior citizens named Centennial Leaders of El Paso.

His writings and art work have earned significant honors too: *Pensamiento y Acción* (thought and action) of the municipality of Juárez honored him in 1959; the New Mexico and Texas Library Associations followed suit in 1977, in a tribute to him, Tom Lea, Carl Hertzog, and

Peter Hurd for their contribution to Southwestern culture. Best of all, his *Riders Across the Centuries* earned the Wrangler Award and a Charles Russell statue from the National Cowboy Hall of Fame in 1985 for Best Western Art Book. The presentation in Oklahoma City was truly a gala affair. He recently recalled that it was, to him, the highest recognition he could ever get.

The Border Regional Library Association also recognized the artist and the book in 1986 for "literary excellence and enrichment of the cultural heritage of the Southwest"; Westerners International gave him a plaque "In Special Recognition" for *Riders Across the Centuries*, plus a certificate of honor in 1985; the El Paso *Herald-Post* entered his name in the Writers Hall of Fame, naming him one of the Authors of the Pass in 1986; and the Texas Catholic Historical Society gave him their prestigious Reverend Paul J. Foik, C. S. C. Award in 1981 for his excellence. And the Doña Ana County Historical Society in Las Cruces, New Mexico, named him Pasajero del Camino Real (traveler on the royal highway) in January 1990.

San Antonio and Bexar County would like to consider José Cisneros as one of their own, to judge by the awards he has received there:

Honorary *Jefe Político de Bejar*, 1974

The José Francisco Ruiz and Erasmo Seguín Award from the Bexar County Historical Commission in 1981

Award of Merit, Bexar County Historical Commission, 1987

Hidalgo de San Antonio de Béjar from the Commissioners Court of Bexar County, 1987

Named *Empresario del Departamento de Béjar* in 1987

Awarded the Silver Spur of Béjar from the Bexar County Historical Commission in 1988

And twice cited by then mayor Henry Cisneros as *Emisario de las Musas*. (The artist points out with a smile that this was not a "brother-in law job." The two Cisneros are not related.)

The many displays of his art work in San Antonio—especially at the Institute of Texan Cultures and the restored San José Mission—keep his name and his art steadily before the people of that city.

The Daughters of the American Revolution recognized his work in 1979 with their DAR Americanism award; Special Greetings with Seal and Ribbons of the State of Texas came from Gov. William P. Clements, followed by a House Concurrent Resolution, in association with José Cisneros Day in the State Capitol, introduced by Representative Nancy McDonald and signed by a host of Texas dignitaries.

The Palace of the Governors Museum in Santa Fe, once the mansion of the Spanish governor of the territory of New Mexico, has recently honored José Cisneros with a solid wall of tiles, nine to a picture, of twenty of his horsemen. Smaller sets, of four tiles each, were given to the artist and to the governor of the state. The artistry of the tile maker

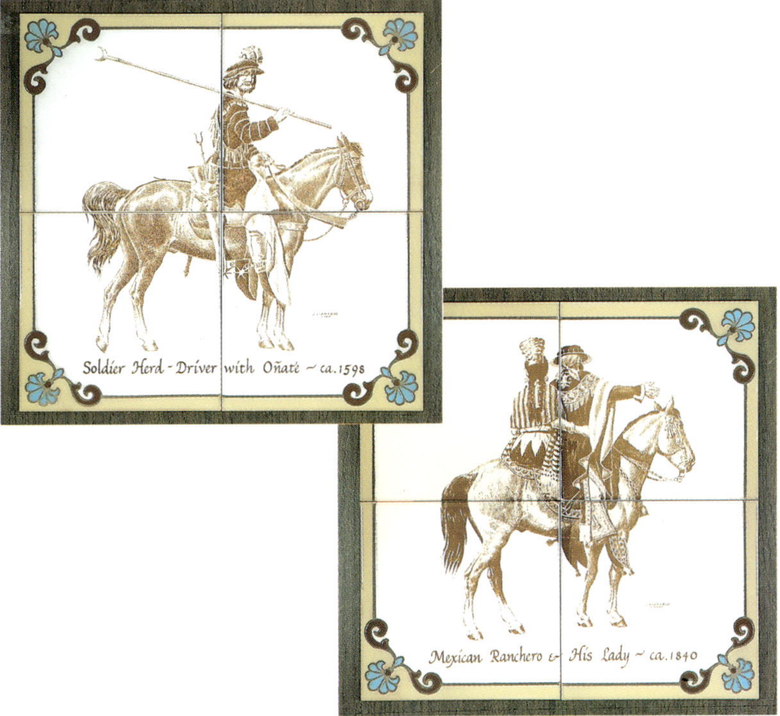

Among the tiles reproduced for display in the New Mexico Palace of the Governors are a soldier with Oñate's expedition and a memorable pair of Mexican settlers—a ranchero *and his lady.*

has rendered the beauty and detail of the originals perfectly, as befits such masterpieces.

As a devout Catholic, José Cisneros takes particular pride in having received Apostolic Blessings from Pope John XXIII in June and again in October 1959; from Pope Paul VI in 1964; and from Pope John Paul II in 1966. Then, in October 1990, he and his wife Vicenta were named Knight and Lady of the Equestrian Order of the Holy Sepulchre, with beautiful plaques in red and gold that rival—almost—some of his own art and calligraphy.

Despite the many honors he has received, the artist continues to be modest. Following a recent conversation with his biographer he wrote quite eloquently on this subject:

> There are events in our lives that cling and remain in our memories forever. On our second visit to the National Cowboy Hall of Fame, through the invitation of the institution for a reunion of the past recipients of the Wrangler's Award, I was able to observe facets of a world that I had seen only in movies or on the television screen. The first time Vicenta and I attended I had been such a nervous wreck that I couldn't eat, couldn't concentrate, and couldn't capture or enjoy the significance of the occasion. This time, however, I felt relaxed, (though awkward in my rented tuxedo) but I felt that I was among a strange crowd in which I somehow did not fit. Unconsciously I began to recall my rustic and humble upbringing and contrasting it with this ebullient and scintillating crowd, immaculately attired and engaged in lively and fluent conversations. The men were almost uniformly dressed in neatly pressed shirts, bow ties, and black party suits, while the ladies sparkled in their diamonds and gold jewelry, leaving behind them a scent of exotic fragrance and wearing an infinite variety of tight and beautiful designer dresses. Hopping from one corner of the reception room to another, tasting the different glasses of spirits in order to gain confidence, we ended up at a table at which we were surrounded by a group of people that

claimed to be from Hollywood. The memories are strong still, but the only tangible thing that remains is a soiled program with a few illegible autographs.

Most recently, in July 1991, the artist was knighted *Caballero de Mérito Civil* by Juan Carlos I, King of Spain, in recognition for his work with respect to the importance of Spanish contributions to the settlement of the Spanish Southwest.

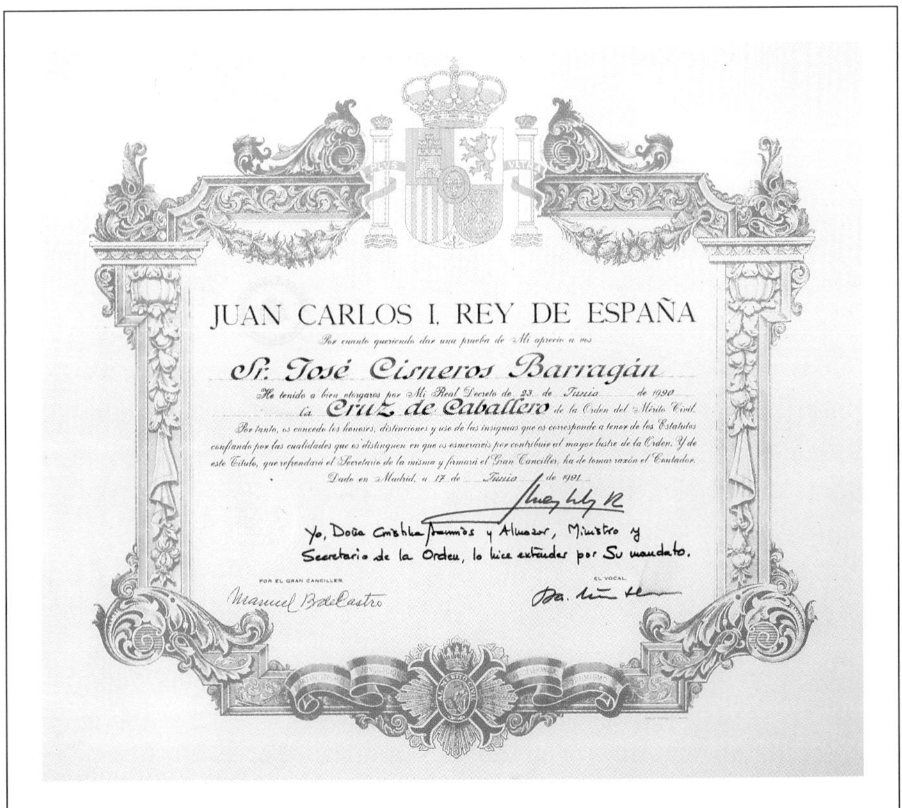

JUAN CARLOS I, REY DE ESPAÑA

Por cuanto queriendo dar una prueba de Mi aprecio a vos

Sr. José Cisneros Barragán

He tenido a bien otorgaros por Mi Real Decreto de 23 de Junio de 1990 la Cruz de Caballero de la Orden del Mérito Civil.

Por tanto, os concedo los honores, distinciones y uso de las insignias que os corresponde a tenor de los Estatutos confiando por las cualidades que os distinguen en que os esmeraréis por contribuir al mayor lustre de la Orden. Y de este Título, que refrendará el Secretario de la misma y firmará el Gran Canciller, ha de tomar razón el Contador.

Dado en Madrid, a 17 de Junio de 1991.

Yo, Doña Cristina [illegible] y Almazor, Ministro y Secretario de la Orden, lo hice extender por Su mandato.

POR EL GRAN CANCILLER

EL VOCAL

With this certificate, Don José Cisneros is certified as a Knight of the Cross.

Less formal, perhaps, but no less real have been two publications that recognize José Cisneros as an outstanding and worthy representative of his Mexican heritage. In 1977 the Continental Press of Elizabethtown, Pennsylvania, released an educational set of *Reading Exercises on Mexican Americans*, gathered by Félix D. Almaráz and María O. Almaráz. Among thirty people who were recognized were singer Vikki Carr, tennis great Pancho González, freedom fighter Father Miguel Hidalgo, actor Anthony Quinn, political leader Benito Juárez, golfer Lee Treviño, labor organizer César Chávez, church leader Patrick Flores, and José Cisneros, artist and historian. In 1989 Sammye Munson brought out a tribute to *Our Tejano Heroes: Outstanding Mexican-Americans in Texas*, featuring such persons as Andrea Castañon Ramírez Candalaria, the nurse of the Alamo; Congressional Medal of Honor winner Roy Benavidez; poet Tomás Rivera; Congressman Henry B. González; and José Cisneros. The compiler cited her collection as being of "outstanding Hispanic leaders of Texas whose lives have helped and are helping to guide its destiny." With such reminders of their heritage as role models before them, students of Hispanic origin will have worthwhile goals to attain.

In March 1992, a reception was held at the University of Texas at El Paso Library, at which the acquisition of the Cisneros library and personal papers was announced. Although several other libraries had expressed interest in obtaining the research materials, books, and correspondence included in the collection, José Cisneros chose the U T El Paso Library for its home, because of his long association with the institution. Here illustrators and historians can study his work, compare his varying styles and growth over the years, and perhaps a budding artist will be inspired to follow in his footsteps.

The permanent collection of one hundred Cisneros horsemen lines the walls of the Library's fourth floor, a magnet for visitors and for alumni who come to see how their university has grown. Young and old find fascination there, with so much detail to study. A student group touring the library recently lingered long by the hundred riders, asking questions of the artist, and marveling that such an important man would take the time to lead a tour for a group of children. One boy asked him, in wonder, "How long did it take you to do all these drawings?"

He didn't hesitate a moment. "All my life," he said.

That life has been rich indeed, and the wealth of his knowledge and artistry has enriched all those who came into contact with the fulfillment of his dreams. Cisneros himself marvels at the frequency of the term *journey* in his pursuit of those dreams: his first publication at fourteen was *"Un Viaje"* (A Journey); his first important book was *The Journey of Three Englishmen Across Texas*; soon after came *The Journey of Fray Marcos de Niza*; the introduction to *Riders Across the Centuries*, a book which he values highly, is entitled "The Artistic Journey of José Cisneros."

The respect of one artist for another is evident in a recent letter from Tom Lea, whose influence Cisneros has always credited for opening the first door to the fulfillment of his dreams:

> I think that in the goodness of your heart you have always given me far too much credit for starting you on the path you would inevitably find; it was the sheer character and quality of your work itself, and certainly no action of mine that set your feet upon the rock and ordered your goings! Yet I am indeed proud that I immediately recognized the great merit of the drawings you showed me that day in 1938 when we were young. And I am immensely proud to share with all your friends and fellows here and afar a happiness in the splendid career you have achieved with your own gifted mind and heart and hand. With affection we all salute you, and we all thank you!
>
> Sincerely your friend
> Tom

In his acceptance speech for the National Cowboy Hall of Fame Wrangler Award in 1985, Cisneros placed those journeys, those dreams in a historical setting:

> Many of the early Spanish explorers of our Southwest carved their names with the points of their weapons on the soft sandstone cliffs of New Mexico. They usually added the words *pasó por aquí*—he passed through here—as testimony and reminder to posterity of their presence at the rim of the Spanish Borderlands.
>
> Standing on the spot where many of the giants of Western art and letters once stood, trying to conceal my emotions, emulating those illustrious caballeros of old, I wish I were worthy to also carve my name in this prestigious hall and add the lapidary words *pasó por aquí.*

José Cisneros has indeed passed through here, and more than many others who had a more fortunate beginning, or were more formally educated, he has left an enduring mark wherever he has turned, not with a sword, but with a fine steel pen. He is a modest giant who came to the Pass of the North and made a difference that will long be remembered.

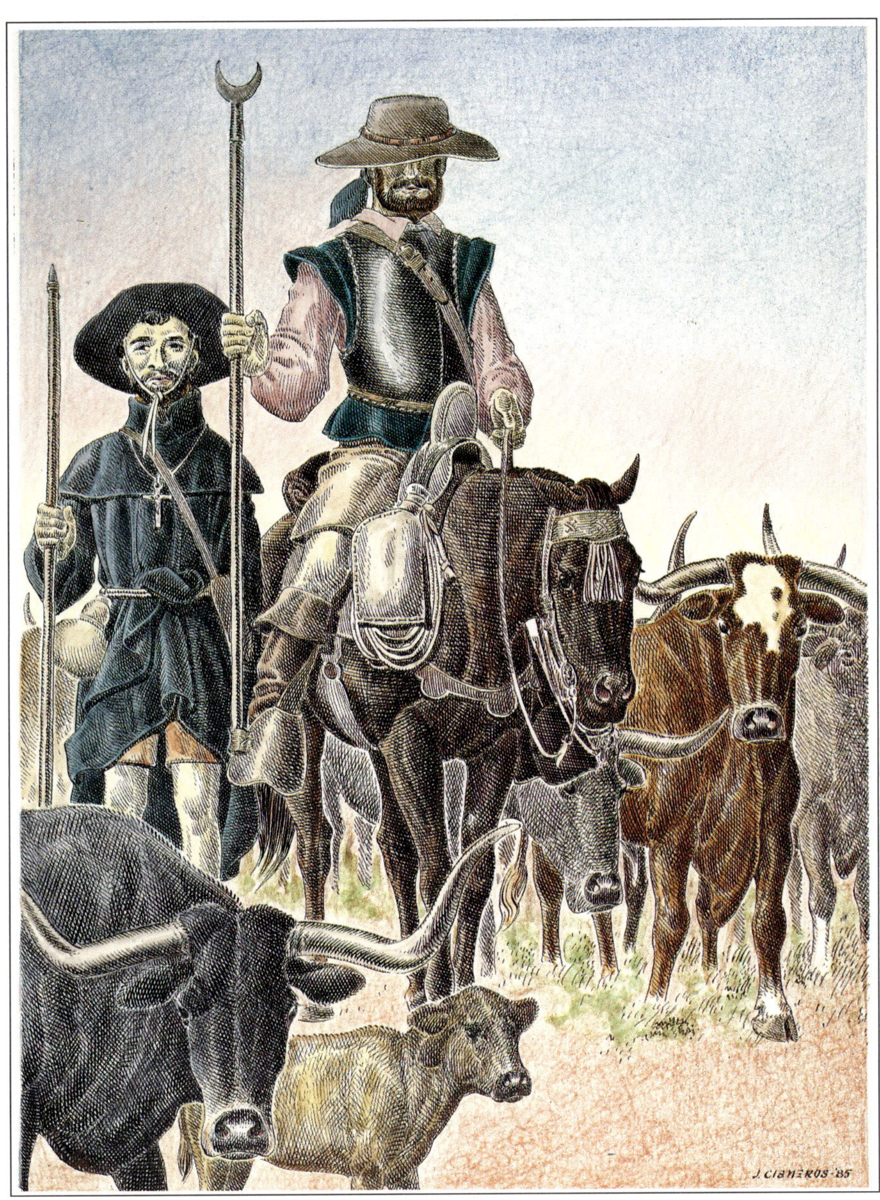

The Texas Sesquicentennial Exhibit at the Hidalgo County Museum, Edinburg, Texas (on permanent display), features this series of scenes from Lower Rio Grande Valley history. The first herds come into the Valley.

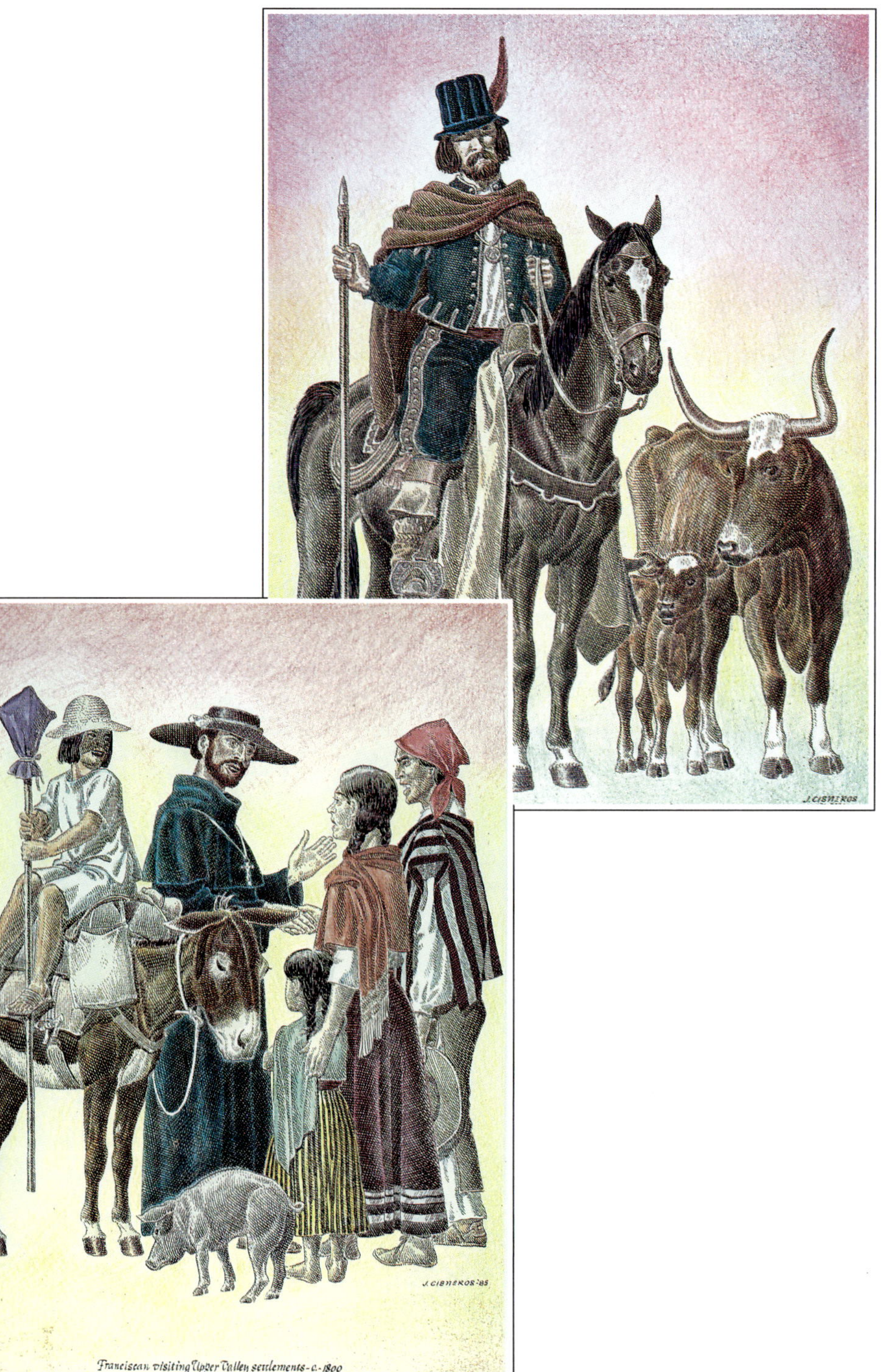

Hidalgo County Museum, Edinburg, Texas
Top: An early ganadero *(herdsman) about 1650; bottom: a Franciscan missionary and Valley settlers.*

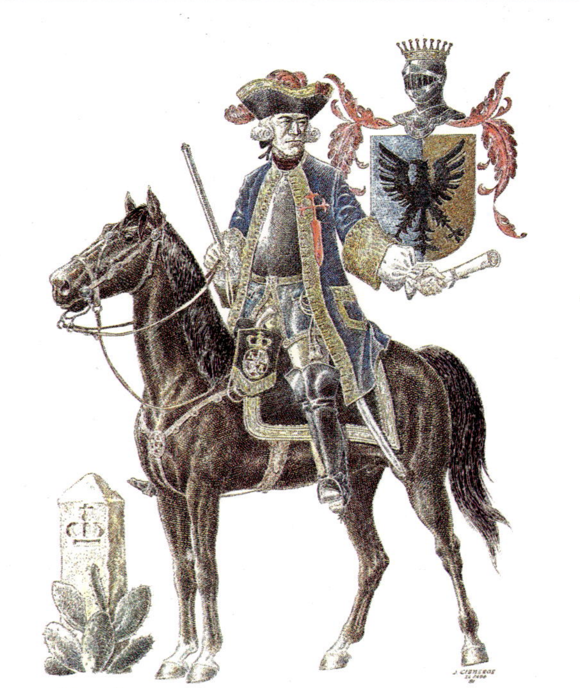

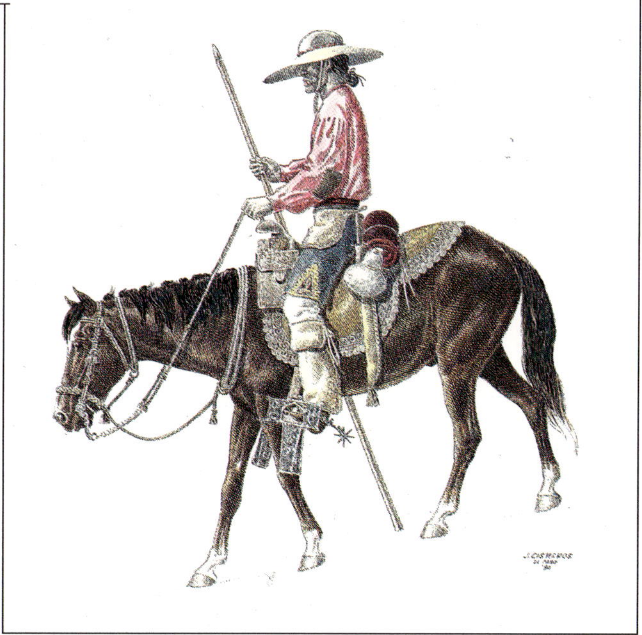

Hidalgo County Museum, Edinburg, Texas
A Spanish 1749 official. A vaquero *(cowboy) about 1750.*

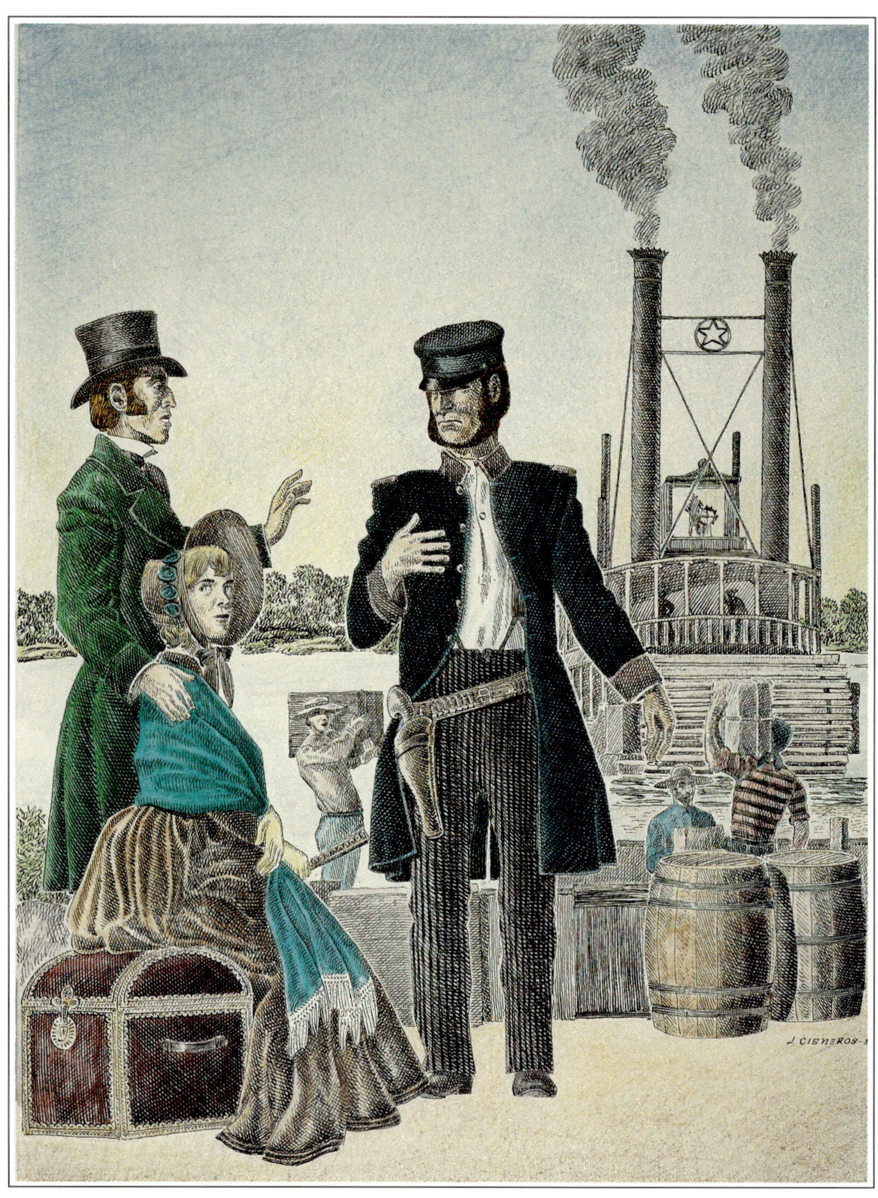

Hidalgo County Museum, Edinburg, Texas
The coming of steamboats, about 1850

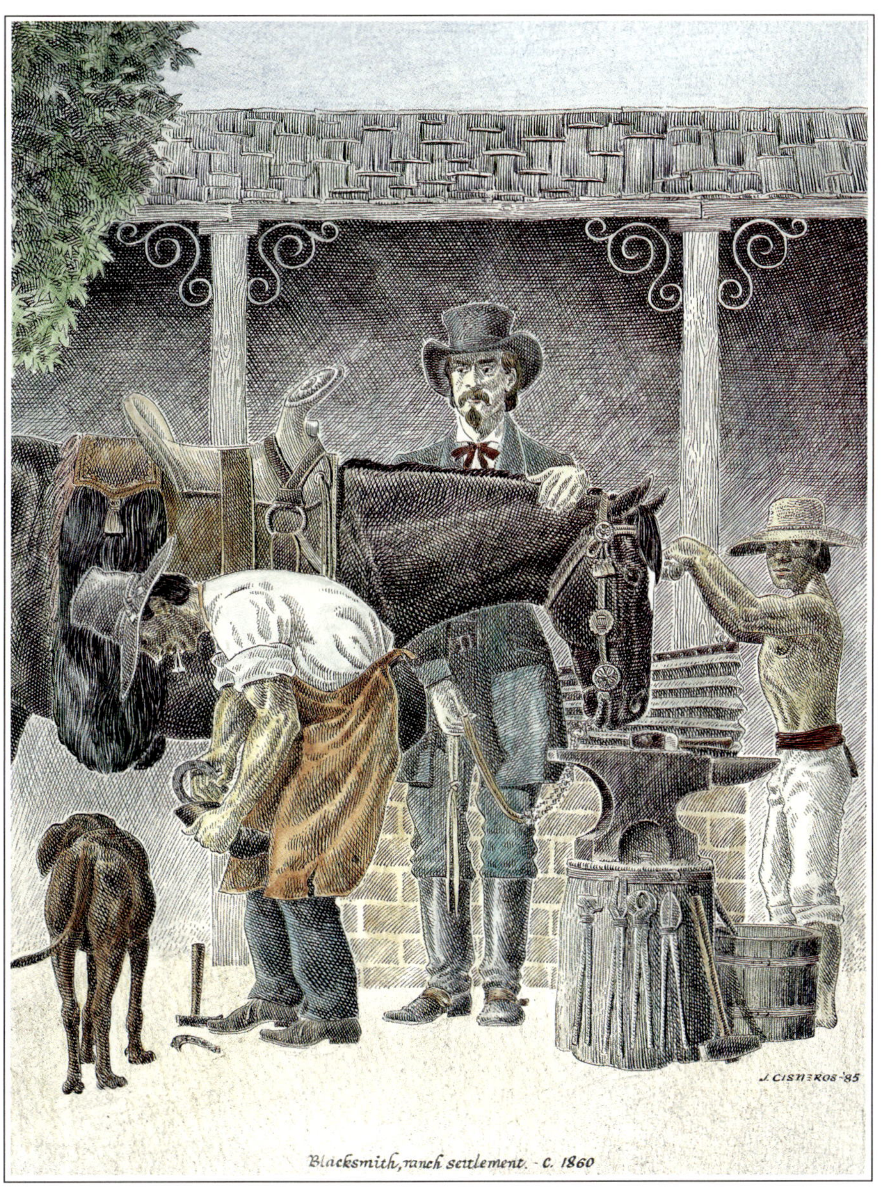

Hidalgo County Museum, Edinburg, Texas
A blacksmith

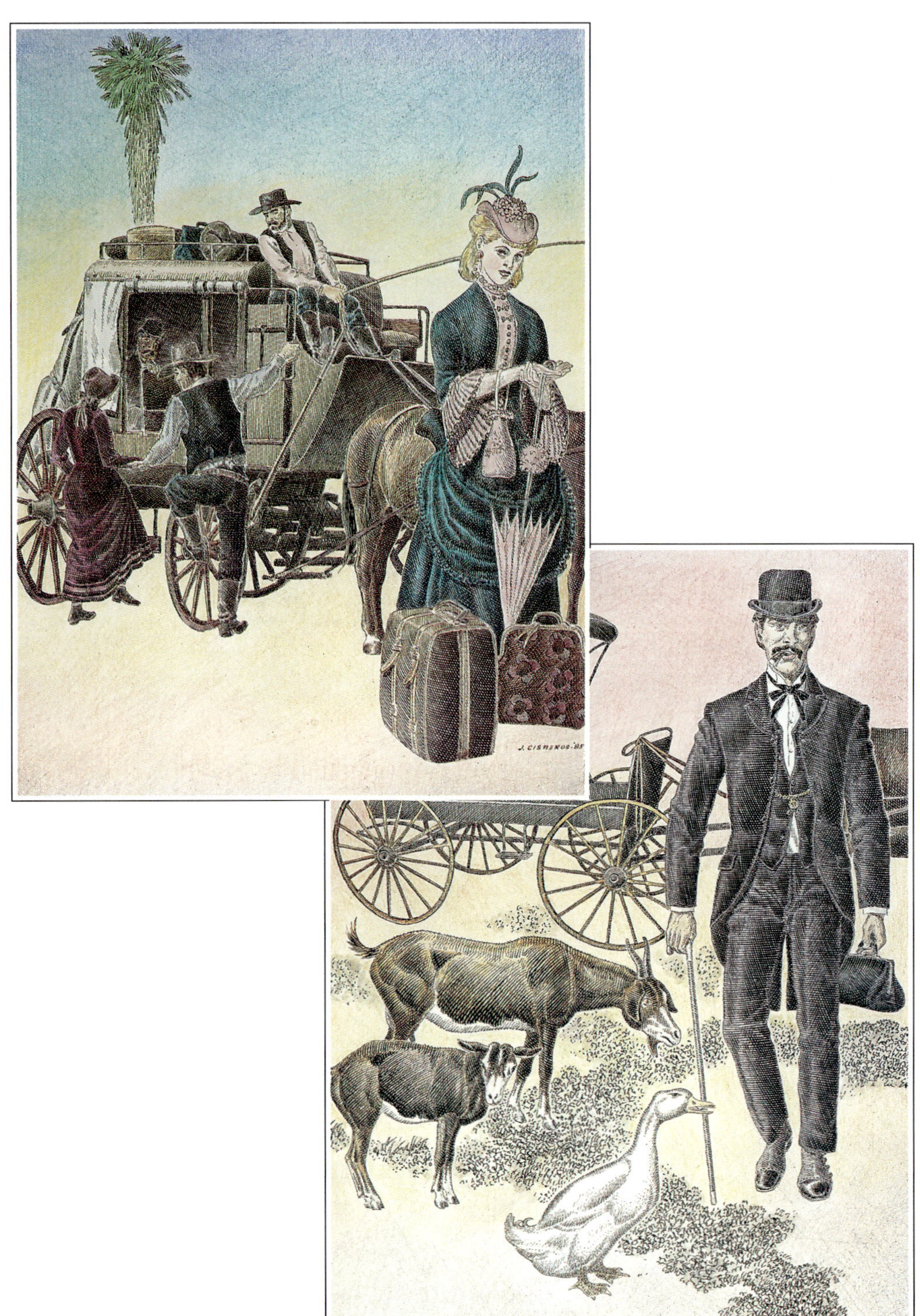

Hidalgo County Museum, Edinburg, Texas
Top: Stagecoaches brought new settlers to the Valley; bottom: A horse-and-buggy doctor

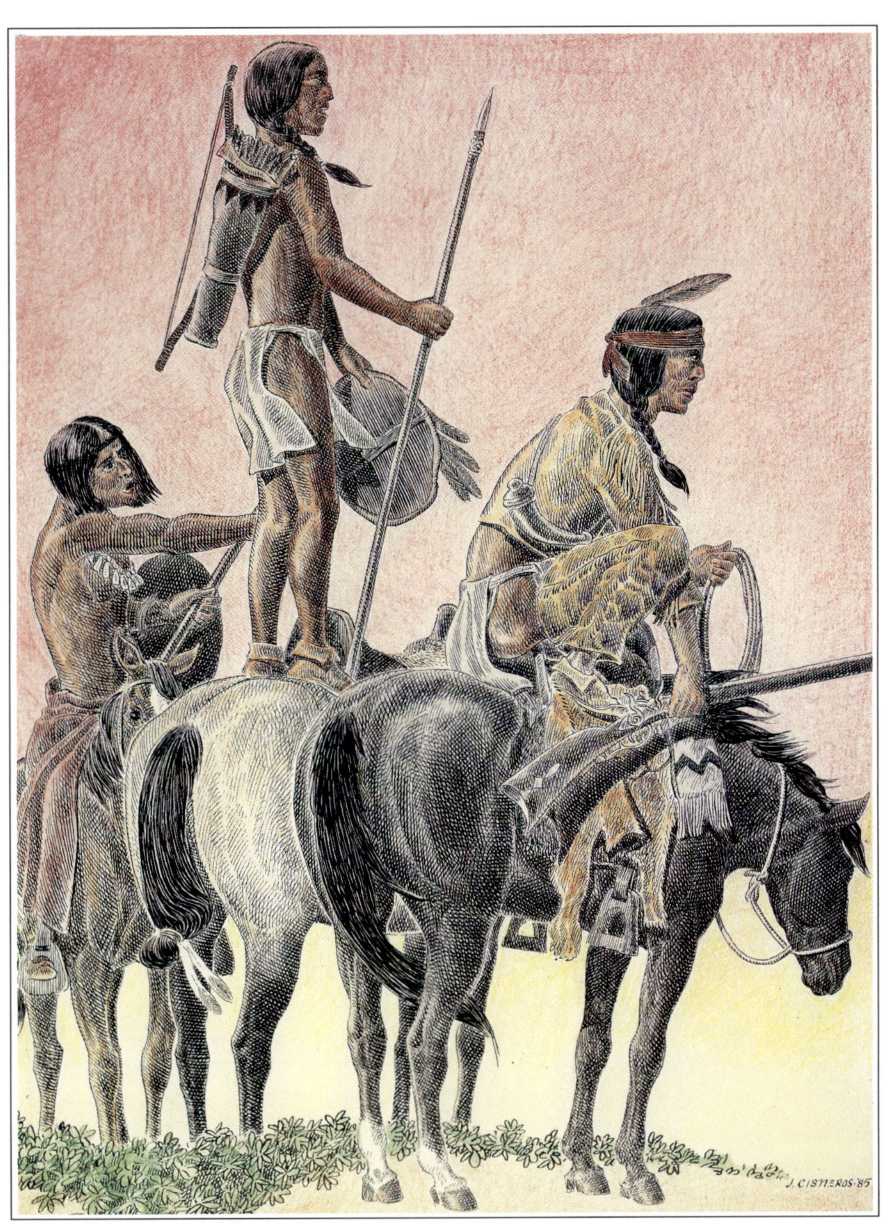

Hidalgo County Museum, Edinburg, Texas
19th century Lipan Apaches

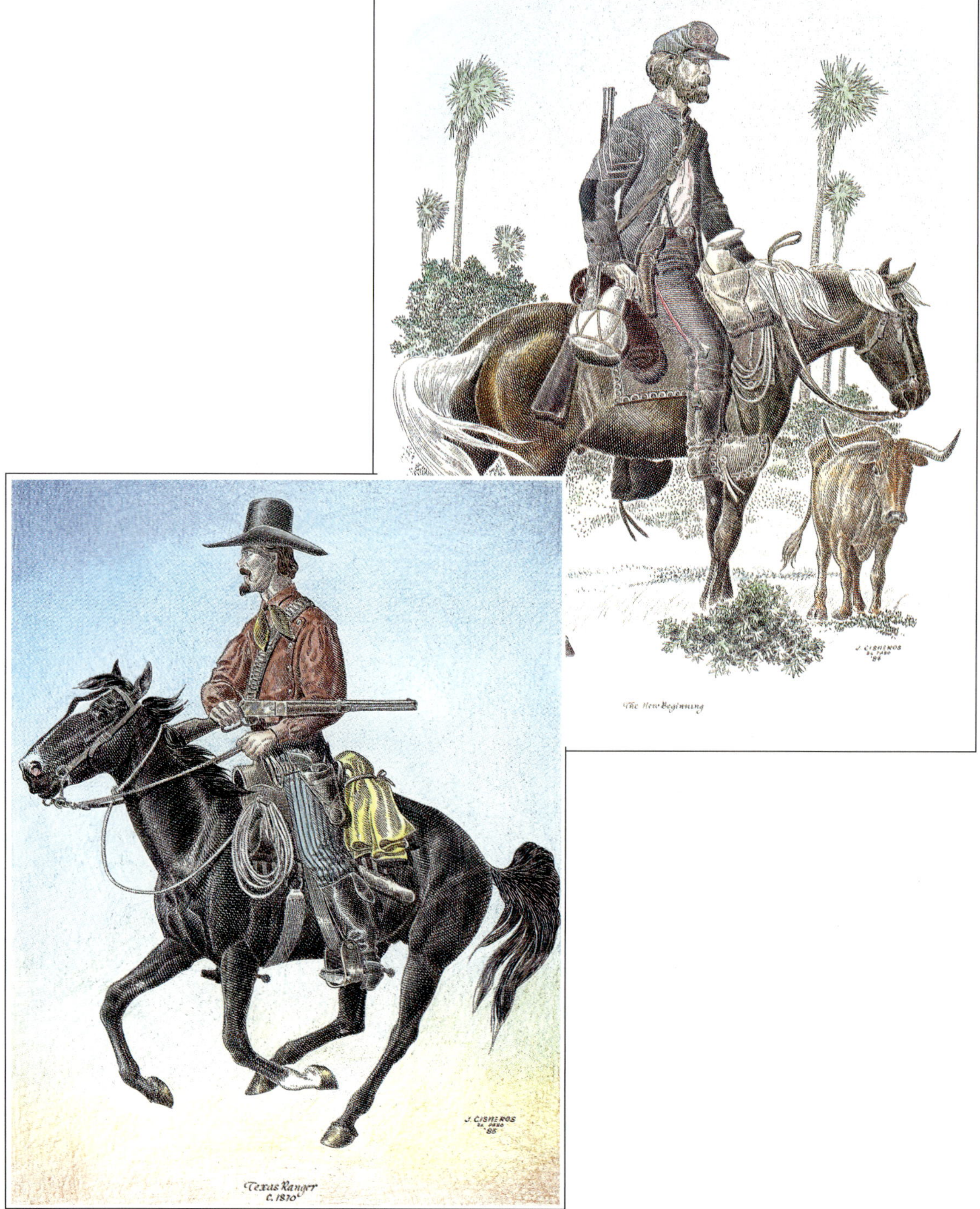

Hidalgo County Museum, Edinburg, Texas
Top: soldiers at Fort Desire; bottom: the Texas Rangers.

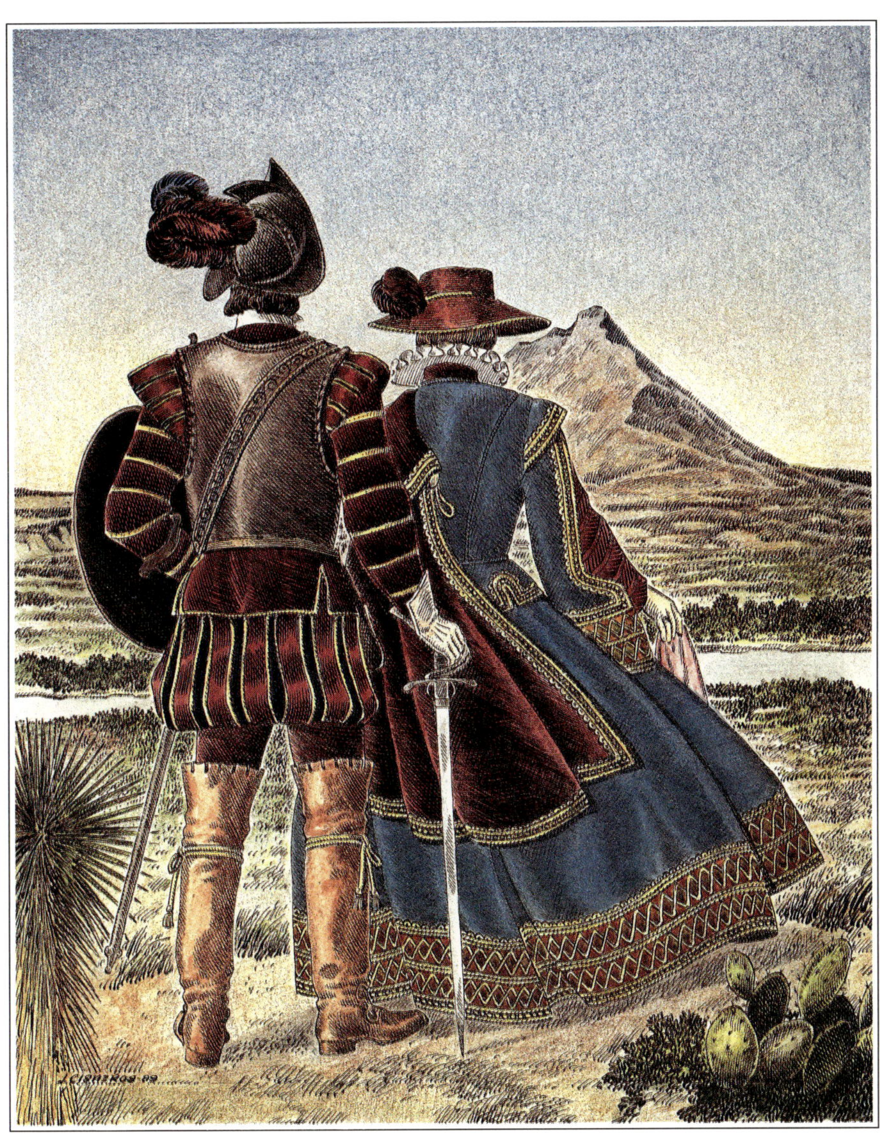

"El Paso Before It Was" graces the cover of El Paso: A Borderlands History *(1990) by W.H. Timmons, one of Texas Western Press' most popular productions.*

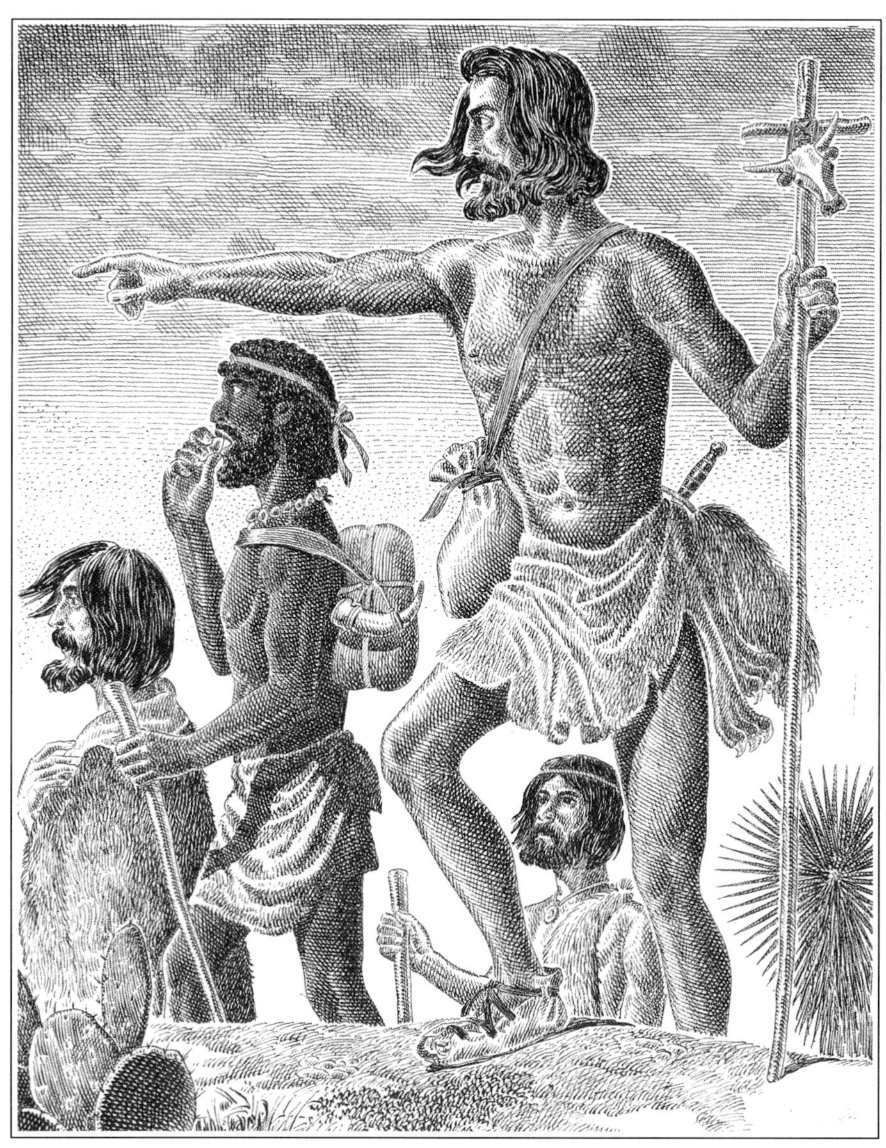

Three pictures from El Paso: A Borderlands History
Alvar Nuñez Cabeza de Vaca and his companions explore the El Paso del Norte region in 1535.

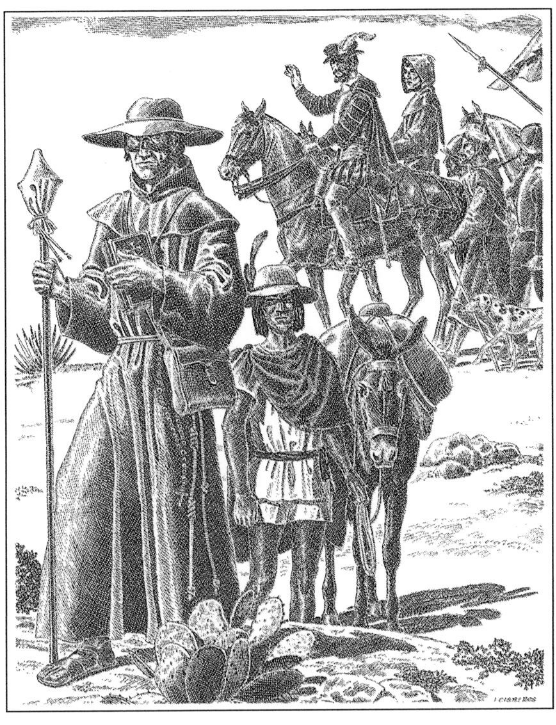

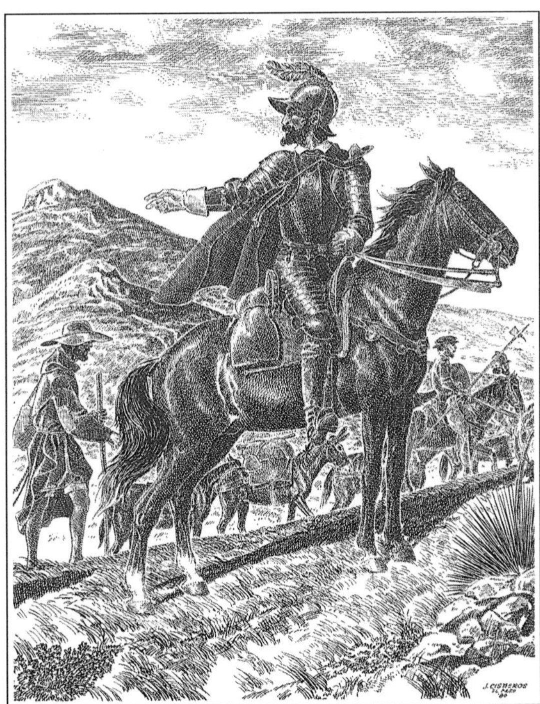

El Paso: A Borderlands History
Top: The Rodriguez-Chamuscado expedition reached the El Paso area in 1581.
Bottom: The Antonio de Espejo expedition came through the Pass of the North in 1582.

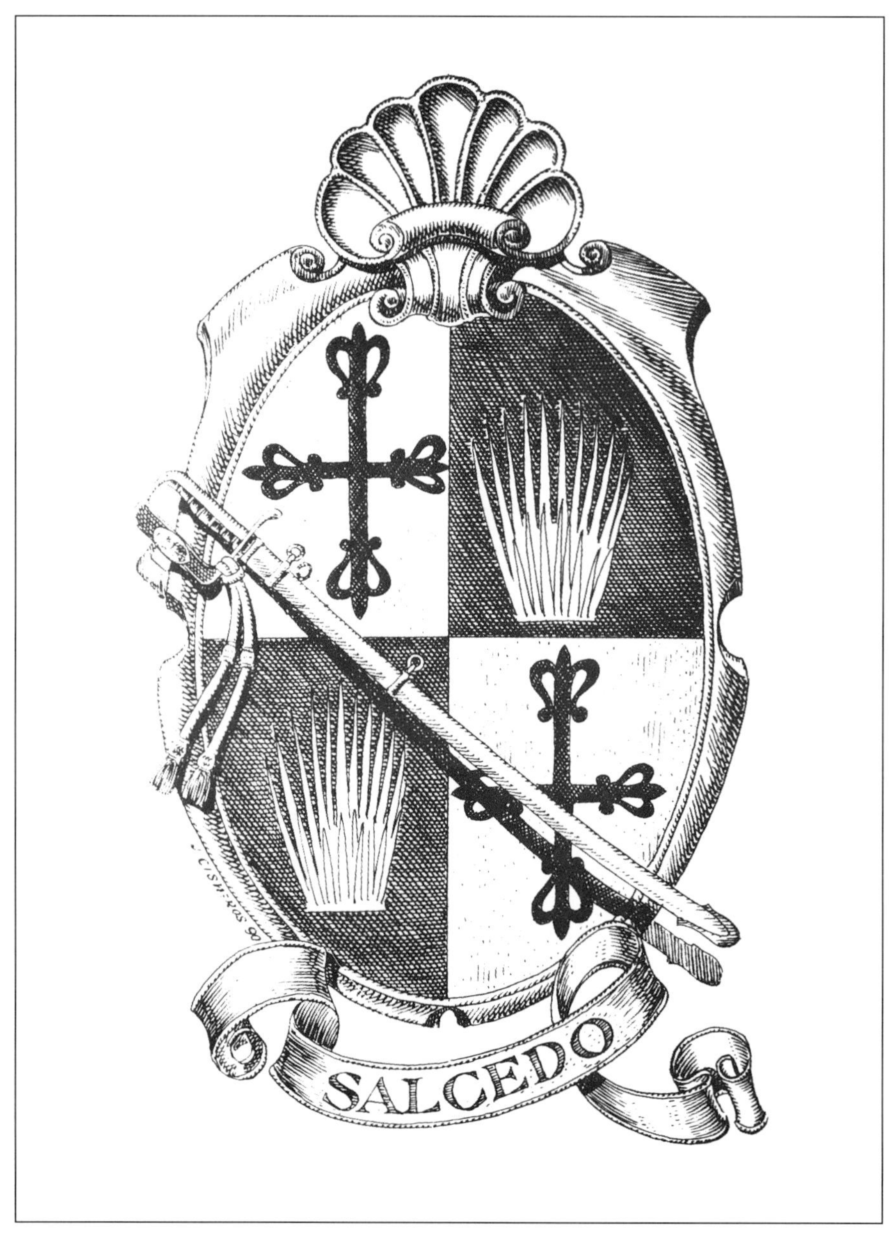

Tragic Cavalier *(1991) by Felix Almaráz describes the disintegration of Spain's empire:*
Coat of Arms *of the last Spanish governor of Texas, Don Manuel Salcedo.*

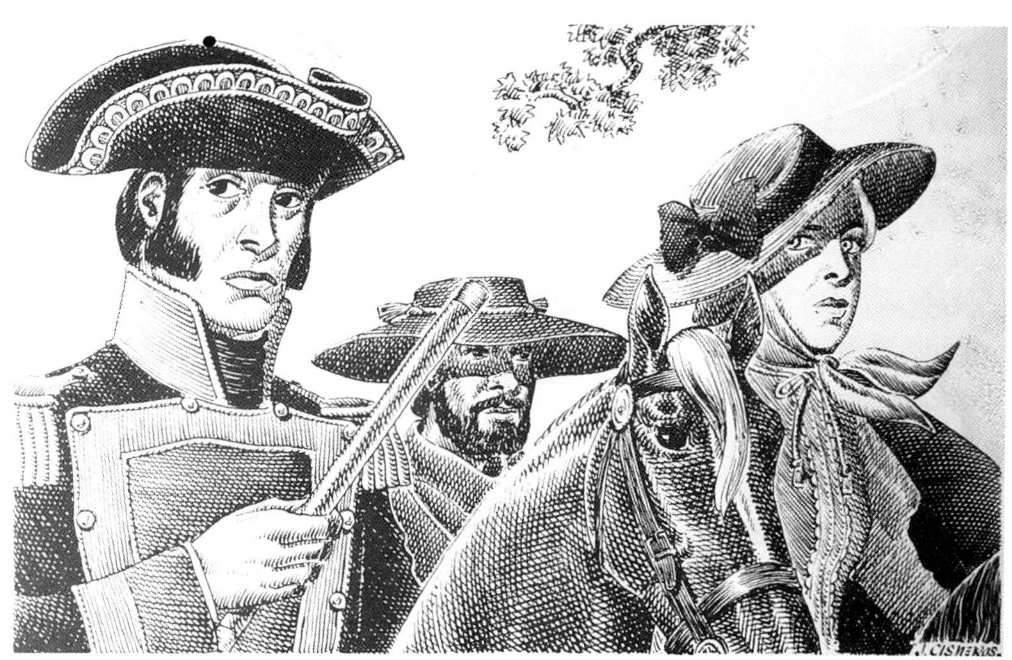

Tragic Cavalier
Salcedo's first year as governor was troubled.

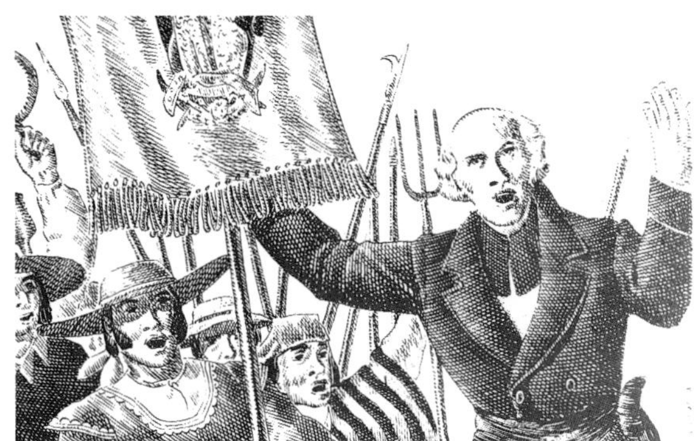

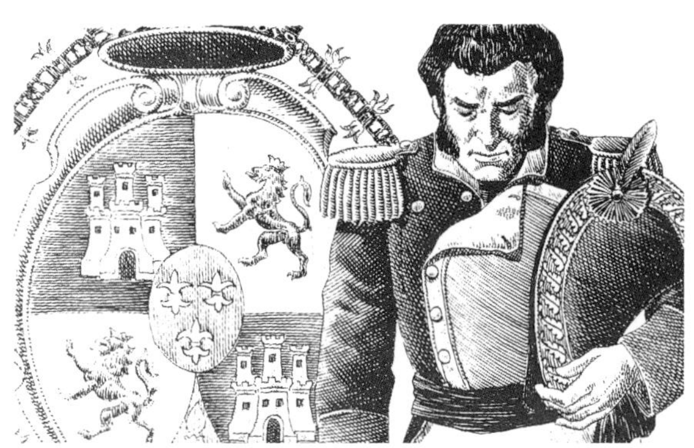

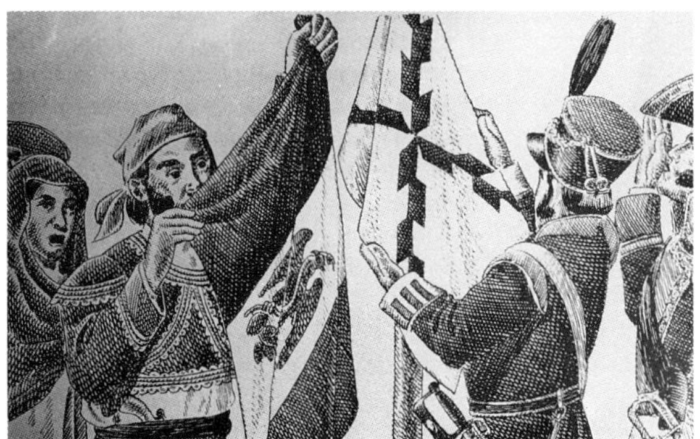

Tragic Cavalier
top: Father Miguel Hidalgo's call for independence was heard in Texas.
center: By 1812, Spanish rule in Texas was in ruins.
bottom: The flag of revolutionary Mexico replaced the flag of Spain.

NEW MEXICO'S

BUFFALO SOLDIERS

1866–1900

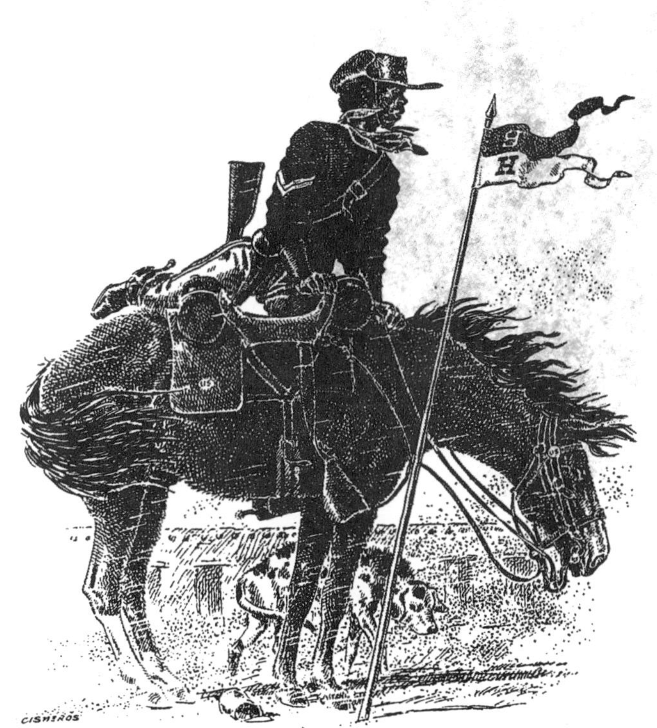

The book jacket for New Mexico's Buffalo Soldiers *(1991) by Monroe L. Billington.*

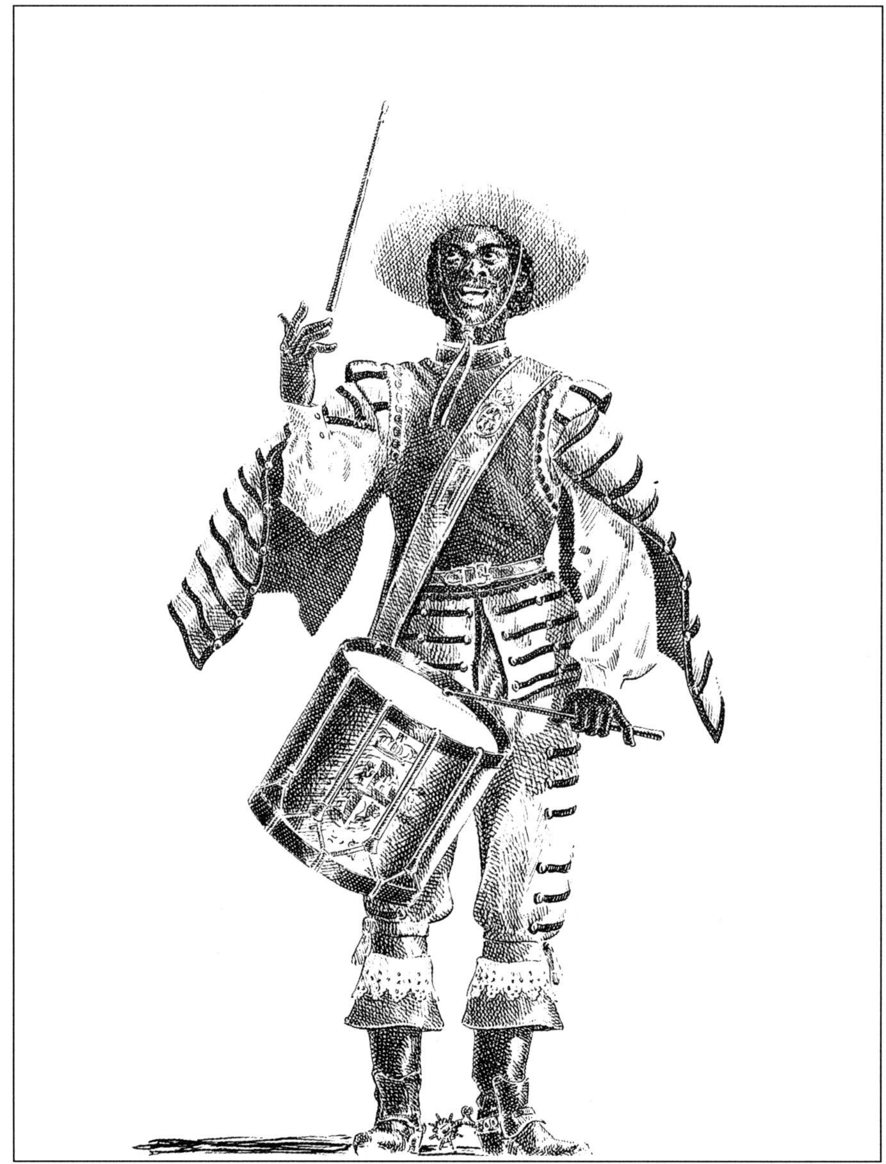

An Angolan who took part in De Vargas' reconquest of New Mexico, featured among Cisneros illustrations for The Black Military Experience *(1971) by John M. Carroll.*

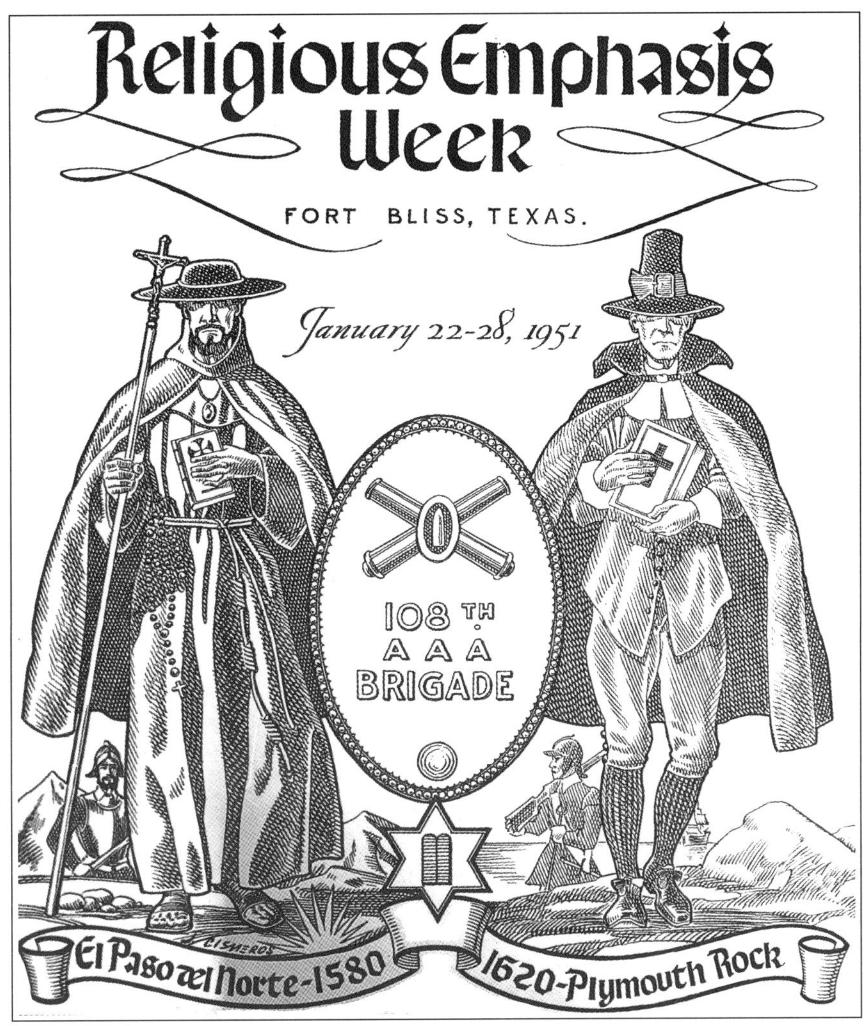

"Religious Emphasis Week" for Fort Bliss in 1951.

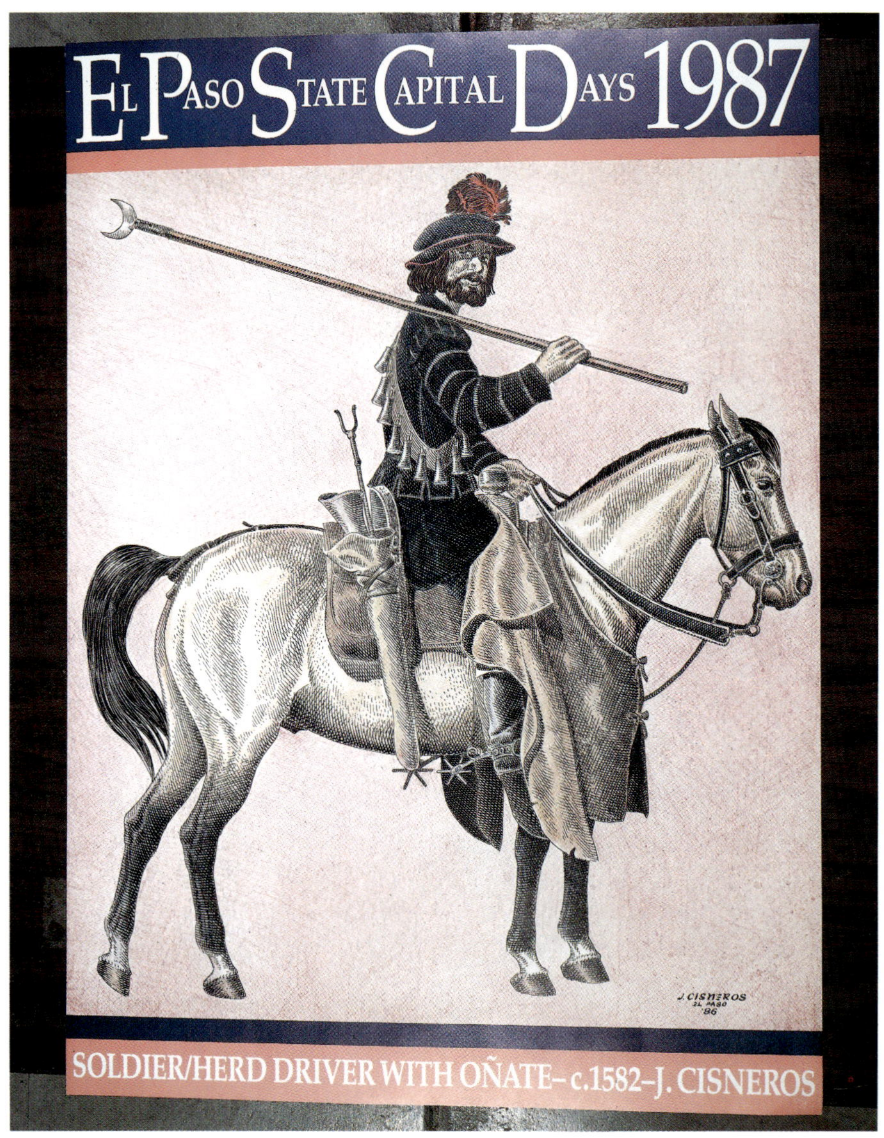

Cisneros poster for El Paso's Day in Austin, Texas.

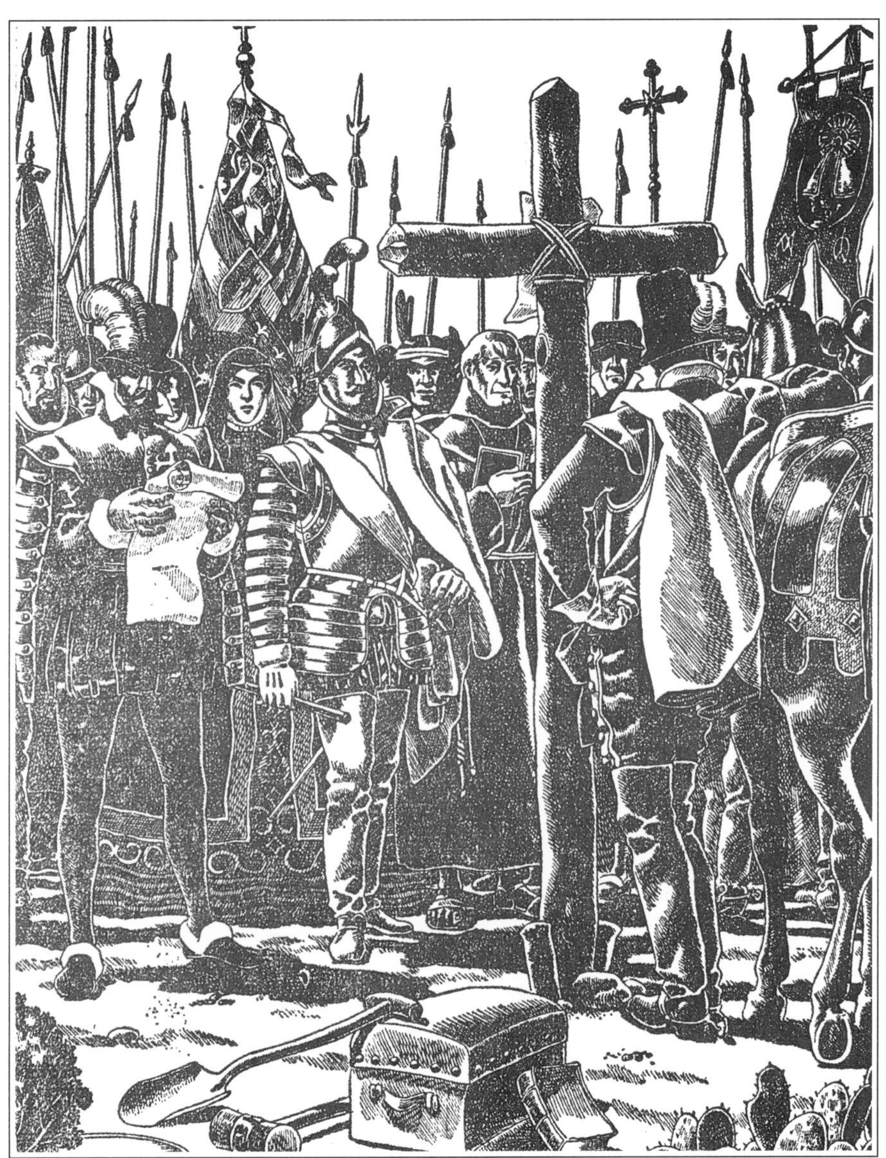

José Cisneros has often been drawn to religious subjects.
The taking of possession of the Spanish Southwest for God and King.

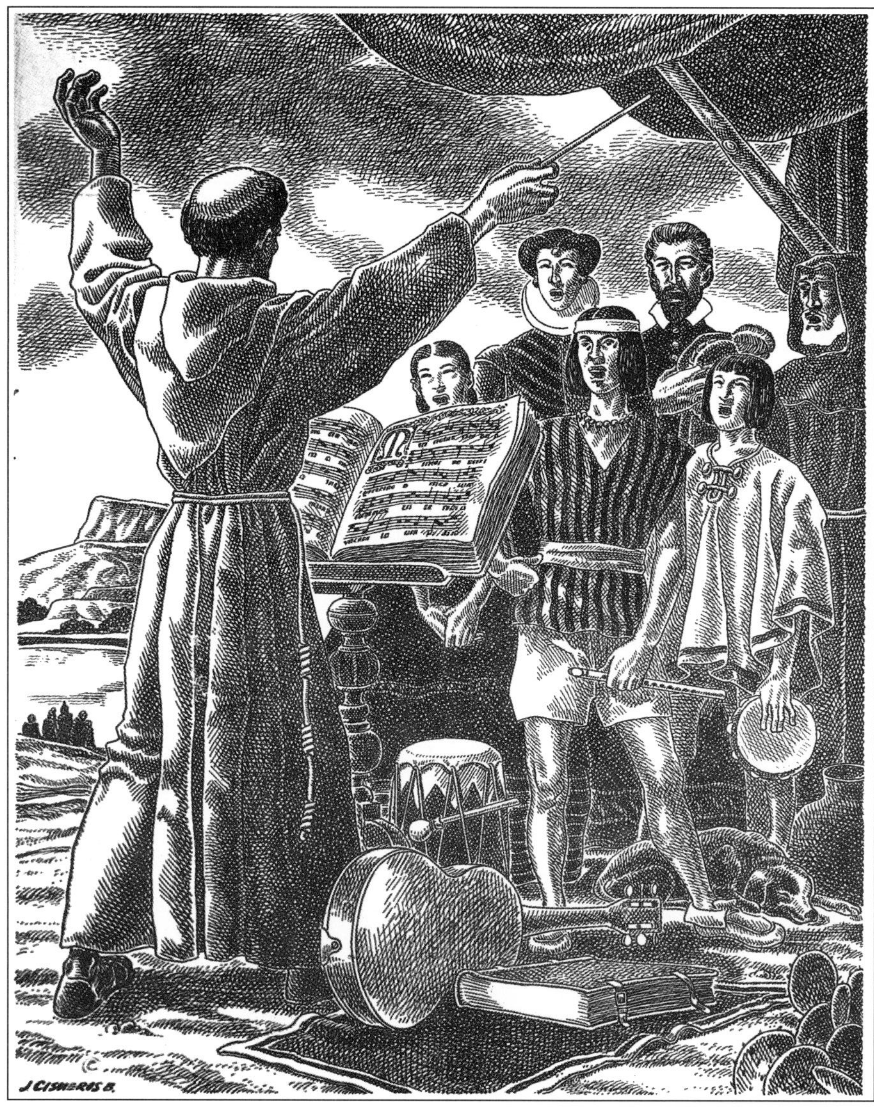

Fray Cristóbal de Quiñones, O.F.M., teaches music to New Mexican Indians and settlers. (Author's collection)

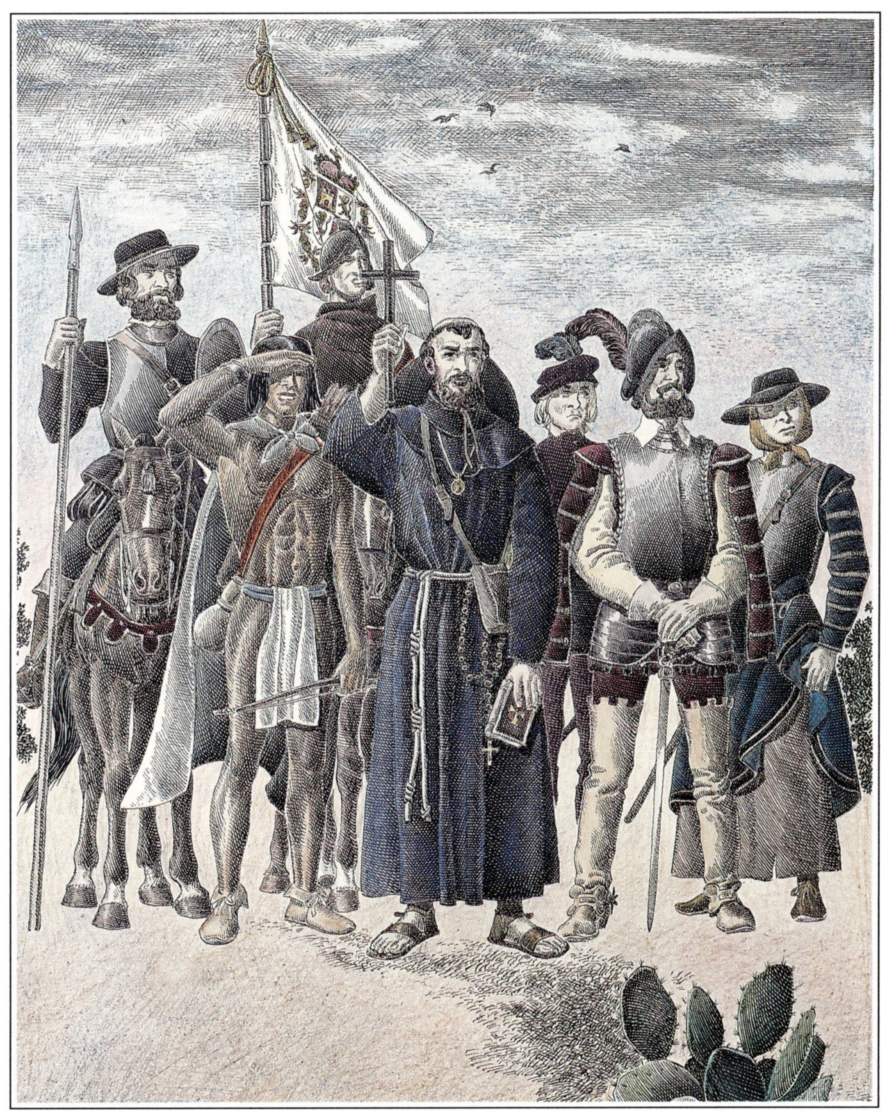

The first Thanksgiving: Conquistadors and settlers gather to give thanks for the safe crossing of the Chihuahua Desert, April 30, 1598.

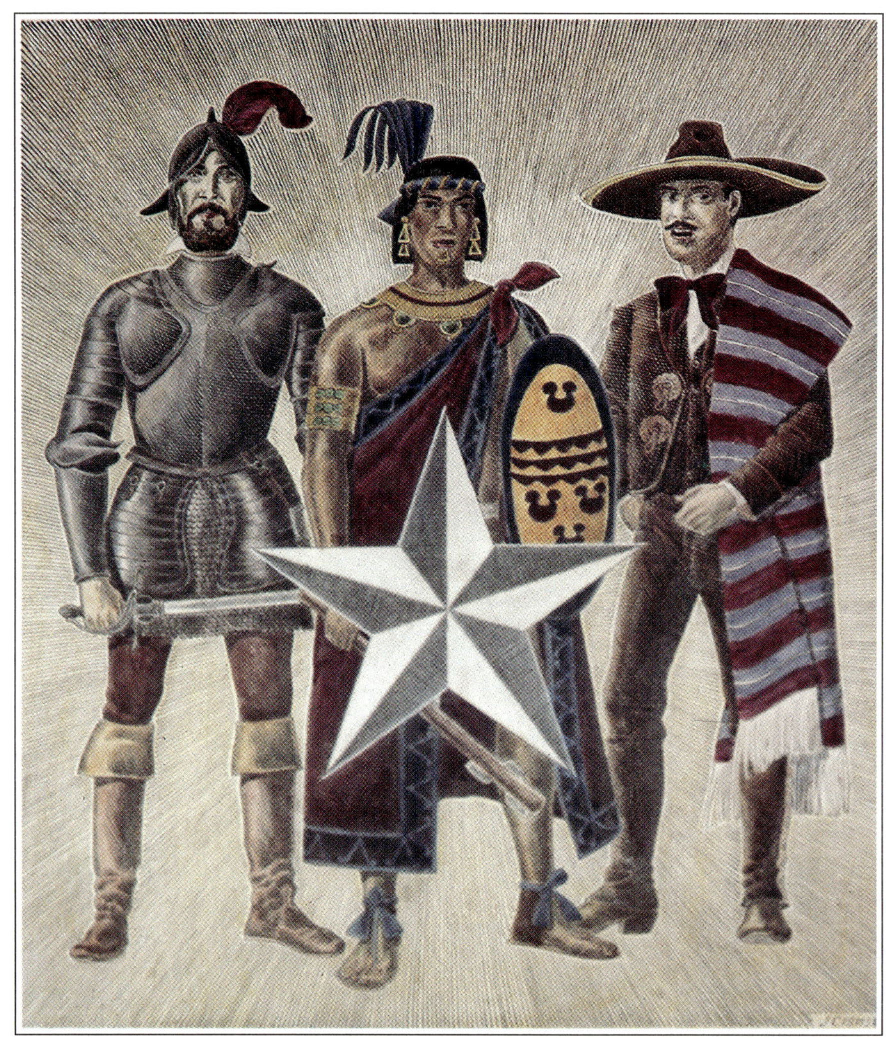

Hispanic Texas, *a 1993 publication by Helen Simons and Catherine A. Hoyt.*

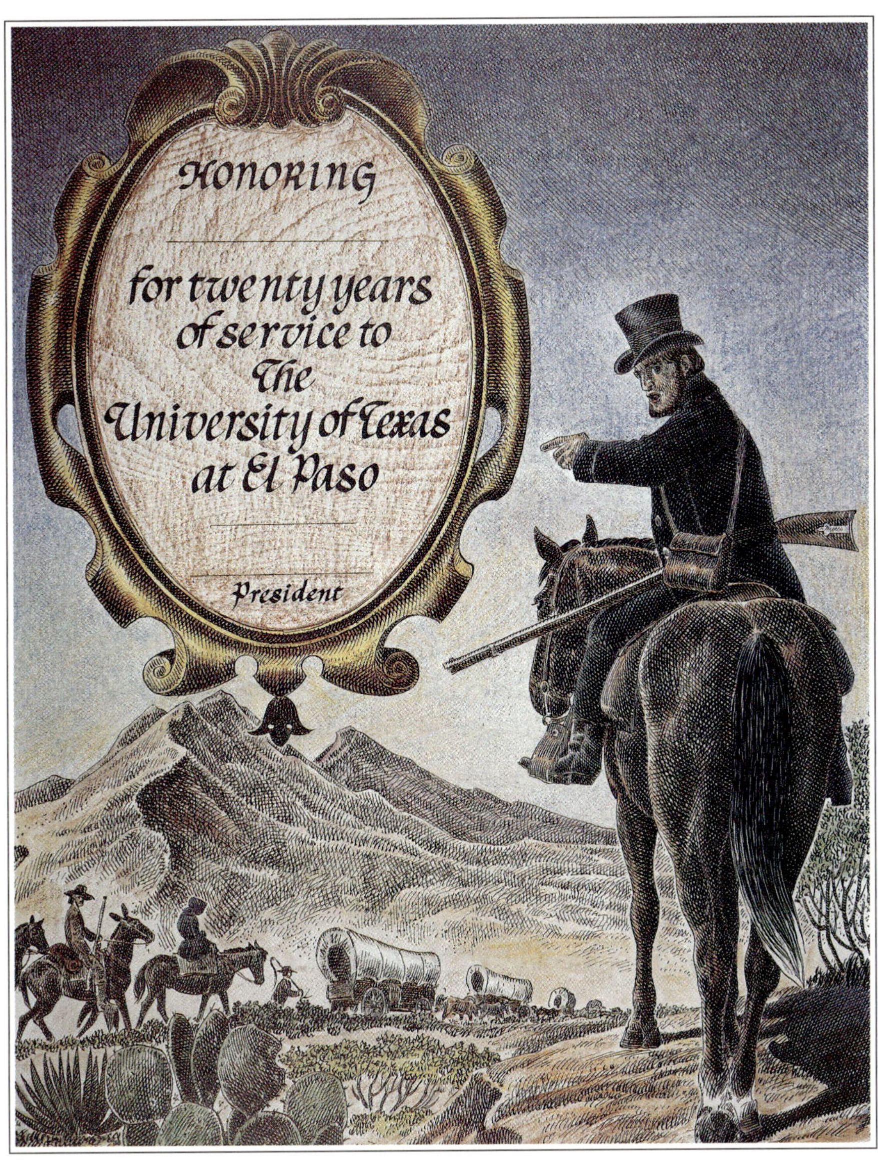

Service awards for University of Texas El Paso faculty and staff

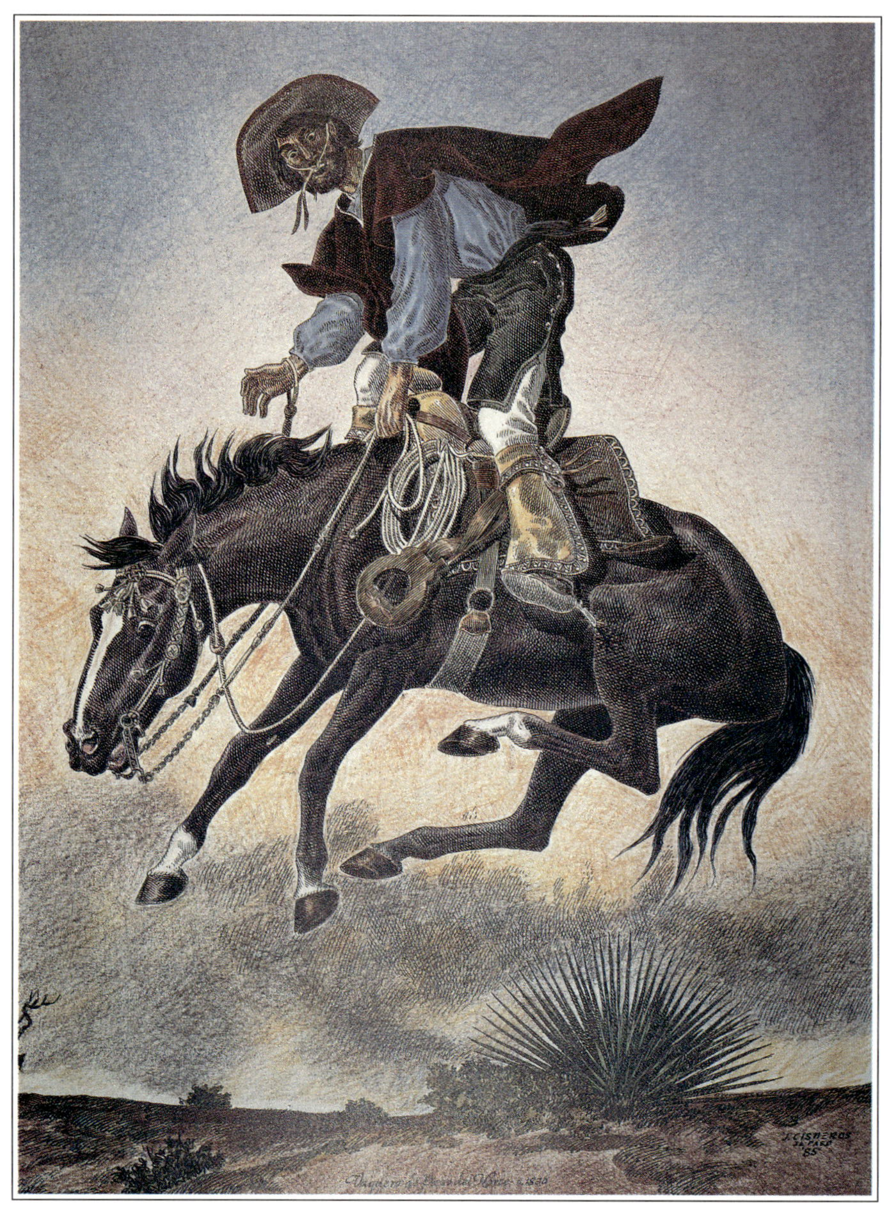

An auction of Texana in 1992, a fund-raiser for the Texas State Historical Association, featured a series of Cisneros drawings.

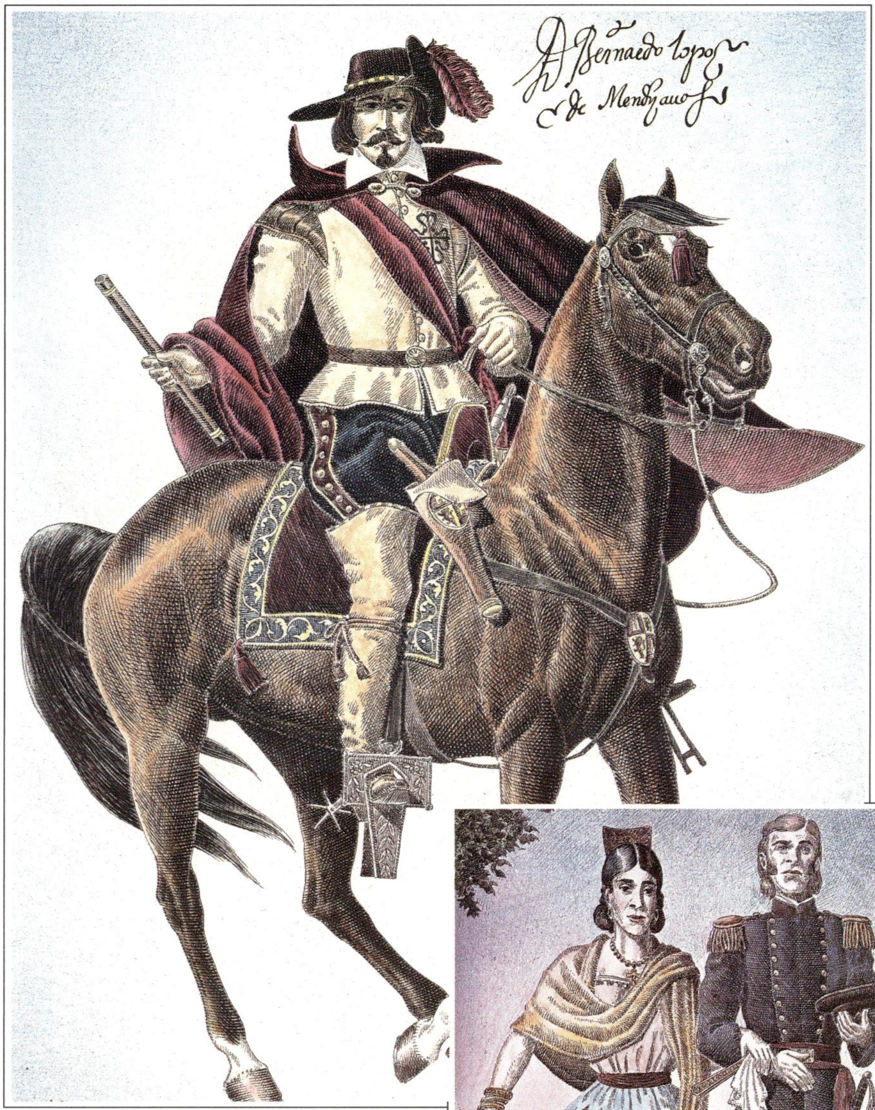

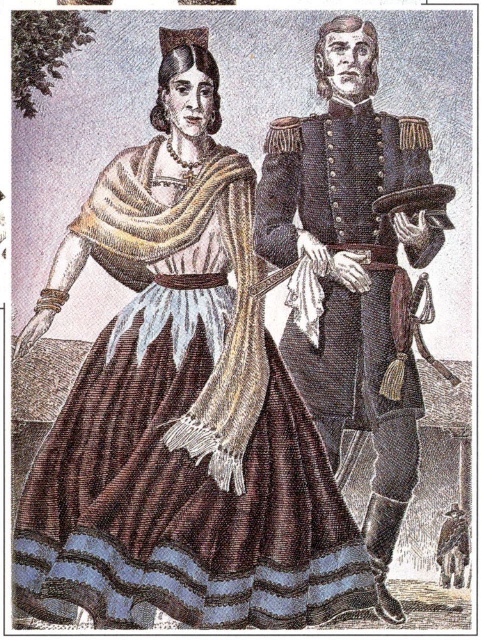

From New Mexico Magazine *: Don Bernardo López de Mendizábal, a Spanish official, and a New Mexican belle with an American army officer.*

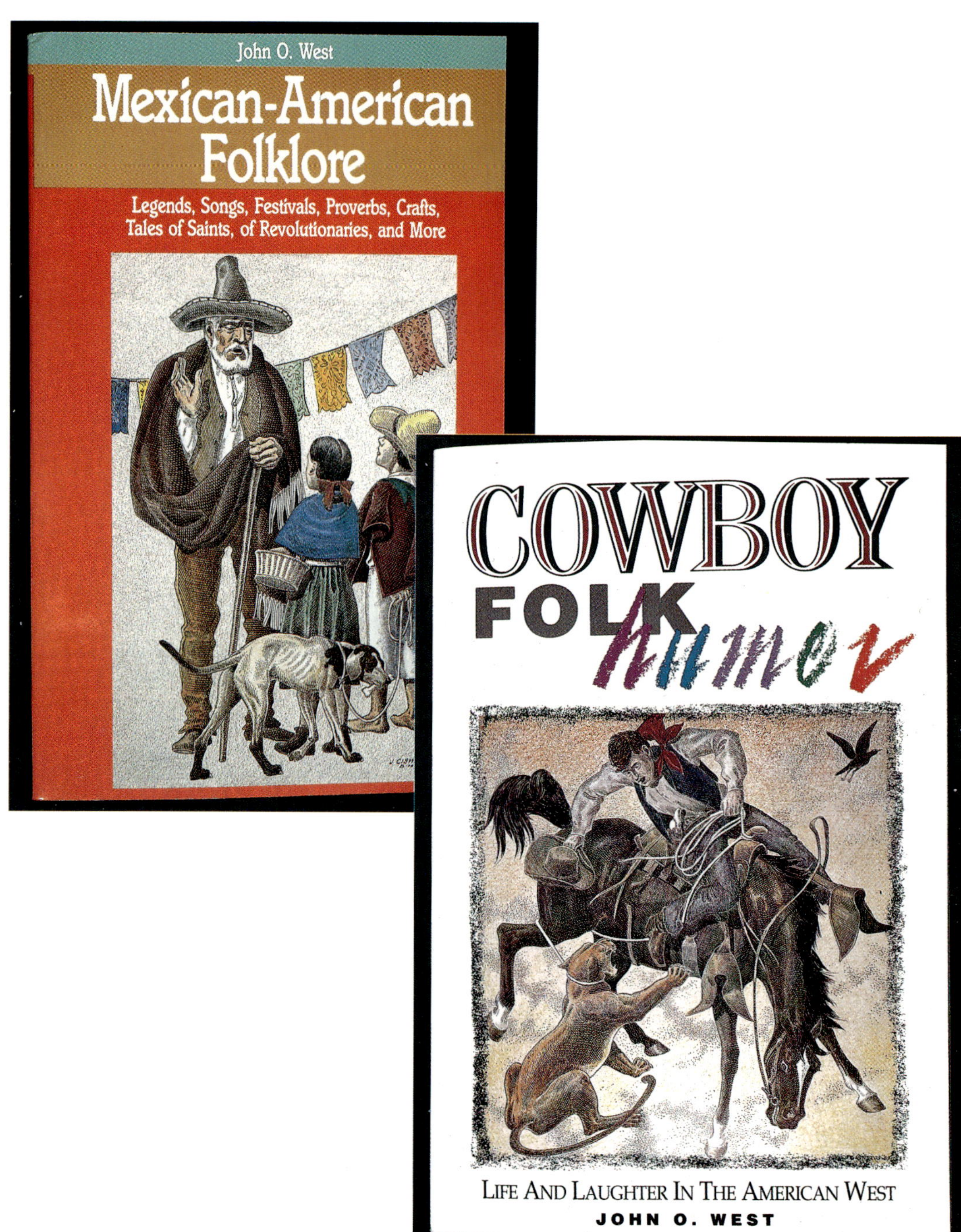

Top: Mexican-American Folklore *(1988) by John O. West;*
bottom: Cowboy Folk Humor *(1990) by John O. West.*

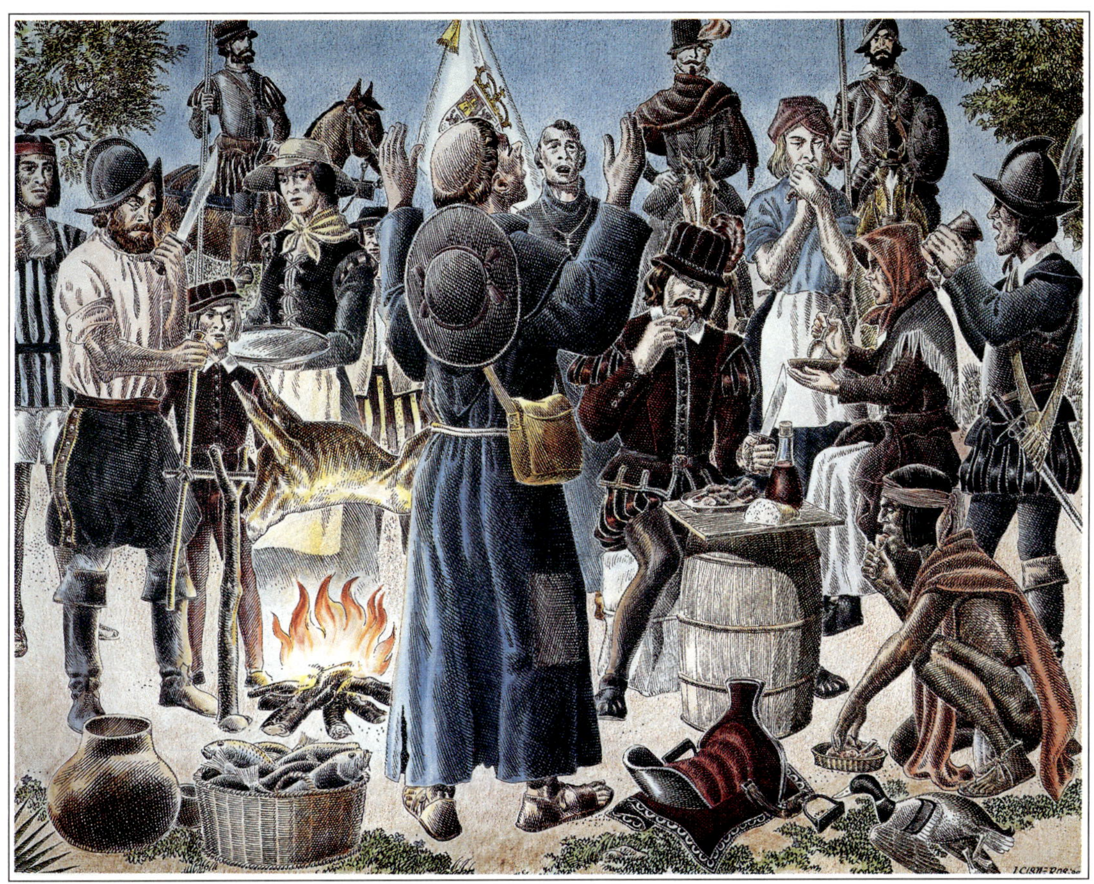

The First Thanksgiving on what is now United States territory. (Courtesy of Sheldon Hall and the El Paso Mission Trail Association)

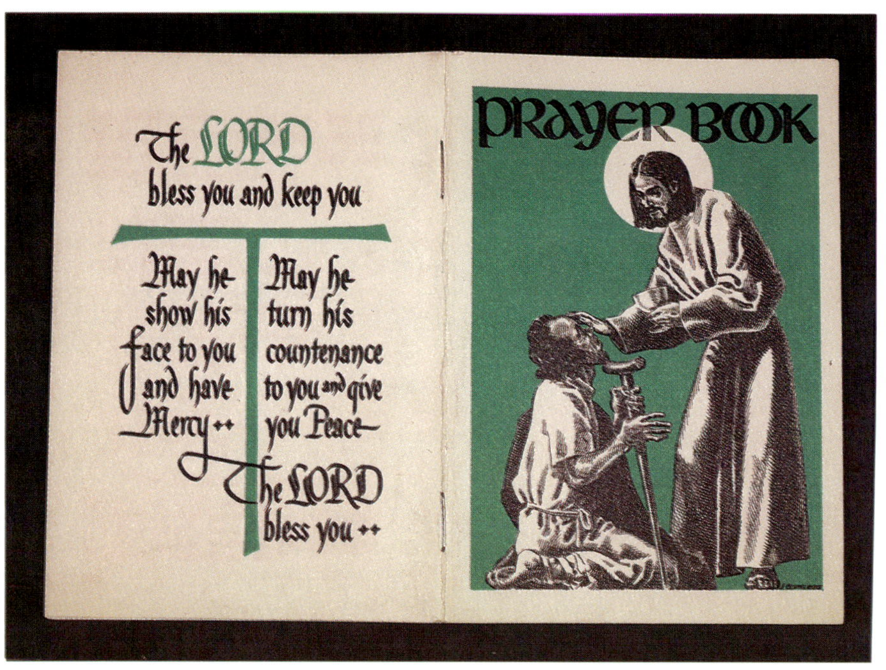

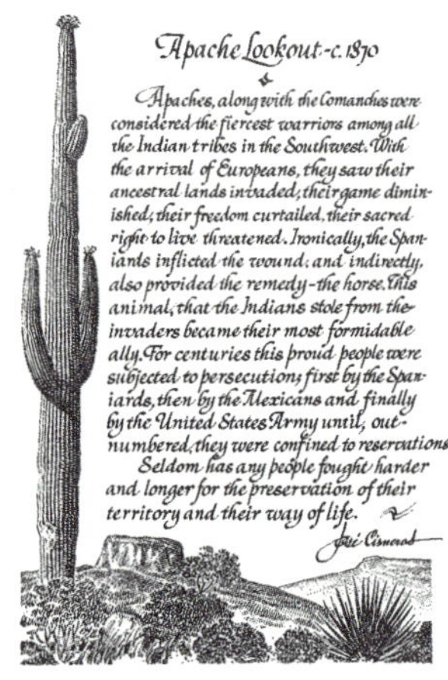

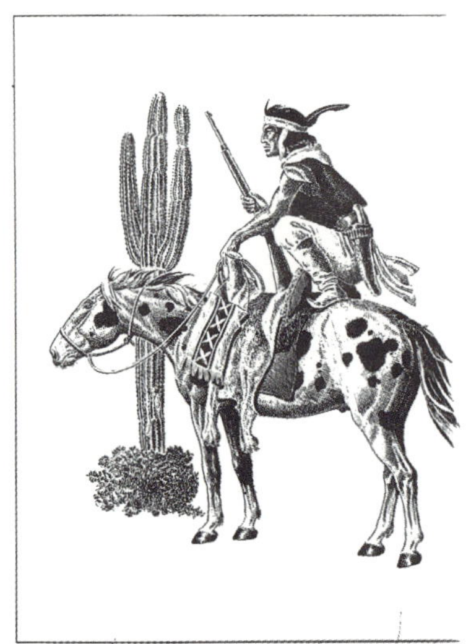

Top: The padre invokes God's blessing.
Bottom: "Apache Lookout," a Christmas card from University of Texas at El Paso's former president, Haskell Monroe

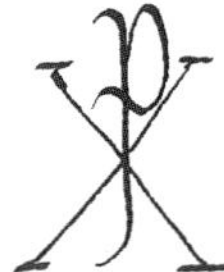

Where there is faith, there is love.
Where there is love, there is peace.
Where there is peace, there is God.
Where GOD is, nothing is lacking.

Transcribed from a wall tile found by Tom Lea in a Baja California home and translated by him. With love and affection for our very dear friends, Lucy and John West.

Vicenta and José Cisneros
ILLUSTRATOR

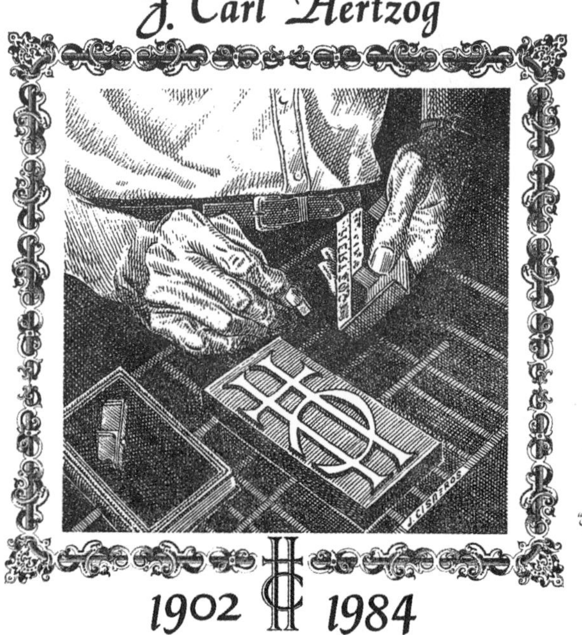

Wattisms.....

"Are you well?" "How you come on?"
"Wayno" "Bravo."
"Plumb alright." "Plumb handy."
"Gollee!"
"Why don't you sell the Charolais now? The price is higher than a tree."
"He is not even a notch on a stick."
"They're about to talk 'em up a storm."
"The fat boys fell out."
"She's a little swole." "She had a rough go."
"Shellin' the woods." "Give it a lick."
"Pay no tensch."

Top: John O. and Lucy West; center: The portrait of the hands of book designer Carl Hertzog and his printer's colophon appear on this University of Texas at El Paso Library Keepsake. (Courtesy of Al Lowman); bottom: "Wattisms" is a collection of quotes from Watt R. Matthews, brought together by Carl Hertzog and published in 1974.

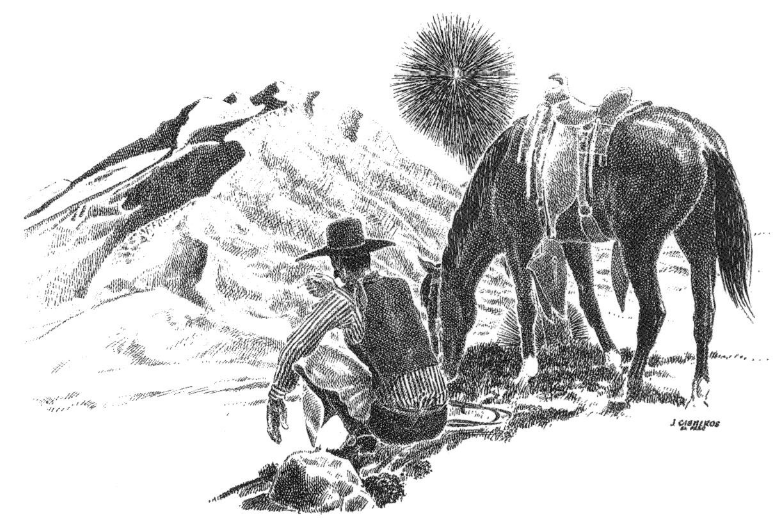

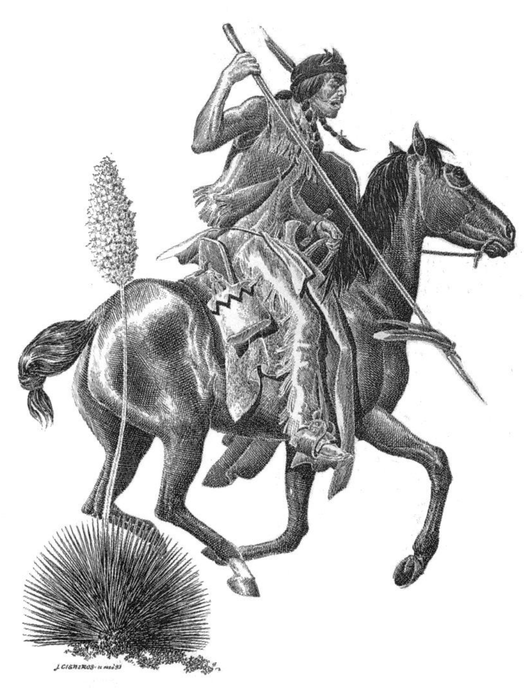

Top: a cowboy contemplates Old Mount Franklin.
Bottom: an Indian lancer on a raid (from Riders Across the Centuries*).*

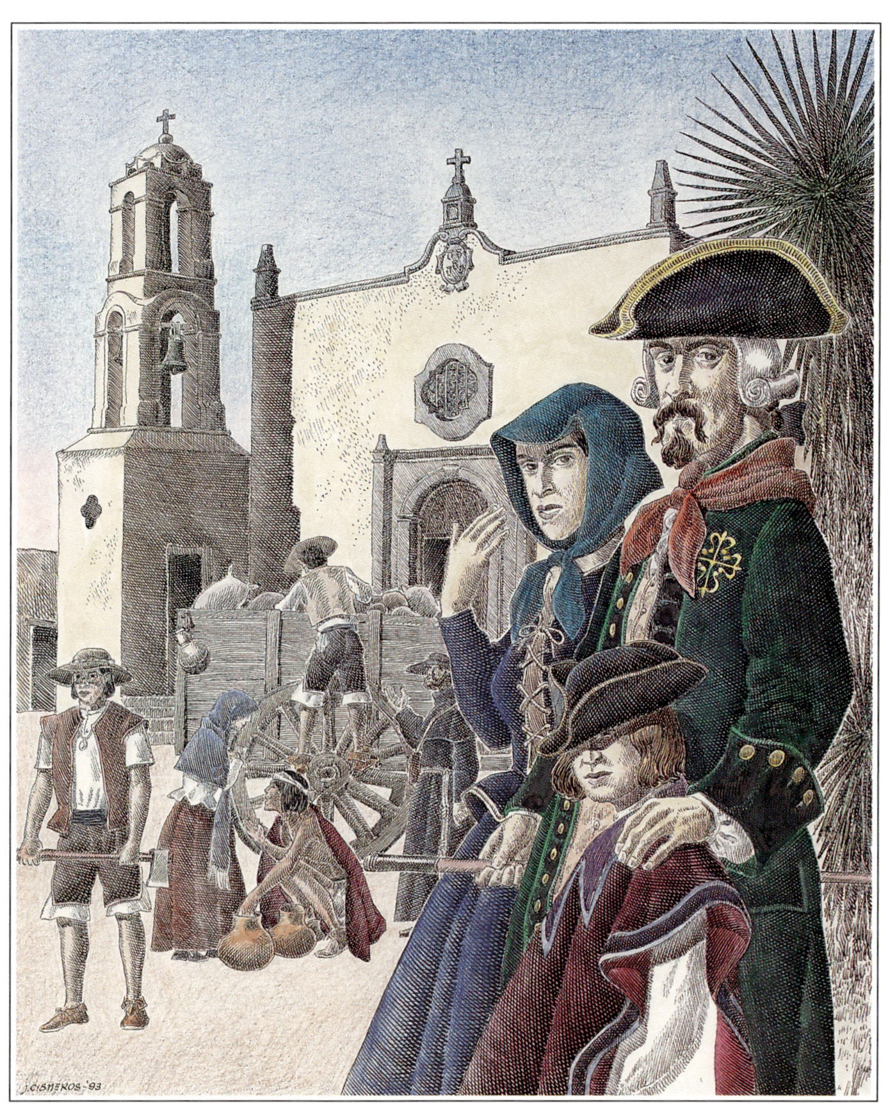

Most Recent Works

Parishioners gather in front of the mission of Our Lady of Guadalupe in Ciudad Juárez, Mexico.

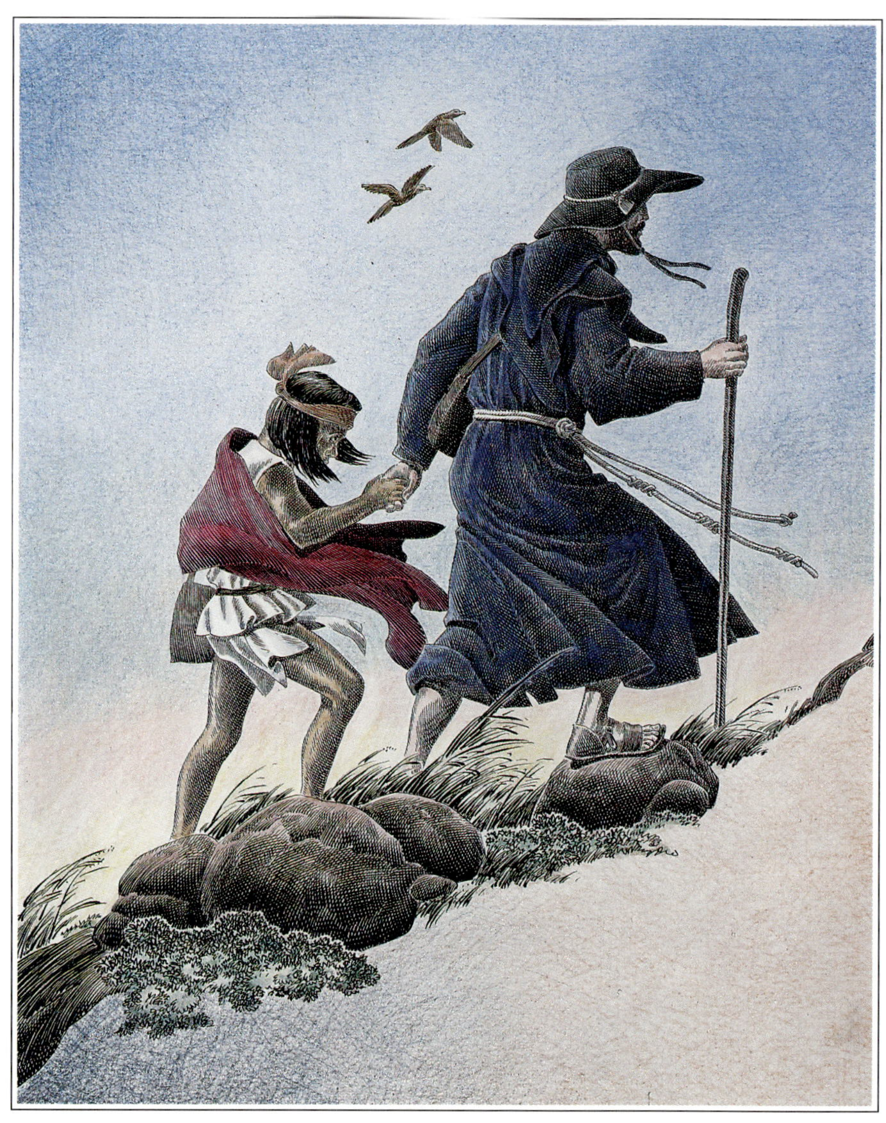

Most Recent Works
"The Short Cut"

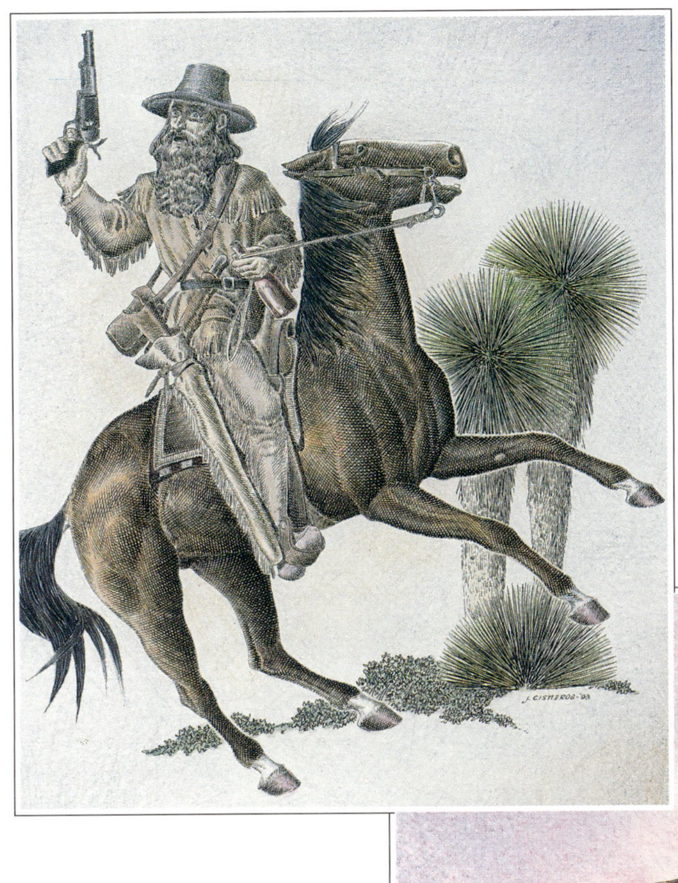

Most Recent Works

Top: a frontiersman; bottom: a Texas cowboy.

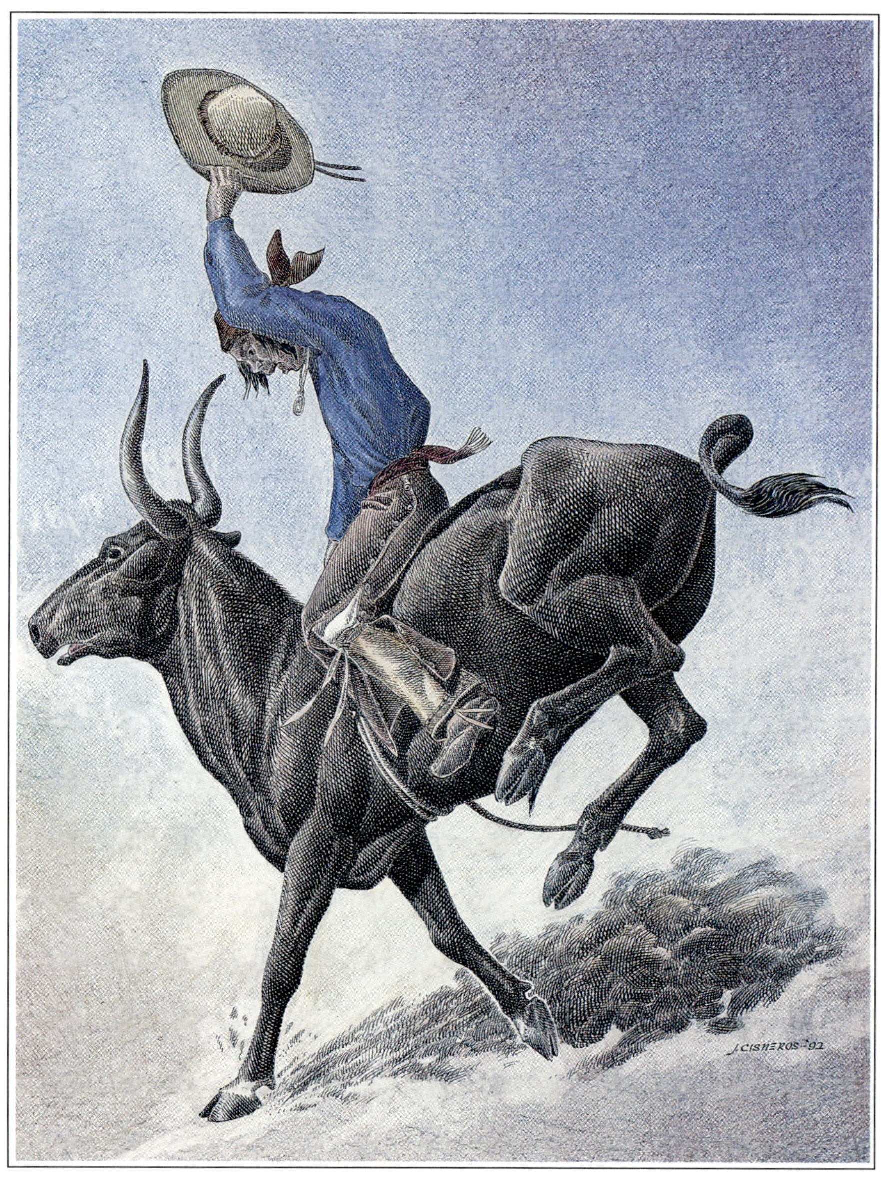

Most Recent Works
A cowboy and steer

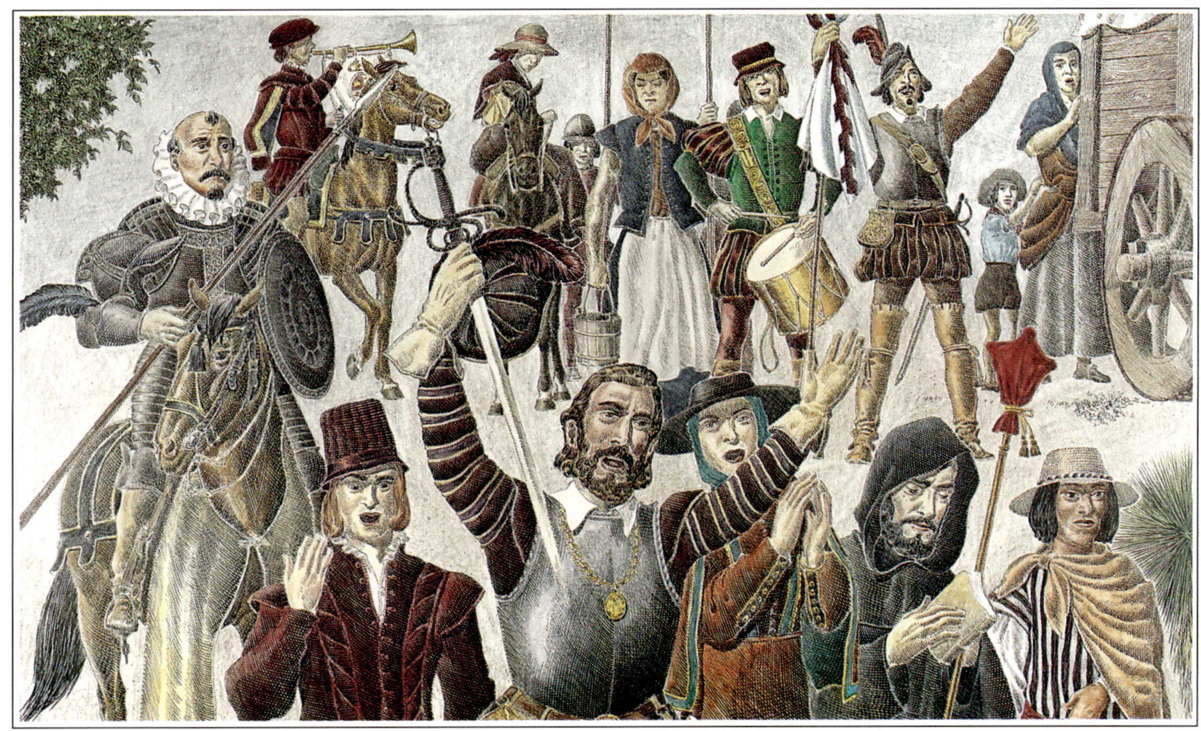

Don Juan de Oñate, The Great Colonizer, dominates this picture, completed July, 1993, with his poet/historian, Gaspar de Villagrá, mounted on the left.

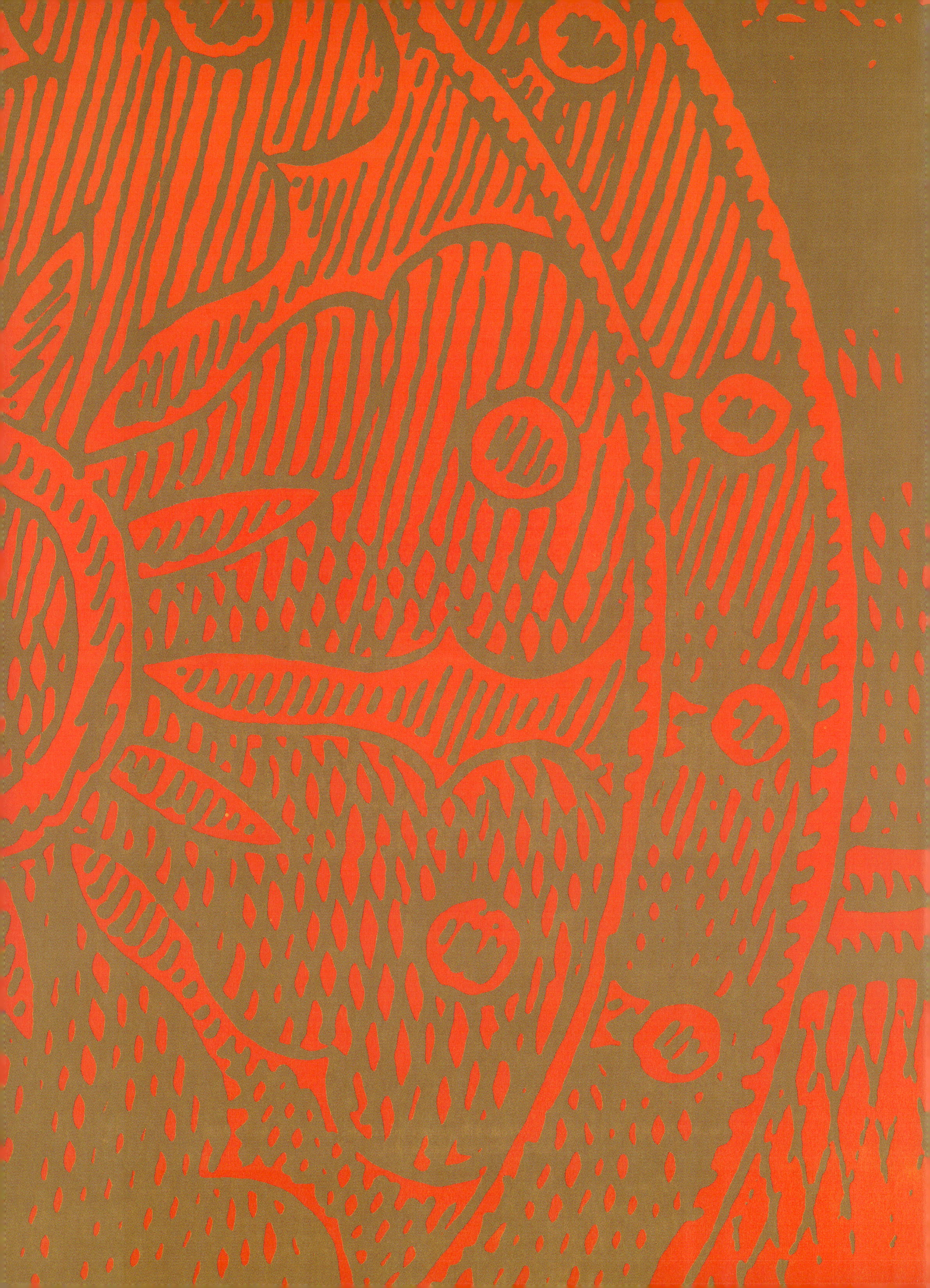

Epilogue

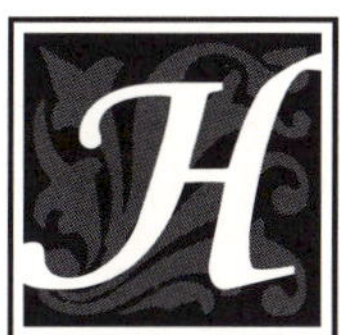

His most recent drawing, completed in July 1993, pictures the varied group of people who accompanied the Great Colonizer, Don Juan de Oñate, and the poet-adventurer Gaspar de Villagrá, who recorded that journey and the remarkable feast of thanksgiving the travelers enjoyed when they finally crossed the Chihuahua desert.

The artist's journey continues for José Cisneros, sparked by his history teacher in El Valle de Allende. He still focuses upon his life-long love of the past of the Spanish Southwest, with emphasis upon the Church, the settler and the conquistador, and the valiant horses that carried those who explored and tamed the vast desert-mountain region.

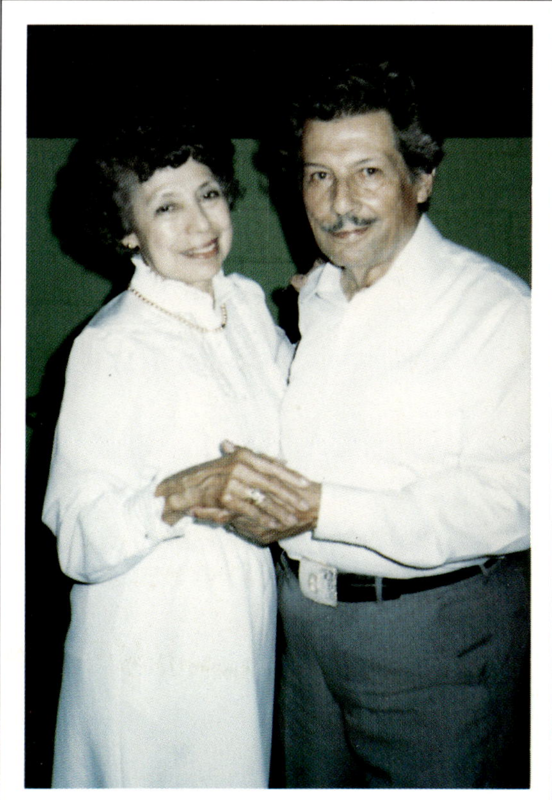